This is a book about the role of culture in social change and the Spanish transition to democracy after Franco. After Franco's death in 1975, Spain witnessed an extraordinary "period of consensus," unique in its own history. Laura Desfor Edles takes a distinctively culturalist approach to the "strategy of consensus" deployed by the Spanish elite at this time, and uses systematic text interpretation (with a particular focus on Spanish newspapers) to show how a new symbolic framework emerged in post-Franco Spain which enabled the resolution of specific events critical to the success of the transition. In addition to uncovering underlying processes of symbolization, she shows that politico-historical transitions can themselves be understood as ritual processes, involving as they do (to use Victor Turner's model) phases and symbols of separation, liminality, and reaggregation.

Symbol and ritual in the new Spain

Cambridge Cultural Social Studies

Series editors: JEFFREY C. ALEXANDER, *Department of Sociology, University of California, Los Angeles, and* STEVEN SEIDMAN, *Department of Sociology, University at Albany, State University of New York.*

Titles in the series

Symbol and ritual in the new Spain

The transition to democracy after Franco

Laura Desfor Edles
University of Hawai'i, Manoa

CAMBRIDGE
UNIVERSITY PRESS

PUBLISHED BY THE PRESS SYNDICATE OF THE UNIVERSITY OF CAMBRIDGE
The Pitt Building, Trumpington Street, Cambridge CB2 1RP, United Kingdom

CAMBRIDGE UNIVERSITY PRESS
The Edinburgh Building, Cambridge CB2 2RU, United Kingdom
40 West 20th Street, New York, NY 10011-4211, USA
10 Stamford Road, Oakleigh, Melbourne 3166, Australia

First published 1998

Printed in the United Kingdom at the University Press, Cambridge

Typeset in 10/12½pt Monotype Times   [SE]

A catalogue record for this book is available from the British Library

Library of Congress Cataloguing in Publication data

Edles, Laura Desfor–
    Symbol and ritual in the new Spain: the transition to democracy
after Franco / Laura Desfor Edles.
        p.   cm. – (Cambridge cultural social studies)
    ISBN 0 521 62140 2 (hardback: alk. paper). – ISBN 0 521 62885 7
(paperback: alk. paper)
    1. Democracy – Spain – History – 20th century.   2. Spain – Politics
and government – 1975–   .   I. Title.   II. Series.
    JN210.E34   1998   320.946′09′045–dc21   97–31040   CIP

ISBN 0 521 62140 2 hardback
ISBN 0 521 62885 7 paperback

Contents

Tables

Figures

Plates

Abbreviations

AP	Alianza Popular, Popular Alliance
CCOO	Comisiones Obreras, Workers' Commissions
CD	Coalición Democrática, Democratic Coalition
CDS	Centro Democrático y Social, Democratic and Social Center
CEDA	Confederación Española de Derechas Autónomas, Spanish Confederation of the Autonomous Right
CiU	Convèrgencia i Unió, Convergence and Union
CNT	Confederación Nacional de Trabajo, National Confederation of Labor
EDC	Equipo Demócrata Cristiano del Estado Español, Christian Democratic Team of the Spanish State
EE	Euzkadiko Ezkerra, Basque Left
ETA	Euskadi Ta Azkatasuna, Basque Homeland and Freedom
ETA-Berri	New ETA
ETA-Zarra	Old ETA
FAI	Federación Anarquista Ibérica, Iberian Anarchist Federation
FDC	Federación de la Cristiana Democrática, Federation of Christian Democrats
FPD	Federación Popular Democrática, Popular Democratic Federation
FRAP	Frente Revolucionario Antifascista Patriótico, Anti-fascist Revolutionary Patriotic Front
GAL	Grupos Antiterroristas de Liberación, Anti-terrorist Liberation Group
HB	Herri Batasuna, Popular Unity
HOAC	Hermandades Obreras de Acción Católica, Workers' Brotherhood of Catholic Action

IDC	Izquierda Demócrata Cristiana, Democratic Christian Left
IU	Izquierda Unida, United Left
JOC	Juventudes Obreras Católicas, Catholic Workers' Youth
KAS	Koordinadora Abertzale Socialista, Patriotic Socialist Coordinating Council
LOAPA	Ley Orgánica de Armonización del Proceso Autonómico, Organic Law to Harmonize the Autonomy Process
MC	Minoría Catalana, Catalan Minority
ORT	Organización Revolucionaria de Trabajadores, Revolutionary Workers' Organization
OSE	Organización Sindical Española, Spanish Syndicate Organization
PCE	Partido Comunista Español, Spanish Communist Party
PDC	Pacte Democràtic per Catalunya, Democratic Pact of Catalonia
PNV	Partido Nacionalista Vasco, Basque Nationalist Party
POUM	Partido Obrero de Unificación Marxista. Workers' Party for Marxist Unification
PP	Partido Popular, Popular Party
PSOE	Partido Socialista Obrero Español, Spanish Socialist Workers' Party
PSP	Partido Socialista Popular, Popular Socialist Party
PSUC	Partit Socialista Unificat de Catalunya, Unified Socialist Party of Catalonia
PTE	Partido del Trabajo de España
SEU	Sindicato Español Universitario, Spanish University Syndicate
UCD	Unión del Centro Democrático, Union of the Democratic Center
UGT	Unión General de Trabajadores, General Workers' Union

Acknowledgements

Like many first books, this book has had a long and seemingly endless gestation, during which time I have accrued enormous intellectual and emotional debts. Above all, I want to thank my mentor, Professor Jeffrey C. Alexander, for his intellectual inspiration and guidance, and unstinting support. In addition, I thank the other members of my doctoral committee: Jeffrey Prager, Duane Champagne, C. Brian Morris from the University of California, Los Angeles, and David Ringrose, from the University of California, San Diego.

A special thanks to Alfonso Pérez-Agote, both for inviting me into his home and to the Basque University when I first began this project, and for sharing his expertise and wisdom. Richard Gunther, Edward Tiryakian, and Juan J. Linz also all took the time to provide extensive comments and suggestions in the early stages of this research. A much belated thank you to them. My colleagues at the University of Hawai'i, Manoa, and Boise State University have been extremely understanding while I was writing this book. I especially thank Professors Kiyoshi Ikeda, Alvin So, and Michael Blain.

In the last few years, many people have read parts of this manuscript or helped make it better in some way. I especially thank Eric Rambo, Juan Amigo, and Josie Bilbao for their camaraderie and help. I also thank Valerie Bunce, Paul Manuel, and the participants of the 1994 National Endowment for the Humanities Summer Seminar on Democratization in Europe; José Alvarez-Junco, Joaquín Fernandez-Castro, and the Harvard-Tufts Iberian Study Group; Miguel Angel Centeno, Hank Johnston, José Rodriguez Ibañez, Benjamin Tejerina, John Torpey, and the anonymous Cambridge reviewers. A special thanks go to Martha Peach, the director of the library at the Instituto Juan March, for her friendly and timely assistance; as well as to Catherine Max and Andrew Humphrys, my exemplary editors at Cambridge University Press.

Financial support for my research was provided by the Del Amo Foundation of Los Angeles, the UCLA Graduate Division, and the University of Hawai'i Research Council. Parts of the book were written as a participant in the National Endowment for the Humanities summer seminar at Cornell University, and parts were presented at seminars at the Center for European Studies at Harvard University, the University of California, Irvine, and the University of the Basque Country. I thank those who invited me. I also thank the Centro de Arte Reina Sofia and the Artists' Rights Society for providing the photograph and giving permission to reproduce Picasso's *Guernica*.

Finally, I thank my parents, Janette and LeRoy Doty and Donald Desfor, for supporting me on my first Spanish journey; and my husband, Michael, who has been with me on my journey since then. I am also extremely endebted to my special family of friends in Madrid: Manuel Willén, Rafael and Asunción Munguira Rubio, and Francisco and Conchita Pulido González. Their warmth and affection over the past fifteen years has been intimately entwined with my warmth and affection for, and understanding of, Spain.

Writing this book and returning (and returning) to Spain has not always been easy. This book is dedicated to Mike and Benny and Ellie for their love and good cheer, often in spite of tremendous inconvenience.

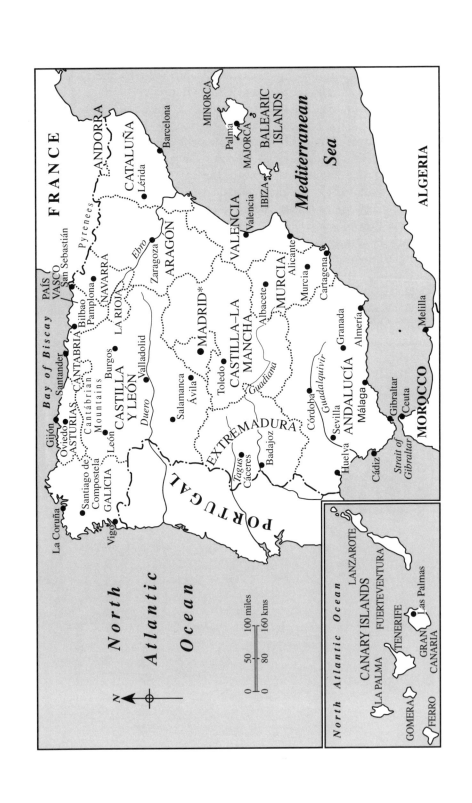

PART I

Interpreting the Spanish transition to democracy

1

Introduction

In his recent book, *In Retrospect: the Tragedy and Lessons of Vietnam*, Robert McNamara suggests that the problem with Vietnam was that we did not understand Vietnam; no one making decisions was conversant with Vietnamese culture; United States' leaders ethnocentrically assumed that Vietnamese values were the same as ours.[1] McNamara says he wrote his book so that we can "learn" from his (and our) mistakes. What he hopes we learn is that we should never enter into war without really *knowing* the country we seek to help, or are fighting against. An "expert" in that country should advise, and be in on the decision.

Interestingly, McNamara also said he could not have "known" this lesson at the time of Vietnam. He said it took him twenty years to write the book because the lesson was so long in coming.

From a culturalist perspective, McNamara's book is intriguing for several reasons. First, McNamara acknowledged something that cultural sociologists and anthropologists take as a given, but that most people tend to forget: that strategic decisions are made in a *cultural* – as well as historical, political, and economic – context; and that in order to understand your own or others' "strategic" interests one must understand the culture of which they are a part. Moreover, in arguing that he "could not have known then" what he knows now, McNamara implicitly admits to his own cultural immersion – as well as to the United States' infamous and long-standing cultural myopia. It was not simply "McNamara in the 1950s," or "America of the 1950s," or even "American interests in the 1950s" – but the specific symbolic frameworks in place in the 1950s and 1960s – that shaped McNamara's perceptions of Vietnam.

McNamara's book is intriguing too because the United States has been trying to "close" the painful and schizophrenic Vietnam event for a long time: through Hollywood movies, through the Vietnam memorials – and now, finally, through the "confessions" of one of Vietnam's critical particapants.[2] But although one often hears that we must not let Bosnia or the Gulf "turn into another Vietnam," "the lesson" from Vietnam is not at all clear. Does Vietnam represent a nation divided? A lack of commitment to war? Does it mean that we should never enter a war we "cannot" win? A war with a people we do not "understand"? Or should we never interfere with someone else's war at all?

Finally, McNamara's book is intriguing culturally, because the process of "rethinking" a national tragedy is a general, global phenomenon. Just as McNamara seeks to understand the "tragedy" of Vietnam and to unearth its "lessons", since at least the 1950s, Spaniards have been explicitly rethinking the "tragedy" and "lessons" of the Spanish Civil War. Yet, in contrast to contentious American attempts to "make sense" of Vietnam, the Spanish collective rethinking of the Civil War has been at once profound, transformative, and nearly universal.

Moreover, this cultural rethinking and reinterpretation of the Civil War has been part and parcel of Spain's recent successful transition from authoritarianism to democracy. Scholars, laypeople, and political leaders alike all point to the Spanish Civil War as the cultural and moral backdrop to the Spanish transition. As the acclaimed Spanish historian Javier Tusell maintains:

> In effect, what the totality of the Spanish people have done collectively in the moment of transition to democracy, is an exercise of looking back so as not to stay back. Throughout the transition, the memory of the civil war, whose fiftieth anniversary was coming close, has been planted on the national body, and there has been a will, more or less explicit, to avoid the reproduction of the war, including procuring the circumstances that contributed without a doubt to the previous destruction of the democratic system.[3]

For a cultural sociologist, the theoretical and empirical questions are clear. Where did this reinterpretation of the Spanish Civil War come from? How did the intricate divisions of the Civil War become subsumed into what has been called a "militant pacifism"?[4] How did this – and other – representations actually inform the events of the Spanish democratic transition?

A New Beginning for Spain

The recent Spanish transition from authoritarianism to democracy is phenomenal not only for "cultural" but political and historical reasons. Historically, the recent democratic transition is phenomenal simply because it is the the first time in Spanish history that parliamentary democracy has worked; i.e. it is the first time that Spanish democracy has been self-sustaining.[5] This is not to say that democracy had never been attempted before. On the contrary, parliamentary democracy in Spain has a long, albeit weak, record. The word "liberal," as part of our political vocabulary, comes from Spain.[6] It was first used to describe a group of radical patriots, cooped up in Cádiz as refugees from the French invasion of 1808. In 1812, they drew up a constitution, which, by enshrining the revolutionary doctrine of the sovereignty of the people, destroyed the basis of the old monarchy; it was to become the model for advanced democrats from St. Petersburg to Naples.

Yet, between 1814 and 1931, there were no less than twenty-five *pronunciamientos* (uprisings) in Spain. Radical intervention by the armed forces was the standard means by which Spanish regimes alternated.[7] Spain twice proclaimed republics – but both ended in civil war. The First Spanish Republic, declared in 1873, broke down into the second Carlist War even before a constitution could be written. The Second Republic, born in 1931 after the demise of the dictatorship of General Miguel Primo de Rivera, survived five tumultuous years before breaking down into the infamous Spanish Civil War of 1936–1939.

As Esenwein and Shubert point out, the term "civil war" conjures up the image of a country divided in two, but the Spanish Civil War (and perhaps all civil wars) was far more multi-faceted.[8] Often mythologized as "the last great cause" (particularly by the West), the Spanish Civil War was actually an intricate coagulation of splits between town and country, constitutionalists and Carlists, new and old Spain, communists and fascists, and clericals and anti-clericals.[9]

The Spanish Civil War began on July 17, 1936 with an attempted military coup d'état (though Franco preferred to call it a "national uprising"). The revolters did not achieve rapid control, however; and the Republican government failed to respond authoritatively to their own army mutiny. Improvised anti-fascist militias began to spring up, sometimes abolishing or supplanting the local *ayuntamientos* (municipal governments). By the end of the first week the state machinery was in total disarray, and "power," in the words of the Communist leader Dolores Ibárruri, "lay in the streets."[10]

The Civil War ended with the Nationalists' victory in 1939, and Generalissimo Francisco Franco set up a traditional dictatorship that lasted nearly forty years, until his death in 1975. The regime consisted of three distinct phases: a first phase, roughly 1939–1951, dominated by fascist policy, including economic autarchy, military repression, unparalleled privilege of the Catholic Church, and the ideology of national Catholicism; a second period, 1951–1959, in which neo-capitalism replaced the outmoded and isolationist model of fascism; and a third period, 1959–1974, characterized by unprecedented economic growth, internal social, political, and religious liberalization, as well as renewed repression by the Franco regime.

Yet, since the death of Franco in 1975, Spain has not only transformed itself from dictatorship to democracy from the inside out; it has done it through a remarkably quiescent process of reform and "strategy of consensus." The Law for Political Reform, passed almost exactly one year after Franco's death, was "a law of the transition for the transition,"[11] which recognized the principles of popular sovereignty, universal suffrage, and political pluralism, and prepared for the legal abolition of the chief Francoist institutions. Other reforms followed shortly thereafter, and in June 1977 the first democratic elections took place without major incident. The elections were the first moment of a "period of consensus" that culminated in the ratification of the 1978 Constitution – "the first constitution in Spanish history that is neither the unilateral imposition of a particular party nor the expression of a single ideology."[12] As Payne maintains:

The democratization of Spain that has occurred since 1976 constitutes a political transformation without any clear parallel or analogy in twentieth-century systems, for an established institutionalized authoritarian system – no mere ad hoc Caribbean military dictatorship – has been totally transformed from the inside out by means of the personnel, institutions, and mechanisms of the regime itself, led by the head of state.[13]

Spain and democracy's "Third Wave"[14]

Since 1989, the Spanish transition from Francoism to democracy has taken on new meaning. Sociologists and political scientists look to Spain to explain not only why the Spanish transition was a "success," but to explain how states transform themselves from authoritarianism to democracy. For many political scientists, Spain is "the very model of elite settlement" – a lesson in "consensual" transition from authoritarianism to democracy.[15]

Yet, regardless of our desire to make sense of our world by applying past "truths," let me forewarn that the Spanish transition does not impart easy "how to" lessons on democratization. Spain is an exemplar – but an exemplar of an extraordinary cultural as well as political process, which is not particularly amenable to imitation.

The central categories of experience differ from one society to another; the weight of cultural, economic, and political factors vary in each democratic transformation. The most important difference between the case of Spain and the former Eastern bloc states is that far more is in transition in on-going post-communist cases. In Spain, the economic and cultural groundwork was laid before authoritarianism came to an end. Occidental capitalism had not only begun, but was institutionalized before Franco's death. Though Spain did experience a significant economic crisis during the transition itself, international economic support allowed the crisis to be deferred until after the consolidation of the democracy. In precisely the same way, regional, social, and international issues were not insignificant after Franco's death (they were very significant), but they were *defined* in basically the same way in pre- and post-Franco society.

By contrast, the post-communist states are dissolving convoluted politico-economic systems at once – before new systems have even been imagined.[16] Whereas Spain was constrained (structurally as well as symbolically) by monetary support and mentoring relationships from the West, today's post-communist states are in a symbolic as well as institutional vacuum. In other words, whether one thought it "good" or "bad," the transcendent goal of the Spanish "democratic transition" was to become a modern western European parliamentary democracy.[17] By contrast, the former Eastern bloc states are neither here nor there: their identity lies in the past rather than in the future. In the cases of "the former Soviet Union," "the former Yugoslavia," and "the former Czechoslovakia," they lack even a clear territorial identity. As Bunce and Csanadi maintain, fluidity is the essential characteristic of the post-communist states: "the structure of post-communism is the absence of much structure although there is a kind of logic to this fluid situation."[18]

I hasten to add that it is not that the Spanish transition to democracy was simply "easier" than that of the post-communist states. Spain is not a case of a political system simply "catching up" with the economic and social system. The Spanish democratic transition was neither "natural" or "inevitable."[19] In point of fact, almost all of the problems that had resulted in democratic breakdown in Spain previously, were still in existence in the 1970s. While the wave of prosperity of the preceding fifteen to twenty years had attenuated economic divisions, the separation between rich and poor was still significant, and could have been used for political ends, even against the workers' economic interests. The regional problem not only remained; it had been made worse by the policies of the Francoist regime – a regime wholly opposed to all regional claims in favor of "centralism" (which, in fact, was not a centralism of Castile or even Madrid, but of the government).[20] In conjunction with threats from the nationalist and non-nationalist left, the far right and the armed forces remained an ever-present danger in post-Franco society.[21] Indeed, several military plots were uncovered between 1977 and 1981; and on February 23, 1981, Lieutenant Colonel

Antonio Tejero Molina led a group of Civil Guards in an attempted coup d'état, which was, in fact, initially a success. It failed because most of the army did not at first respond, and the king persuaded the remaining forces to stay loyal.[22] The Spanish transition is phenomenal precisely because so much could have – and historically has – "gone wrong." The purpose of this book is to explain what did not go wrong and why.

Outline of the Book

This book is divided into three parts. Part I provides a theoretical and historical backdrop to the Spanish transition; Part II delineates the spirit of consensus at the heart of the transition; Part III demonstrates how this generalized system of meaning enabled the institutionalization of Spanish democracy.

Specifically, in the following chapter I critically analyze existing models of democratization – i.e. functionalist/modernization, structural/Marxist, and elite/rational choice paradigms. I will show that, despite the diversity within and between these approaches, they all tend toward the theoretical problem of rationalism, i.e. they overemphasize conditions and factors external to the individual actor. In the latter portion of chapter 2, I outline a cultural theory and methodology that is designed to correct this theoretical and empirical deficiency. This culturalist approach focuses on symbolization – the subjective, non-rational realm behind and within seemingly "rational" political processes and "objective" socio-economic structures.

Chapter 3 places the Spanish transition to democracy in historical perspective. This is a history rife with religious, regional, and class divisions, as well as a long but weak history of democracy. This history of division and democracy is epitomized in the Spanish Second Republic (1931–1936), in which Spain was literally split between a conservative/monarchist/religious right and a republican/socialist/anarchist anti-clerical left. The Second Republic ultimately broke down into the infamous Spanish Civil War (1936–1939), and the victory of the Nationalists led by General Francisco Franco.

Part II of this book explores the core symbols of the so-called "period of consensus" at the heart of the Spanish transition. In chapter 4, we will see that four core symbols: "a new beginning," "national reconciliation"/"*convivencia*," "democracy," and their symbolic opposite "Civil War," emerged and penetrated Spanish society after Franco's death and became generalized throughout that society. We will also see that these core symbols provided the ground rules of the "politics of consensus"; in addition, they represented the ritual process of transition. In short, following the model of Victor Turner, who first pointed out that all rites of passage (or transition) contain three stages – separation, liminality, and reaggregation – I will argue that representations of "a new beginning" symbolized separation from the old social state (authoritarianism); "national reconciliation" and *convivencia* ("living together with others") represented the communality of the liminal phase; and "democracy" represented reaggregation to the new social state (parliamentary democracy).

Chapter 5 explores the first critical transitional "moment of consensus" – the democratic elections of June 1977. We will see not only that the newly emerging core symbols enabled the successful resolution of this pivotal event, but that the core symbolic framework affected the outcome of the elections. Moreover, I will argue that as the "debut" (or "new beginning") of democracy, the June 1977 electoral event symbolized separation from Francoism in the ritual process of transition.

Chapter 6 focuses on a second critical consensual moment: the drafting of the Moncloa Pacts in October 1977. The Moncloa Pacts were a set of important political and economic agreements, designed as temporary palliatives until a new constitution could be drafted. In this chapter we will see that the drafting of the Moncloa Pacts was both enabled by and reaffirmed the emerging Spanish transitional symbolic framework. The specific generalized strands of shared meaning of a "new beginning," "democracy," and "national reconciliation" engendered the very notion of a "strategy of consensus" (the process of elite negotiation used to construct the Pacts as well as the 1978 Constitution). In other words, pacting "made sense" – given that "democracy" was the ultimate (sacred) goal, and violence was an unthinkable (profane) means by which to achieve it. Moreover, the Moncloa event, in which former enemies sat side by side in the Palace of the Moncloa in order to resolve historically volatile politico-economic issues, ritualized (or acted out) "national reconciliation" and the communal state of liminality, in the ritual process of transition.

In Part III we see that the construction and maintenance of a shared symbolic framework is neither autonomatic nor easy. Chapter 7 focuses on the complex and polemical process of drafting the 1978 Constitution. We will see that the drafting of the 1978 Constitution was far more complicated and volatile than the drafting of the Moncloa Pacts. Yet, once again, the core transitional symbols helped resolve crucial political debates, including the historically explosive issue of the role of the Church in Spanish society. Moreover, the "new beginning" of "democracy" and "reconciliation" was institutionalized in the 1978 Spanish Constitution. The successful drafting of the Constitution symbolized the closing of the ritual process, and the "success" of the Spanish transition.

Yet, the crucial exception in terms of Spain's historic "politics of consensus" is the Basque nationalists, who did not in fact embrace consensual bargaining, and who did not endorse the 1978 Constitution. Chapter 8 focuses on this crucial exception, by exploring Basque nationalist transitional symbolization. We will see that while the core transitional symbols of a "new beginning" of "national reconciliation" and "democracy" emerged also in the Basque Country, this symbolic framework was complicated by Basque nationalist representations, which at times directly opposed the dominant symbolic framework of the transition. Specifically, in contrast to the Catalan nationalists, who tended to link "autonomy" with "democracy" and the core transitional symbols, Basque nationalists tended to portray the recuperation of the Basque *Fueros* (historic local laws) as symbolically opposed to the "democracy" embodied in the 1978 Constitution. Nevertheless, we will also see that this exception underscores the central theme of this book – that the previously discussed (Spanish) transitional symbolic framework was hegemonic in the post-Franco period.

In sum, this book shows how the dominant symbolic framework of the Spanish "period of consensus" enabled the successful resolution of key democratic moments, and thus the success of the Spanish transition. It also shows the way culture works in processes of social order and social change. Chapter 9 recaps these empirical, theoretical, and methodological points, and provides a brief synopsis of Spanish culture and politics since the ratification of the 1978 Constitution.

2

Theories of transition and transitions in theory

Since the Second World War, analysts have taken basically four different approaches to the issue of democratization. In the 1950s and 1960s, political cultural and modernization perspectives were dominant; in the next decade, neo-Marxist and structural models largely replaced modernization models; and since the 1980s, elite and rational choice models have been increasingly popular. This chapter critically examines the theoretical orientation of these three perspectives, focusing on recent elite and rational choice models of transition, and the case of Spain. In the latter portion of the chapter, I introduce a fourth model, which explicitly seeks to rectify the theoretical dilemmas of earlier perspectives. This model is part and parcel of the burgeoning new interest in culture in political sociology, as well as in the social sciences and humanities in general.

Sociological theory after the Second World War: the functionalist–structuralist divide

In the 1950s and 1960s, structural functionalism was, in many respects, the theoretical modus operandi of sociology. Propelled by the work of Parsons and Merton, functionalists portrayed society as an intelligible system, a sum of symbiotically connected parts. Structural functionalism emphasized the existence of common value systems in societies, and the social mechanisms that maintain consensus. In the 1970s, Marxist-inspired analysts challenged the functionalist hegemony. Parsons was dethroned, and functionalism became known as a conservative apology for liberal capitalism. Structure replaced culture at the center of society; and politics was viewed as conflict over material resources, rather than the construction and maintenance of a shared system of values.[1]

The substantive area of democratic transition has been part and parcel of sociology's "systems" and "conflict" phases. In the first period, analysts such as Lipset, Almond and Verba, and Pye and Verba developed important, provocative political cultural models of democracy and democratization within the functionalist tradition.[2] These theorists conceptualized democratization as symbiotic and evolutionary; they used the Parsonian pattern variables to categorize "political cultures" (cognitive, affective, and evaluative orientations to political phenomena), and they argued that a specific value orientation (or "civic culture"), as well as level of economic development, is necessary for democratization.[3]

In the 1970s, structural theorists challenged the modernization and political cultural approach to democratization. Marxist-inspired analysts such as Poulantzas, Gunder Frank, and Tilly, to name a few, quite rightly argued that modernization models overemphasized cultural and underemphasized external economic and internal class variables; and that they suffered from Western-centrism and ahistoricism.[4] However, conflict and structural theorists not only replaced the study of values with the study of power and material resources; they largely replaced the study of democracy and democratization with the study of (violent) social revolution and/or imperialism. Thus, not only the causal variables, but the substantive field changed in the conflict period. Value-driven, consensual social change and (subjective) political culture were "out"; conflictual social change (i.e. revolution) and (objective) material and/or structural conditions were "in."[5]

In short, by the 1970s, political sociologists had not only abandoned modernization models; they had abandoned the substantive area of democratic transition. Thus, another theoretical alternative, with roots in political science and economics rather than sociology, came to the fore. Corporatist, elite-centered, and rational choice models became the theoretical modus operandi in what became known as, significantly, "transitology" (the study of political transitions). Today, analysts such as Burton and Higley, and Przeworski explicitly champion an elite or rational choice approach; while others, such as O'Donnell and Schmitter, and Diamond, Linz, and Lipset, purport "atheoreticism" and/or implicitly adopt the elite-centered model.[6]

I will call this rational choice/elite approach the "pact school." The pact school includes corporatist, elite-centered, and rational choice models of transition that highlight the construction of elite "pacts" in "consensual" transitions from authoritarianism to democracy. There are several different versions of this school, and there is significant debate among pactmen.[7] Nonetheless, pactmen share a specific theoretical logic and present a similar image of democratic transition. In the following section, I will explain and critically analyze the theoretical orientation of the pact school.

Table 2.1. *Theoretical presuppositions of structural sociology, the pact school, and exchange theory*

Approach	Action	Order	Empirical unit
Structural sociology (Skocpol, Tilly)	Rational	Collective	Class/interest group

Pact school
   Elite (Higley and Burton)
   Rational choice (Przeworski)
   Corporatist (O'Donnell and
   Schmitter)
	Rational	Individual	Elite

Exchange theory (Homans)	Rational	Individual	Actor

The pact school approach to transition

As shown in Table 2.1, the common denominator between structural sociology and the pact school is the presupposition of rationality.[8] Both structuralists and pactmen hold that beneath any substantive normative commitment the real motivating factor is the desire on the actor's part to maximize utility. Both structuralists and pactmen reject "subjective" or "soft" cultural arguments, in favor of a more "objective" focus on material conditions. Of course, for both structuralists and pactmen, this theoretical logic is rooted in a rejection of functionalism.

As Table 2.1 also shows, however, unlike structural sociologists, pactmen assume an individual rather than a collective level of analysis. Pactmen explain social arrangements in any given historical moment as built up principally through the action of the individuals in that particular interaction. Przeworski, for example, criticizes the literature following Moore's seminal work because "history goes on without anyone ever doing anything." He counters with "a micro approach [to transition] in which actors have choices and their choices matter." [9] In this way, pactmen are similar to micro-sociologists of the 1970s, who also solved the problem of order through individualism. Indeed, at the presuppositional level pactmen are most similar to exchange theorists (see Table 2.1). Cooperation, rather than community, is the intended model – something which can be achieved through individuals acting on the principle of "I'll scratch your back if you scratch mine." [10]

Of course, it is the individualistic and rationalistic focus on elites that differentiates the pact school from functionalist, structuralist, and micro-sociological perspectives. Unlike structural sociologists, who see elites as representatives of various organized interests, pactmen see elites as individual, well-placed actors: they believe that *only* elites, defined as the "top leadership in all sectors," are able to affect national political outcomes.[11]

This individualistic, rationalistic focus on elites is readily apparent in the popular pact school concept "elite settlement."[12] It is also readily apparent in that, as pactmen themselves state, the pact school image of transition is that of a "complex game." Indeed, "game theoretic perspectives," "game analogies," and even a chess parlance saturate the substantive area of transition.[13] In accordance with this game image, pact school analyses of transition are post-hoc reconstructions of the *strategic* reasons that elites may have had for engaging in pacts or settlements and sometimes making extraordinary compromises in transitions to democracy.

The case of Spain

For pactmen, Spain is "the very model" of elite settlement;[14] it is "the country to be studied": it epitomizes "transition from above" or "transition through transaction."[15] Why did Spanish elites engage in pacts? And why did Spanish elite negotiations work? Pactmen maintain that (1) pacting was inherently strategic for Spanish elites; (2) Spanish elites had extraordinary abilities and skills, owing to their pragmatic personalities, or the fact that they had "learned" pragmatism from the "experience" of the Spanish Civil War; and (3) Spanish elites were "able" to pact because they were relatively "free from mass pressures."

First, pactmen maintain that Spanish elites had an *"interest* in achieving consensus." Pacting was a "natural" strategy for Spanish elites – a "requirement of day-to-day politics" for the government, and a "tool to win social power and legitimacy" for the opposition.[16] But if consensus was just a means to an end, what did Spanish elites want? How was it that polarized elites whose ideologies ranged from fascism to communism could all get what they wanted through pacting?

Interestingly, what we see when we attempt to answer this question is that it is *not* that regime and opposition elites' external interests were both met through consensus. Rather, as pactmen themselves note, regime and opposition elites came to define their interests (and the appropriate means by which to attain them) in a new way during the transition. Spanish elites "defined their *goals* not as the maximization of the interests of their respective clienteles, but rather the creation of a legitimate and stable regime within which their supporters' interests would merely be 'satisficed'." Spanish consensus was based on a "general moderation in respect to the traditional political demands of the radicals and a commitment to a minimum of welfare state policies by the conservatives."[17] In other words, both regime and opposition elites came to define *democracy* as their most important goal, and both regime and opposition elites – and the masses – came to define violence as an inappropriate means to achieve it.

How and why did Spanish elites come to define their means and ends in this way during the transition? Pactmen maintain that Spanish elites had extraordinarily pragmatic "personalities," and/or that the "experience" of the Spanish Civil War "taught" Spanish elites moderation ("to avoid block action and majoritarian principles in making basic decisions about political institutions").[18] For Morlino, the case of Spain (as well as Greece) demonstrates that the experience of civil war "tends to have a moderating impact on the behavior of the elites of the future democracy."[19] Similarly, for Share, the "exemplary elite behavior" of the transition was a function of "the widespread awareness of [Spain's history of extremism and violence] and the ability to learn historical lessons from it."[20] Medhurst concurs: "'a learning process' was at work. On all sides there was a determination to avoid the violence that had given rise to Franco's regime and the oppressive rigidity characteristic of his brand of stability."[21]

But, of course, there is no a priori reason for the "experience" of civil war to lead to moderation. The experience of civil war can just as easily lead to revenge – as it so often has in Spanish (and world) history. Yet, the notion that moderation was just one possible lesson of the Civil War opens up pactmen to a subjectivity they seek to avoid. Then pactmen have to explain why Spanish elites learned this particular lesson.

The case of the Basques

These theoretical problems become even more apparent in the case of the Basque nationalists, however, because Basque nationalist elites did not embrace consensual bargaining. Pact school arguments as to why Basque nationalists did not embrace consensus are circular and contradictory – if the Basque exception is even acknowledged.[22]

First, pactmen maintain that disunity among Basque elites made pacting virtually impossible. States Gilmour, "the difficulty with the Basque Nationalist Party (PNV [Partido Nacionalista Vasco]) was that it was still divided – as it had been ever since the end of the nineteenth century – into moderate regionalists and extreme nationalists."[23] Similarly, Gunther, Sani, and Shabad maintain that, "intense divisions made it extremely difficult for the largest and the historic Basque party, the PNV, to make binding

commitments."[24] Yet, as we will see in subsequent chapters, every major
political party suffered serious internal schisms between its more radical
and conservative members during the Spanish transition. Indeed, the
government "party," the UCD (Unión del Centro Democrático – Union of
the Democratic Center), was a coalition rather than a genuine party.[25] If
elites agree to pact (as did Spanish communists, socialists and centrists as
well as Catalans), pactmen maintain that elites put aside their internal divisions in order to achieve their "ultimate" aims. Elites are said to act in
accordance with their "perceptions of success, as well as their interest."[26] If
elites do not pact (as in the case of the Basques), however, pactmen suggest
that elites' interests were simply irreconcilable.

Secondly, pactmen maintain that Basque elites simply lacked the "personality," "ability," "character," or "will" to embrace consensual bargaining. Gilmour, for example, maintains that PNV leaders were not prepared
"to accept political responsibility," and that "on nationalist questions there
was very little difference between this group of highly reactionary people
and the 'maoist,' 'third world' leaders of ETA."[27] Gunther, Sani, and
Shabad argue more subtly that the problem was one of leadership selection.
In contrast to other opposition elites, who explicitly took the "personality
characteristic" of "pragmatism" into account in the appointment of representatives to the constitutional drafting committee, the PNV chose the
former Jesuit Xabier Arzallus, "reputed to be one of the least moderate,
least flexible members of the party hierarchy." For Gunther, Sani, and
Shabad these and other "departures from the politics of consensus" explain
the failure of the Basque–government negotiations.[28]

Yet, whether they focus on elite personality or leadership selection, these
arguments are patently circular. Why did Basque elites fail to learn (or lack
the ability to learn) the "lesson" of pragmatism from the Civil War – especially given that Basque "costs" in the war (and the aftermath of the war)
were so enormous? Why did Basques select the "nonpragmatic" Arzallus as
their representative? This same circularity is also evident in Gunther, Sani,
and Shabad's comment that, while other elites sought to secure a constitutional consensus, "conversely, representatives of the Basque Nationalist
Party (PNV) did not regard endorsement of the Constitution by consensus
as an important political objective." "Departures" from the politics of consensus are symptomatic of – they do not explain – the failure of Basque
elites to embrace consensual bargaining.[29]

This circularity turns into outright contradiction, however, when
pactmen attempt to (more equitably) blame Basque and government elites
for the failed negotiations. For instance, Maravall and Santamaría state:

Neither the government nor the nationalists were clear in spelling out the ultimate logical and temporal limits to the process. Lingering negotiations between them led frequently during 1979 to changing strategies, alternating and "unnatural" alliances, blackmail, deadlock and confusion.[30]

Though they eschew subjective variables, here Maravall and Santamaría maintain that "unnatural alliances" (i.e. alliances not based on common interest), as well as "blackmail, deadlock and confusion" demarcate Basque–government negotiations. Of course, this contradicts Maravall and Santamaría's own earlier assertion that government elites "learned" "pragmatism" from the Civil War (see above). Theoretically, the point is that "objectivity" within a rationalistic and individualistic frame of reference necessarily gives way to subjective residual categories.

Non-elites in the Spanish transition

Finally, pactmen maintain that Spanish elites were "able to pact" because they were relatively free from mass pressures. This follows the pact school theoretical premise that pacting is a mutually rewarding (rational) strategy, and that "elites are disposed to compromise *if at all possible.*"[31] In a most extreme version of this argument, López Pintor maintains that the Spanish masses were an "absent majority" or a "soft cushion" over which government and opposition elites could negotiate.[32] Gunther, Sani, and Shabad more subtly argue that a crucial ingredient of the politics of consensus was that "negotiations took place in private, and not in public arenas. Privacy shields party representatives from the scrutiny of their respective supporters and electoral clienteles, and thus facilitates the making of concessions central to compromise agreements."[33]

But were Spanish non-elites as passive as pactmen claim? Were Spanish elites indeed relatively autonomous? Though pactmen portray the Spanish masses as "apathetic" and "demobilized" and thus irrelevant to the transition, they also maintain that the "extraordinary moderation" of the masses "facilitated" the Spanish transitional process; and that "pressure" from extremists induced elites to compromise.[34] Moreover, inconsistencies abound as to why non-elites were "passive," "moderate," or "demobilized." For example, although López Pintor, and McDonough and López Pina both describe the Spanish masses as demobilized during the Spanish transition, López Pintor traces demobilization to the economic prosperity and consumerism of the 1960s, whereas McDonough and López Pina trace demobilization to the economic insecurity caused by the 1970s' world-wide economic crisis.[35] Meanwhile, Fishman challenges the demobilization thesis but concurs that the world-wide economic crisis of the late 1970s made workers "fearful"; while Przeworski maintains that prosperity followed by economic stagnation causes the masses to mobilize.[36]

Furthermore, the case of the Spanish socialists challenges the elite autonomy argument altogether. Analysts of socialist working-class organizations have found that socialist elites were not "disposed to compromise" at all – they became moderate, in large part because of pressure from "rank-and-file workers."[37] According to Fishman, "the impetus for restraint came from below, from the rank-and-file workers, with the workplace leaders participating reluctantly in the limitation of conflict rather than serving as the lieutenants of a politically orchestrated demobilization from above."[38] Similarly, Foweraker finds that the Spanish democratic project began with, and continued because of, the labor movement.[39] Yet, my point here is not the empirical one, as to the "exact" amount of "mass" participation in the Spanish transition. My point is that while instrumental calculation must be considered part of every act, subjective considerations pervade every calculation.[40]

The emergence of cultural sociology

Since the early 1980s, sociologists have begun to rejoin the "systems"/"conflict" divide; they are returning to synthesis. In this new period the battle between "conflict" and "order" is not only considered old hat, but wrong; conflict and order are seen as two sides of the same coin, and the nuances of both "structure" and "contingency" are explicitly addressed.[41]

At the forefront of this new trend toward synthesis is the burgeoning new disciplinary speciality of cultural sociology. Recent cultural works not only reintroduce the notion of culture into politics and economics, but build on the structural sociology of the 1960s, which emphasized material contingencies.[42] Thus today cultural analysts explore "struggles over meaning" rather than shared values. They emphasize that people are active, skilled users of culture, and that they have the capacity to resist and redefine the messages of culture producers.[43]

In other words, in contrast to political cultural sociologists within the functionalist tradition, who sought to demonstrate how (internalized) "values" shape "behavior" – a static (and often deterministic) way to conceptualize the relationship between culture and action – today cultural sociologists seek to show how culture shapes action by enabling the construction of "reality" itself. Yet, as Alexander points out, cultural projections of agency do not necessarily escape the concretist and empiricist mistakes of other models. Some recent cultural analysts erroneously portray action as a process that often, or even typically, positions itself over and against culture. But action is a constant process of exercising agency through, not against, culture. Agency is inherently connected to representational and symbolic capacity; agency is inherently related to culture.[44]

In the case of the Spanish transition, this problem is readily apparent in Victor Pérez Díaz's recent, highly acclaimed book, *The Return of Civil Society in Spain*. On the one hand, Pérez Díaz differentiates himself from pactmen by focusing not on the political machinations of Spanish elites, but on "the institutions and values in civil society [that] preceded, and prepared the way for, the political transition of the 1970s."[45] Moreover, in contrast to his (functionalist) political cultural predecessors, Pérez Díaz emphasizes the "*invention* of tradition," rather than the mere internalization of democratic values. Pérez Díaz emphasizes that Spaniards "*constructed* a set of quasi-sacred texts, discourses, myths, rituals and icons that pervade everyday politics."[46]

Yet, empiricist and concretist problems are readily apparent in Pérez Díaz's conceptualization of "tradition" as "a set of beliefs, rules and values and an institutional setting," as well as his conceptualization of civil society, as "markets and voluntary associations," in general. For example, Pérez Díaz maintains:

> Spaniards were exposed to institutions and cultures . . . which were simply *far more efficient* than their own in achieving some of their traditional objectives as well as other objectives which they were rapidly learning to appreciate . . . In this way, Spaniards learned from, imitated, and wound up identifying with the people of Western Europe.[47]

That traditions are " invented" and/or "learned" because of "efficiency" in "achieving objectives" makes cultural innovations simply calculations about utility, which (as we have seen in the pact school) not only obliterates the moral realm, but results in determinism.[48]

Put in another way, actors do not *simply* "invent" traditions and "use" culture as an instrument with which to interpret and solve problems.[49] Actors are not nearly so heroic. Culture exists within the actor him/herself, rather than external to him/her. In order to explain how and why democratic traditions are "invented" we need a more robust theory of symbolization. For this, we must turn to symbolic anthropology, semiotics, and literary analysis.

Toward a dynamic theory of culture

One of our most important cultural theorists, in my view, is semiologist Umberto Eco. For Eco, culture is a system of "multicontiguous" representations, which does not proscribe specific behaviors, but merely frees a series of possible readings. According to Eco, while the cultural system may be likened to an enormous box of marbles, in which shaking the box forms different connections and affinities among the marbles, the cultural system is more analogous to a box of magnetized marbles, which establish a system of attraction and repulsion, so that some are drawn to one another and others are not. Better yet, we could imagine that every marble emits given wave-lengths, which put it in tune with a limited (though possibly very large) number of other marbles. But these wave-lengths can change according to new messages emitted and therefore the possibilities of attraction and repulsion change over time.[50]

In other words, symbols are multi-vocal (not uni-vocal); they are not all of the same logical order but are drawn from many domains of social experience and ethical evaluation. Moreover, components of meaning are not closed in number or frozen into a system of relevant units, but form an open series. Thus the existence of cultural codes does not at all make us "cultural dopes"; on the contrary, it enables the generation of both factual messages, which refer to original experiences, and messages which place in doubt the very structure of the code itself. The aesthetic function of art as well as language is to create connections which as yet do not exist, which thereby enriches the code's possibilities. And original interaction and experience create unique configurations in the formation of a complex conceptual arena. At the level of the individual, a certain symbol (and/or meaning) can be shared across a cross-section of groups, and at the same time be intertwined in other, less consensual representations. This allows for (micro-level) rational action and individual agency, without undermining the collective structure of systems of meaning.

Eco uses diagrams to help illustrate the creative use of collective structures of meaning. For instance, Eco shows how apparent leaps of metaphoric substitution are in fact short circuits of a preestablished path; e.g. a "long white neck," being a property of both a beautiful woman and a swan, means that a woman can be metaphorically substituted for by the swan.[51] States Eco:

A metaphor can be invented because language, in its process of unlimited semiosis, constitutes a multidimensional network of metonymies, each of which is explained by a cultural convention rather than by an original resemblance . . . The imagination is nothing other than a ratiocination that traverses the paths of the semantic labyrinth in a hurry and, in its haste, loses the sense of their rigid structure.[52]

In precisely the same way, in this study I use "cultural maps" to demonstrate the complex interpenetration of symbols in the "period of consensus" at the heart of the Spanish transition. These "cultural maps" (first presented on p. 43) do not represent individual shared "values" or internalized "ideologies" at the level of personality; rather, they exemplify cultural *patterns* that are commonly intelligible and widely accessible. Like linguistic systems, these cultural patterns tend to work at a relatively unconscious level (what Giddens calls "practical consciousness"[53]). In other words, just as a speaker unknowingly draws upon a range of syntactical and other rules in order to utter a sentence and in the process of drawing upon those rules reproduces the overall totality which is the language, so is there a massive conceptual arena geared into the continuities of day-to-day social life and whose knowledgeability is expressed in practice.

Yet, for both Eco and myself, these diagrams have a purely orientative value. A bidimensional graph cannot wholly reproduce – indeed, it impoverishes – the associations in terms of both number and dimensions. I illustrate this fluidity and multivocality in my maps by using curved lines and few fixed points. The idea is that each symbol can and is linked to various other symbolic networks; these maps merely show a rough estimation of one dimension of symbolization at a fixed point in time.[54]

Thus far I have proposed that we take sense-making seriously, and systematically explore the subjective as well as objective dimensions of motivation and action. But of course, "culture," is a methodological as well as a theoretical morass. The obvious question is, how do we rigorously analyze "root beliefs," "symbols," or "ultimate values"?

Today cultural sociologists have increasingly turned to discourse analysis to get a handle on subjectivity. As Ricoeur first pointed out, the premise of textual analysis is that writing elevates "saying" to "what is said." Writing frees itself from its author and the narrowness of the dialogical situation; from this "objectivity" derives the possibility of explaining the text.[55] Thus, the goal of discourse analysis is not to "rejoin the author," but to understand the non-ostensive reference – "the world of the text." Most importantly, this world is not hidden behind the text, it is "disclosed in front of it."

The media is a particularly important site for cultural analysis because the media is both a major forum for the dissemination of news and a major forum for the construction of meaning.[56] In Durkheimian terms, the parameters of the media are not only political and economic, but are also "religious" – the media reflects and reworks the basic categories of the sacred and the profane. The "sacred" is the emotionally charged symbol of the good; the "profane" is its symbolic opposite, the emotionally charged symbol of the bad, which in the religious realm is denoted by evil. These emotionally charged symbols contrast with routine signs that lack this heightened affect.[57]

This processing function of the media works alongside – it is intertwined with – the media's more obvious institutional parameters. But this processing function is especially significant in times of crisis or rapid social change. In ambiguous, rapidly changing situations, people look to the media to establish reality, and to define and interpret events going on around them.

In the case of the Spanish transition, this processing function of the media was particularly salient. Newspapers and magazines began to appear in the twilight of the Franco regime that explicitly sought to redefine Spanish society. The name of one of the leading journals in the process of democratization, *Cambio 16* ("Change 16"), established in 1972, explicitly proclaims this goal (sixteen people focused on change).[58] As the president of *Cambio 16*, Juan Tomás de Salas stated:

> We were more than a publication, we were more than simple witnesses, because in our pages was a true parliament: the free parliament that had been prohibited by Franco . . . We were never impartial. We spoke of reality and pursued the facts with the obsession of newspapermen in normal conditions, and only formally hid the fact that the regime had to fall.[59]

A cultural analysis of the Spanish transition

This book is based on the systematic analysis of several different Spanish newspapers during the so-called "period of consensus" at the heart of the Spanish transition (April 1977 – December 1978). The most important newspaper in this study as well as the transition itself is *El País*. *El País* was begun in May 1976 by a group of investors who formed a company specifically for this purpose.[60] It self-consciously set out to be *the* newspaper of the democratic transition. *El País* sought not only to educate the Spanish public in democratic matters by providing articles on the mechanics of voting and commentaries by prominent political leaders, etc., but explicitly pushed the government in a democratic direction. On the second anniversary of *El País*, editor-in chief Juan Luis Cebrián wrote:

> Today one can say without doubt that the press has been an effective instrument of dialogue and social collaboration at the moment of change and that there has been an honest and sincere effort of media professionals in order to help in establishing a regime of public liberties. It [*El País*] was able to popularize and promote, often alone, demands for political amnesty or for legalization of the Communist Party, both of which were necessary conditions for the establishment of a democracy.[61]

The other newspapers in this study – *El Alcázar, El Socialista, Mundo Obrero, Deia,* and *Egin* – were less widely read papers with specific political ideological and/or regional affiliations.[62] These newspapers are important not so much for the numbers of people they reached, but because they reflect a specific political or national/regional textual "world," and enable the comparison of specific and generalized symbols and meanings.

In analyzing these newspapers, I focused on three crucial moments of consensus: the three months preceding the first democratic elections of June 1977; the month of the drafting of the Moncloa Pacts in October 1977; and the last four months of the drafting of the 1978 Constitution. For each of these periods, I read and analyzed every article or editorial that (1) was by or about any political, ecclesiastical, or other (e.g. royal, trade union) elite; (2) indicated the official or unofficial position of major or minor political parties, groups, or unions; or (3) concerned the specific event at hand. Of utmost importance were the leaders and ideological position of the four major political parties during the transition: the conservative Alianza Popular (Popular Alliance, AP), founded in 1976 by former Franco ministers and led by Manuel Fraga Iribarne; the Partido Comunista Español (Spanish Communist Party, PCE), founded in 1920 and led by Santiago Carrillo; the Partido Socialista Obrero Español (Spanish Socialist Workers' Party, PSOE), founded in 1879, but newly emerged in the transition period and led by Felipe González; the centrist government party, Unión del Centro Democrático (Union of the Democratic Center, UCD) formed in 1977 under the leadership of Prime Minister Adolfo Suárez.

In the first stage of analysis, I summarized each article or editorial, and pulled out salient symbols and representations. Of course, even at this early stage I was aware that I was selecting what *I* thought was important about each text. In my view, this awareness is crucial in the process of text interpretation. The text interpreter must consciously go back and forth, reading, interpreting, and rereading each text. He or she must continually ask if what s/he finds "most important" about a particular text is at the center of what the article is "about," and if she has construed the text in the "best" way (because there are many ways of construing a text). This specific plurivocity of the text means that it is possible to argue for or against an interpretation, to confront interpretations, to arbitrate between them. Analysis does not "prove" that a particular interpretation is true; it shows that "an interpretation is more probable in light of what is known."[63]

In the second stage of analysis, I reread my notes, reviewed the original sources, and revised my analytical categories. While there were many different symbols for analysis, four different, albeit intertwined, representations clearly stood "in front of" the texts. These were abstract, generalized symbols, employed in different ways, in different situations, by different authors, but which nevertheless exemplified a transcendent strand of shared meaning. These symbols were: (1) "a new beginning," (2) "Civil War," (3) "national reconciliation"/"*convivencia*," and (4) "democracy."

In this book, we will see that the symbols of "a new beginning," "national reconciliation"/"*convivencia*," "democracy," and "Civil War" were intertwined in competing political ideologies in distinctive ways – thus causing important divisions. Nevertheless, these symbols contained strands of shared meaning, which became the specific tenets or ground rules of the politics of consensus. In addition, these strands of shared meaning (or symbols) became representations of the ritual process of transition.

The ritual process of transition

Victor Turner is probably the most important anthropologist to follow Durkheim in pointing out the parallel between primitive ritual processes and those of contemporary society.[64] Expanding on the work of Van Gennep, Turner points out that, in conjunction with their individual purposes, all rites of birth, initiation, marriage, and the like have an overall goal: to ensure a change of condition or a passage from one magico-religious or secular group to another. Three phases make up this generic ritual process: separation, liminality, and reaggregation. The first phase, separation, comprises symbolic behavior signifying the detachment of the individual or group from an earlier fixed point in the social structure. During the intervening "liminal" period, the characteristics of the ritual subject are an ambiguous blend of lowliness and sacrality, or homogeneity and comradeship. In the third phase, reaggregation, the passage is consummated. The ritual subject is expected to behave in accordance with the norms and ethical standards of the new social state.[65]

What I am proposing here is that, like individual rites of passage, politico-historical transitions are a ritual process consisting of phases of separation, liminality, and reaggregation. Specifically, like their individual counterparts, a political transition is by definition a "liminal" stage between two distinct social states, and the goal of political transition is the successful putting behind of the old, and the consummation of the new social state.

Yet, there are two crucial differences between primitive rites of passage and politico-historical transitions. Modern politico-historical transitions are not predetermined structural processes; they occur largely through representations of separation, liminality, and reaggregation. In addition, modern societal transitions are far less linear and far more contingent than individual rites of passage. Modern ritual processes are not proscribed; they are achieved, often against great odds.

In the case of the Spanish transition, we will see that the newly emerging sacred transitional symbols enabled the completion of the ritual process of transition. Specifically, the "new beginning" came to symbolize the ritual aspect of separation, as the sacred new beginning meant the putting behind of the old Francoist era, and setting out on a new course for the future. "National reconciliation"/"*convivencia*" came to symbolize the sacred homogeneity and communality of the liminal state. And "democracy" came to symbolize the sacred end social state of reaggregation.

Where did the core symbols of the Spanish transition come from? How did they become embedded in what became known as the "politics of consensus"? Before we further explore Spanish transitional symbolization, we need to place the Spanish democratic transition in historical context.

3

Spain: a history of divisions and democracy

The sacred transitional representations that emerged and penetrated Spanish society after Franco's death were rooted deep in Spanish history. This is a history rife with religious, regional, and class divisions, and long epochs of political instability.[1]

Early Spanish history

The Iberian peninsula has been inhabited and reinhabited by many different peoples in the last 5,000 years, and overall, as Strabo first noted, the Iberian peoples have tended to be "bad mixers."[2] In the third century, Roman legions came and captured the peninsula (which had been inhabited by Nordic Celts in the upper third of the Peninsula and tribes from Africa in the south) and dominated it for four centuries. The Romans were followed by various Germanic tribes, until the Arabs came and defeated the Germanic Visigoths in AD 711 and dominated the peninsula throughout the Middle Ages.[3]

The Arabs failed however, to conquer the least Romanized peoples of the remote areas of the Cantabrian mountains. And it was in these mountains that the eight-century-long "*Reconquista*," or "Reconquest," of the Iberian peninsula began. The *Reconquista* fused the two great driving forces of medieval times – war and religion – into one mammoth religious war. According to Crow, no other European country experienced a similar period.[4]

In 1480, King Ferdinand and Isabella the Catholic attempted to complete the religious unity of Spain by setting up the infamous Spanish Inquisition. Originally designed for the express purpose of examining the sincerity of Jewish converts (called *marranos*), the Inquisition quickly gathered momentum and eventually led to the persecution of the entire Jewish population of the peninsula, and later, under the pretext of a Moorish incursion in Spanish territory, the slaughter or expulsion of the entire *Morisco* (Moorish) population. Yet the ignominy of the "Spanish Inquisition" was not merely its proportions but its length: the Inquisition spanned over four centuries, and was not officially abolished until 1820.[5]

Under the reign of *los reyes católicos*, Ferdinand and Isabella, Spain blended the religious and Catholic unity of medieval days with the centralization of power in the crown and the hegemony of the Castilian region.[6] But even in its "golden age" Castilian power was never as absolute as many history books maintain.[7] Isolated communites in the north (e.g. Aragon, Navarre, and the Basque Country) held fast to their own traditions; Catalonia (an imperial empire in its own right in the previous era[8]) retained its own independent institutions, currency, customs, and tax system throughout the sixteenth and seventeenth centuries; and rebellions against the Spanish monarchy broke out in both the Basque Country and Catalonia in the seventeenth and early eighteenth centuries. In 1640, a full-fledged revolution in Catalonia turned into a twelve-year war (called the "War of Separation"), in which the Spanish Viceroy was assassinated, and Catalonia declared its independence from the King of Spain. The War of Separation ended with Catalonia's defeat; but it enabled Portugal to cut free from Spain.[9]

The nineteenth century was one of continuous political turmoil in Spain. The Bourbons brought in French, liberal ideas, but the attempt to "Europeanize" Spain was resisted by many Spaniards. The struggle between French liberalism and traditional Spanish monarchy became manifest in 1808, when Napoleon made his own brother, Joseph Bonaparte (José I), King of Spain. The idea of a foreign king enraged the Spanish populace, and on May 2, 1808, they rose in revolt. The bloody rebellion (memorialized in Goya's masterpiece *Executions of May 3, 1808*) turned into the Peninsular War, called the War of Independence in Spain.

A long series of wars, known as the Carlist wars, raged from 1833 to 1874. These wars pitted rural Basque and Catalan peasants who sought to defend their local liberties against liberals who controlled the government in Madrid and were trying to centralize Spanish administration. The Carlist wars ended with the Carlists' defeat, but a military *pronunciamiento* in 1868 quickly put an end to the liberal government. A monarchy was established, but it failed, and a republic was set up. Four republican presidents and less than one year later, the army took over and established a military dictatorship.[10]

The chaotic alterations in the Spanish government in the nineteenth century were transported to the Spanish colonies. By the turn of the century, the Spanish empire had completely collapsed. Cuba, Puerto Rico, Guam, and the Philippines were lost, and the Spanish military was humiliated by Cuban rebels. Basque and Catalan industrialists lost their foreign markets, and the alienated intelligentsia and workers throughout Spain grew increasingly hostile.[11]

Part and parcel of the political turmoil in Spain in the nineteenth century were serious economic divisions. Class was a particularly salient category in the industrializing northern as well as the agrarian southern regions. While throughout the 1800s most farms in the north were less than 10 hectares, the south was dominated by large estates (more than 100 hectares) worked by a large population of landless laborers, hired mostly on a daily basis – at wages usually half or less than the national average. This system of patent exploitation resulted in frequent protest and conflict in agrarian Spain. Robberies, crop burnings, and banditry, as well as intermittent revolts – e.g. Seville in 1857; Loja (Granada) in 1861; Montilla (Córdoba) in 1873; Jerez de la Frontera (Cádiz) in 1892 – were rampant.[12] Meanwhile, in northern cities, particularly Barcelona, anarchism (and later anarchosyndicalism) emerged and gained ground.[13] Although anarchosyndicalism did not gain a mass base until after the First World War, anarchist "propaganda deeds" resulted in the death of Prime Ministers Antonio Cánovas del Castillo in 1897 and José Canalejas in 1912, and there were anarchist attempts to kill Prime Minister Antonio Maura in 1904, and King Alfonso XIII in 1905 and 1906.[14]

In the socially polarized agrarian south, as well as in the major urban centers and industrial zones, the Church was considered the property of the ruling class; and the agrarian as well as industrial poor grew increasingly anti-clerical in the late nineteenth and early twentieth centuries. The situation was more complex than a wealthy Church versus working-class anti-clericals, however. Rural poor tended to support the Church, especially in Castile; and anti-clericalism was also rampant among the upper classes, particularly the urban intellectuals. To complicate the situation even further, class and clerical issues intersected with regional ones, especially in the northern regions of Catalonia and the Basque Country.[15]

Nowhere were the volatile intertwined issues of Church, class, and region more evident than in *Semana Trágica* ("Tragic Week"), the last week of July 1909. During this week a general strike called by workers in Barcelona turned into a mass revolt, in which over fifty churches, convents, church schools, and welfare institutions were burned, and some eighty-three people lost their lives.[16] *Semana Trágica* ended with the public execution of the anarchist intellectual Francisco Ferrer, but a severe repression followed and after that anarchosyndicalism grew even more volatile. According to Esenwein and Shubert, Barcelona was the scene of an "all-out class war" between 1919 and 1923, featuring massive general strikes, lockouts, and *pistolerismo* (gang warfare).[17]

In 1923 General Primo de Rivera took matters into his own hands by declaring a military *pronunciamiento*. Primo de Rivera's "temporary dictatorship" (originally stipulated as "ninety days") turned into nine long years, however, during which time Primo de Rivera not only lost the support of his former allies, but important sectors of the military. With part of the military actively conspiring against him, Primo de Rivera consented to a royal request for his resignation in 1930.[18] In April 1931, a leftist Republican–Socialist alliance won the national elections, and King Alfonso XIII fled from Spain. Without bloodshed, Spain had begun its "first democracy."[19]

The Second Republic (1931–1936)

The republicans won the national elections of 1931, but Spain was virtually split between a republican/socialist/anarchist left and a conservative/monarchist/religious right. Consequently, "the Second Republic" actually consisted of three distinct, reactionary moments: the Republic of the Republicans (1931–1933); the conservative *bienio negro* ("black biennium, 1934–1935"); and the short-lived Popular Front (1936).

In the first period, the victorious Republican–Socialist alliance headed by Manuel Azaña acted quickly and aggressively to grant Catalan autonomy, institute agrarian reform, and separate Church and State. Between April 28 and July 14, 1931 the Republicans issued six decrees dealing with agrarian reform, announced freedom of religion, prohibited public processions for Corpus Christi, and ended compulsory religious education. The Republicans also established an autonomous executive power, the Generalitat, in Barcelona for all four Catalan provinces.[20] The 1931 Constitution eliminated the government's financial support of the Church, restricted the amount of land the Church could own, required the Church to inform the government of all their investments and to pay taxes, prohibited Church involvement in education, and stated that Spain had no official religion – the first such declaration in the country's history.[21]

The Church hierachy reacted harshly to the new Republican government. The Archbishop of Toledo referred to the Republican victory as a triumph of "the enemies of the Kingdom of Jesus Christ,"[22] and the Church issued a declaration saying that the new Constitution was not binding on Catholics, as it forced them to violate the laws of the Church (in particular, parents' obligation to have their children educated in Catholic schools), and implying that Catholic deputies who had voted for the new law were in danger of being excommunicated. Meanwhile, the Catholic monarchist right encouraged landowners to "declare all out war on the Republic" by ignoring the new land reform rules, not paying wages owed to workers, and by refusing to cultivate their land.[23]

In February 1933, a conservative coalition called the Confederación Española de Derechas Autónomas (CEDA – Spanish Confederation of the Antonomous Right) was formed; fighting in its first election in November 1933, the CEDA emerged as the single largest party with 115 seats, and the Radicals (a right-wing group) improved from 89 to 104.[24] The Spanish Socialist Workers' Party (PSOE) were reduced from 117 to 58 deputies, the Republicans were all but wiped out, and the Radical Socialists, who had split into three factions before the elections, disappeared.[25]

Thus, while in the spring of 1931, the left had been united and euphoric with the creation of the Republic and the right had been discredited and in disarray, two years later the tides had turned. Now the alliance of the left had disintegrated while the right had a well-organized and well-financed party with a charismatic leader.[26]

The Republic of the Right (1934–1935) is known as the *bienio negro* – a period of polarization and confrontation, a rehearsal for the coming Civil War. This period is epitomized by the Asturian revolt of October 1934, an event since deemed the "most substantial revolutionary episode in twenti-eth-century Europe after the Russian Revolution."[27] The revolt began in the coal mines in Asturias but quickly turned into a full-fledged revolution. Approximately 1,200 rebels lost their lives, as did approximately 450 members of the army troops, coordinated by General Francisco Franco.[28]

The October revolution was immediately followed by a fierce and wide-ranging repression. At least 30,000 were imprisoned, the socialist press was banned, and municipal governments far from the insurrection were left suspended, as was the Catalan autonomy statute. The harsh repression abetted the coalescence of the various leftist groups, however. In February 1936, a leftist coalition called the Frente Popular (Popular Front) won the national elections, and Manuel Azaña again became prime minister. The pendulum swung back to enforcement of the Republican laws (which had never been repealed). Agrarian reform, the closure of religious schools, and the confiscation of Jesuit property took place at a more rapid pace than ever before, while in the cities, church burnings and other anti-clerical attacks continued.[29]

The Spanish Civil War

The Spanish Civil War began on July 18, 1936 with an attempted military coup. The revolt was not completely successful, however, and it quickly turned into civil war. In Madrid and Barcelona, the working classes, supported by members of the *Guardia Civil* (Civil Guards) and *Guardia de Asalto* (shock troops/riot police), successfully resisted the insurrection despite the fact that the President of the autonomous Catalan government in Barcelona, Lluis Companys, and his counterpart in Madrid, Prime Minister Casares Quiroga, adamantly refused to issue arms to civilians. Anarchists and left-socialists interpreted the government's reluctance to arm them as actions typical of a bourgeois government, and became determined not to simply defend the bourgeois government, but to instill a new society.[30]

Except for the Basque country, which was largely undisturbed, industrial collectives sprang up in nearly every corner of the Republican zone, including the urban centers of Barcelona, Madrid, and Valencia, and the rural regions of Aragon, the Levante, and Andalusia. A new morality manifest itself in a multiplicity of ways: taxi drivers, barbers, and waiters refused tips with pride; luxury hotels were converted to barracks or communal dining halls (as in the case of the famous Ritz Hotel in Barcelona). Worker management was proclaimed on large signs on countless cafes, shops, and businesses. Taxis, cars, kiosks, and trams were emblazoned with the initials and identifying colors of the different workers' parties (CNT–FAI, Confederación Nacional de Trabajo – Federación Anarquista Ibérica, UGT, Unión General de Trabajadores, POUM, Partido Obrero de Unificación Marxista, PSUC, Partit Socialista Unificat de Catalunya). As far as the revolutionaries were concerned the days of privilege, egoism, hate, envy, and other "bourgeois values" had been banished forever.[31]

Yet, the new morality of the revolution was juxtaposed with the old axiom of violence and a belief in the necessity of purging the rearguard of undesirable elements. Literally thousands of "class enemies" were executed in the first months of the Civil War; some estimate that as many as 80,000 people were assassinated during the Republican or "Red" repression. Another of the tragic consequences of the "revolutionary excesses" was the vicious assault on the Catholic Church, a grisly onslaught that resulted in the destruction of countless religious buildings and the deaths of over 6,800 members of the clergy (inluding some 280 nuns).[32]

Of course, the Nationalists had their own forms of unmitigated brutality. Their acceptance of the concept of "total war" resulted in the deaths of thousands of civilians. The rebel officers declared martial law in occupied territories, proclaimed that all opposed to "the Movement" were in a state of rebellion, and sent thousands to the firing squads via hastily set-up military courts. Thus, the horrors of the Civil War are marked by their seeming rationality as well as irrationality: if the "Red" repression tends to be perceived as (irrational) "frenzied clerical bloodletting"; the horror of the "White repression" was that it was "systematically carried out under the ubiquitous gaze of the recognized authorities."[33] This perception as to the "the horrors of the Spanish Civil War" (on both sides) will be discussed further in the next chapter.

Francoism

When the Spanish Civil War ended in April 1939, hundreds of thousands of Spaniards and tens of thousands of foreigners had died, and Franco had achieved total military and political victory.[34] Nevertheless, April 1939 saw not the beginning of peace or reconciliation but the institutionalization of full-scale vengeance against the defeated left. Hundreds of thousands of Republicans were subsequently imprisoned, tortured, or killed; the last official victim, Julián Grimau, was not executed until April 20, 1963.[35]

The Civil War continued to permeate Spanish life in other ways too. Franco introduced a plethora of war holidays, including April 1, "The Day of Victory"; April 17, "The Day of Unification"; July 18, "The Day of the Uprising"; October 1, "The Day of the Caudillo"; and October 29, "The Day of the Fallen." Franco also constructed obtrusive monuments to the War, such as the Victory Arch at the entrance to the University City in Madrid, and the massive mausoleum, monastery, and basilica (with 500-foot cross) Valle de los Caídos (Valley of the Fallen), carved into the hillside of the Valle de Cuelgamuros in the Sierra de Guadarrama outside Madrid.[36]

From economic autarchy to occidental capitalism

Spain was a poor, agricultural country before the Civil War. After the War was over, Franco instituted a policy of economic autarchy and protectionism. The result was that prices rose faster than wages in the 1940s, and per capita income was cut by nearly one-fifth compared with 1936.[37]

Beginning in the early 1950s, however, Spain began to emerge from her economic and political isolation. Anti-communism created a basis for establishing relations with the United States. In 1952, Spain entered UNESCO (United Nations Educational, Scientific, and Cultural Organization); in 1953, Spain entered the International Labor Organization and sent a contingent to fight with the anti-communist forces of the Korean War; and in 1955 Spain was admitted to the United Nations. Between 1953 and 1963 American economic aid (including credits) would come to $1,688 million, to which was added $521million in military assistance.[38]

Yet, despite the influx of American dollars, Spain faced serious economic problems.[39] In 1957, Franco completely reorganized his cabinet and brought in the technocrats of the lay Catholic institute, Opus Dei: Alberto Ullastres at the Ministry of Commerce, Mariano Navarro Rubio at the Ministry of Finance, and Laureano López Rodó in the key post of head of the Technical Secretariat of the Presidency of the Government. The model the technocrats adopted was, as Carr and Fusi state, "taken from the recipe book of orthodox capitalism."[40] The technocrats opened the country up to foreign investment, froze wages, and limited credit, and forced Spain into greater reliance on export earnings.[41]

Economic liberalization allowed Spain to participate in the global boom of the 1960s. From 1959 to 1973, real GNP (Gross National Product) grew at an annual rate of 7.3 percent, the highest in the OECD except for Japan and Greece. Per capita income more than doubled in real terms.[42] The Spanish economy was refueled from abroad: by tourist earnings, by the remittances of émigrés working abroad, and by foreign loans. By the early 1970s, southern Spain had become northern Europe's "sun playgound"; and one out of every five jobs in Spain was financed by foreign investment.[43] But Spanish corporations such as El Corte Inglés (the department-store chain, "The English Cut"), emerged and grew as well. Today one of the richest and most solid private companies in Spain, El Corte Inglés became a "market success" by instituting long shopping hours, instigating prolific advertising campaigns (especially billboards), and, as its very name attests, capitalizing on (and reaffirming) the bourgeois and Western aspirations of Spaniards.[44]

From National Catholicism to Vatican II

The explicit goal of the Nationalist crusade was to reinstitute the pre-eminence of the Catholic Church, and by the end of the war in July 1939 all vestiges of the separation of Church and State had been wiped out. The Catholic Church was put back in charge of education; and from 1939 to the 1970s all private relationships and public rituals had to be conducted in accordance with Church doctrine.[45] A rigorous system of censorship was established, although, significantly, the Church itself was exempt, and Catholic Action groups were allowed to "freely carry out their apostolate."[46] A Concordat between Franco and the Vatican signed in 1953 affirmed the exalted role of the Catholic Church, and brought Francoism a measure of international respectability.

For the first two decades of his regime, Franco enjoyed the explicit support of the Catholic Church. But Franco's relationship with the Church changed profoundly after the death of one of his closest allies, Pope Pius XIII. The successors to Pope Pius (Pope John XXIII and Pope Paul VI) took a very different approach to the pontificate. In his final encyclical in 1963 (*Pacem in terris*), Pope John XXIII advocated peaceful co-existence, freedom of speech, freedom of communication, freedom of association, and basic civil rights, including the right of a people to choose those who govern them – an indirect (if not a direct) criticism of Francoism. Of even more impact than the encyclical was the Second Vatican Council of October 1962. The Council made no alterations in formal theology, yet it accepted the modernist critique of the Church and espoused many of the values of secular liberal society, including religious liberty.[47]

Ironically, the privileges of the Church established by the 1953 Concordat allowed younger clergy as well as regional clerics who were dramatically influenced by Vatican II to question the intimate relationship between the Catholic Church and the Francoist state and pointedly to condemn Francoist society. Thus, in May 1960, 339 Basque priests signed an open letter to the regional bishops protesting the Church's close alliance with the Francoist state. In 1963, the Abbot of Monserrat, Dom Aureli Escarré, publicly denounced the regime as it prepared for its celebration of "Twenty-five Years of Peace." While the Abbot was subsequently forced to retire, thereafter younger clerics became increasingly militant.[48]

Beginning in the late 1960s, divisions between Church and State became more profound as the Vatican began systematically to bypass the elderly, conservative clergy for younger, more liberal priests in making senior appointments. In 1969 Pope Paul VI appointed the moderate Mgr. Enrique Tarancón Archbishop of Toledo and Primate of Spain; and shortly thereafter, Tarancón became Archbishop of Madrid, and president of the Episcopal conference. While Tarancón was certainly no radical, he would become a critical source of moderation in the post-Franco period.[49]

In sum, the most striking aspect of the Spanish Church in the late 1960s and early 1970s was its tremendous ambiguity. Large numbers of clergy were abandoning the Church or in open revolt, but the formal structure of Catholicism remained largely the same.[50] Over 90 percent of Spanish bishops present at Vatican II had been ordained before the Civil War, and most came out against the new teachings. The Franco regime blithely sustained its national Catholic identity to its dying day: three bishops sat as Franco's personal appointees in the regime's last parliament, and an archbishop sat in the government's Council of State and Council of the Realm.[51] Most paradoxically, a special jail (*cárcel concordatoria*) was set up in Zamora in 1969 to house renegade clergy.[52]

Put another way, Vatican II impacted the social, cultural and spiritual bases of Spanish Catholicism far more deeply than it impacted the "institution" of the Catholic Church. And, ironically, many of the lay organizations that Franco helped set up grew to oppose him. Such is the case with the apostolic workers' organizations HOAC (Hermandades Obreras de Acción Católica, Workers' Brotherhood of Catholic Action) and JOC (Juventudes Obreras Católicas, Catholic Workers' Youth), started in 1946 to "recuperate the working world for Christ," i.e. co-opt the militant workers' organizations where anarchosyndicalism and socialism had been predominant. In the 1960s, dissident activists from HOAC and JOC began to abandon their service orientation and merge with dissident workers from the single Francoist syndical organization, the Organización Sindical Española (OSE, Spanish Syndicate Organization). Workers committees (called *jurados*) had begun to emerge out of the OSE as early as 1947; and by the late 1950s, the legal *jurados* evolved into clandestine "workers' commissions" (Comisiones Obreras, CCOO) and increasingly engaged in decentralized collective bargaining.[53]

In 1966, the CCOO "came out" and became a permanent and national movement affiliated with the Spanish Communist Party (PCE, Partido Comunista Español). The result was both an increase in worker militancy and the broadening of the workers' agenda. Workers fought not only for higher wages and better conditions of work, but also for "democracy." In 1966, Spain lost 1.5 million working hours through strikes; this number grew to 8.7 million in 1970, and 14.5 million in 1975, making Spain the third-highest country in Europe in strike activity, even though nearly all strikes were still illegal.[54]

Not only workers, but students "came out" against the regime as well. As early as 1956, strikes broke out in Madrid University and a number of students were arrested. Franco dismissed the Minister of Education, the progressive Catholic Joaquín Ruiz Giménez, as well as the Rector of Madrid University, Laín Entralgo (a Ruiz Giménez appointee). But many of these student protestors (as well as Ruiz Giménez and Laín Entralgo) would go on to become important members of the democratic opposition.[55]

The high point of the opposition was the Congress of Munich of 1962, in which 118 delegates agreed to work for "the establishment of institutions authentically representative and democratic which will guarantee that the government is based upon the consent of the people."[56] Yet, the Congress of Munich did not have significant organizational effects; and the opposition was no more organized in the early 1970s than it had been in the late 1940s.[57]

Moreover, predictably, the rise of the student opposition and the "coming out" of the CCOO led to a wave of repression. Indeed, in the years from 1967 to 1973 Spain witnessed the most heavy and widespread repression since the early years of the regime. Between 1968 and 1973 at least 500 workers' leaders were imprisoned; and the regime declared three States of Emergency. In the first two months of 1974, 24,817 workers were laid off without pay and 4,379 were dismissed for political reasons.[58]

More ominously, the harsh repression spurred on militant opposition groups, most importantly, the Basque nationalist group ETA (Euzkadi ta Azkatasuna, Basque Homeland and Freedom) founded in 1959, and the Marxist terrorist organization of Madrid, FRAP (Frente Revolucionario Antifascista Patriótico, Anti-fascist Revolutionary Patriotic Front), founded in 1968. In 1968 a series of gun battles between ETA members and Civil Guards culminated in the assassination of Melitón Manzanas, a hated police commissioner. The Spanish government imposed a "State of Exception," (whereby certain rights are suspended), arrested more than two thousand Basque residents, and sentenced six *etarras* (ETA activists) to death.[59] This was the beginning of a "spiral of violence," which led to more arrests, trials, shootings, kidnappings, and bombings, and ultimately, the assassination of Prime Minister Luis Carrero Blanco in 1973.[60]

The twilight of the Franco regime

From 1936 to 1973, Francisco Franco was Head of State, Prime Minister as well as *Generalísimo* (Supreme Commander) of the Armed Forces. His right-hand man and confidant throughout most of those years was Admiral Luis Carrero Blanco. Carrero Blanco proclaimed "absolute loyalty" to Franco; he was Franco's *"alter ego."*[61] In 1969, Franco appointed Carrero Blanco Vice-President; in June 1973, now 80 years old and ailing, Franco made Carrero Blanco President (Prime Minister).[62] But on December 20, 1973 Prime Minister Carrero Blanco and his two Civil Guard escorts were assassinated in Madrid by the Basque separatist group ETA. This was the most serious governmental crisis in the history of the Franco regime. Forced immediately to choose another Prime Minister, Franco finally decided on a relatively obscure member of Carrero Blanco's cabinet, Carlos Arias Navarro.

In the twenty-three months between his appointment in December 1973 and Franco's death in November 1975, Arias Navarro fluctuated between encouraging speeches promising reform, and repressive, reactionary measures. For instance, on February 12, 1974, Arias Navarro made an impressive speech promising an immediate democratic "opening up" of the regime, which led to the coining of the phrase "spirit of 12 February" to refer to reform. Yet, merely weeks later, the government placed the Bishop of Bilbao, Mgr. Antonio Anoveros, under house arrest for a moderate homily about Basque cultural freedom; executed a young Catalan anarchist, named Salvador Puig Antich; and dismissed the Chief of the Army General Staff, a leading advocate of the political neutrality of the army.[63]

By the spring of 1975, it seemed the "spirit of 12 February" was completely dead. Arias Navarro rejected any suggestion of constitutional reform, and, after a series of terrorist actions, declared martial law in the Basque Country. Martial law unleashed a repression unlike anything seen before. On August 27, 1975, the government passed a new Anti-terrorist Law, which made the death penalty mandatory for terrorists. One month later the new law was applied to five ETA and FRAP militants.[64]

The transition to democracy

Franco died on November 20, 1975, after a long and drawn-out illness. In the first year after Franco's death, it was not clear in which direction Spain was headed. Although Franco had declared Spain a monarchy in 1947, he rejected the true heir to the throne, the son of Alfonso XIII, Don Juan de Borbón, in exile in Portugal, because Don Juan was an open supporter of liberalism. Franco did not officially resolve the monarchy problem until 1969, when he chose Don Juan's son, Juan Carlos, as Prince of Spain.[65] Juan Carlos had lived under Franco's aegis for more than a decade, and, in addition to his university studies, he had received training in all three branches of the armed forces. On his deathbed in November 1975, Franco finally handed over his powers to Juan Carlos, and Juan Carlos swore personal loyalty to Franco and the principles of the Movement (the Movimiento, the only legal political party under Franco).[66]

Certainly, the first disappointment for many Spaniards was the king's reappointment of Arias Navarro as prime minister. Arias Navarro's infamous ambiguity infuriated both Francoist reformists (*aperturistas*) and hardliners (*continuistas*), as well as the democratic opposition. By early 1976, most of the hitherto clandestine political parties had come out into the open, and were holding congresses, distributing manifestos, and calling for the pardon of political prisoners. In the first three months of 1976 alone, there were reportedly 17,731 strikes and street demonstrations.[67] At the same time, however, the terrorist campaigns of ETA and FRAP continued to increase. In March 1976, five protestors died after police opened fire on a crowd in Vitoria, provoking a general strike in the Basque Country.

In July 1976, King Juan Carlos finally forced Arias to resign. He was replaced by the king's own designee, Adolfo Suárez, who headed a completely new cabinet. Suárez was a political unknown; he had never held a high position in the administration of the State, though he had risen within the Movimiento hierarchy to the position of secretary. Opposition leaders had grave doubts about Suárez's reformist intentions, while Francoists were reassured by his appointment, based on his success in the Movimiento.[68]

Nevertheless, under the leadership of King Juan Carlos and Adolfo Suárez, Spain made significant strides toward democracy. The Suárez government replaced Arias Navarro's dubious "reform" strategy with a consensual strategy of reform, called significantly, *reforma-pactada* ("negotiated reform") by the government, and *ruptura-pactada* ("negotiated break") by the opposition. The first major accomplishment of the Suárez government was the Law of Political Reform, which was passed by the Cortes (parliament) in November 1976 and submitted to the Spanish people in a referendum on December 16, 1976. Some 78 percent of the electorate took part in the referendum, and 94.2 percent gave their approval.[69]

The Law of Political Reform paved the way for a "period of consensus" unlike anything seen previously in Spanish history – a relatively peaceful, quiescent period of moderation and reform, which resulted in the first democratic elections of June 1977, and the successful drafting of the 1978 Constitution. In the remaining chapters of this book, we explore the symbolic impetus of this pivotal "consensual" period. The question is, in light of Spain's turbulent history, forty years of dictatorship, and the ambiguity of the post-Franco state, what was the basis of this extraordinary, historic "militant pacifism"?

PART II

The symbolic basis of Spanish consensus

4

The spirit of consensus: the core representations of the Spanish transition

The spirit of the Spanish "politics of consensus" was rooted in four core intertwined symbols: "a new beginning" of "democracy" and "national reconciliation" and their symbolic opposite, (profane) "Civil War." These core symbols are illustrated in Figure 4.1. As discussed in chapter 2 (pp. 20–21), this "cultural map" illuminates the central cultural pattern, or basic conceptual arena, of the transition. These core symbols are linked to, but not at all the same as, shared "values." Symbols (unlike "values") are multivocal and contingent; symbols can be manipulated, reworked, and interchanged. The term "representation" is often used synonomously with "symbol." However, as reflected in Table 4.1, "representation" refers not only to symbols, but ritual processes and events (e.g. the first democratic elections). Thus "representation" is more inclusive than "symbol"; and it reflects the *process* of perception and cognition (or "symbolization"). As we will see, these four intertwined symbols were the basis of both the *strategic* ground rules of the politics of consensus, and the *ritual process* of the Spanish transition (see Table 4.1).

The new beginning

Times of crisis are opportunities to reaffirm as well as to rethink and reformulate fundamental values.[1] This generalization away from the specificity of everyday life often takes the form of expressions of a new temporality. Hunt, for example, points out the centrality of symbols of "rebirth" in the French Revolution.[2] Turner describes the state of liminality that exists during transitional periods as a "moment in and out of time."[3]

In the case of Spain, the valuation of Franco's death – whether it was good or bad – was hardly consensual, but Franco's death evoked a transcendent understanding of temporal separation. Franco's death was

Table 4.1. *Core representations of the Spanish transition*

Ritual phase	Core ritual event	Core symbol (sacred)	Core symbol (profane)
Separation	1977 Elections	*New Beginning*	*Civil War*
Liminality	Drafting of Moncloa Pacts	*National Reconciliation Convivencia*	*Civil War*
Reaggregation	Drafting of 1978 Constitution	*Democracy*	*Civil War Dictatorship*

universally interpreted as "the close of a chapter, and the beginning of a new one" in Spanish history. Recall that Franco had been the Head of the Government, Head of State, Generalissimo of the Armed Forces, and Chief (*Jefe*) of the only legal political party ("The Movement") for nearly forty years. As Franco moved in and out of illness (he died when he was eighty-two years old), everyone was asking, "Después de Franco, qué?" ("After Franco, what?").[4] What everyone knew, however, was that "after Franco" was a whole new era.

For most moderate leftists and centrists, a temporal break with the past was embodied in appeals to "look forward, not back" at the time of the transition. As Tierno Galván, the leader of the Partido Socialista Popular (PSP, Popular Socialist Party) was quoted as saying, "the muscles in our neck hurt, from looking back so much; it's time to think of the future."[5] Similarly, an article by Julián Marías – renowned literary journalist and disciple of Generation of '98 philosopher Ortega y Gasset – entitled, "The Curtain Rises," discussed the "debut" of democracy. Both the title, "The Curtain Rises," and the word "debut" affirm that democracy was a genuine new beginning.[6] The new democracy was neither a reform nor a continuation of Francoism, nor a return to the Second Republic (with its incumbent polarization). Of course, in terms of the ritual process, "a new beginning" reflects separation from the old social state of Francoism (see Table 4.1).

For Spaniards of virtually all political persuasions, "the new beginning" was also represented by the "new generation" of the transition. The most popular and important leaders of the transition – Don Juan Carlos, Adolfo Suárez and Felipe González – were all in their thirties or early forties at the time of the transition; and other young political aspirants emphasized that they too were men "of the generation of the King and the President of the Government," as the new minister of Public Works, Luis Ortiz González, explicitly stated.[7] While, generally, "youth" represents hope, the future, and

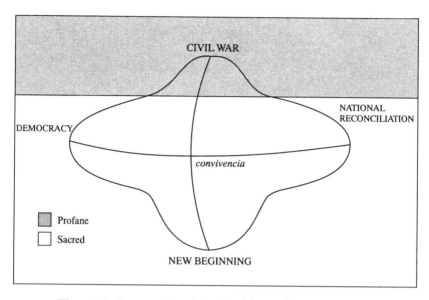

Figure 4.1. Core symbols of the Spanish transition

the optimism of a fresh, new beginning, the new generation in the Spanish transition had been infants or children during the Civil War; they symbolized innocence, and the potential for *convivencia*, as they did not "participate in either of the two bands of the Civil War, nor in its consequences."[8]

In other words, what Spaniards were not supposed to look back at during the transition was the Spanish Civil War, and the fraternal division, polarization, and strife of the Civil War and Francoism. The "new beginning" meant literally both the debut of "democracy" and the debut of "national reconciliation." This is illustrated in Figure 4.1, in which (sacred) democracy and (sacred) national reconciliation stand in symbolic opposition to (profane) civil war.

Civil War and national reconciliation

The "new beginning" marked by Franco's death was the sacred symbolic opposite of the Civil War, the "debut" not only of democracy, but of "national reconciliation" and "*convivencia*." "National reconciliation" meant putting an end to the fraternal division, polarization, and confrontation characteristic of the Spanish Civil War: an end to horizontal (political, regional) and vertical (class), as well as clerical vs. anti-clerical, divisions. *Convivencia* means, literally, "living together with others," but it also connotes peace and tolerance. *Convivencia* was the social – rather than the

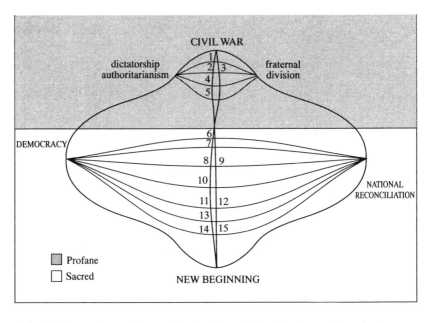

1 irrationality	4 extremism	7 rationality	10 *convivencia*	13 moderation
2 confrontation	5 violence	8 pluralism	11 pact/dialogue	14 modernization
3 polarization	6 nonviolence	9 tolerance	12 compromise	15 new generation

Figure 4.2. Linkage of "democracy" and "national reconciliation" in symbolic opposition to "Civil War"

political – expression of reconciliation. These symbolic linkages are shown in Figure 4.2, which is a more detailed rendering of the core representations illustrated in Figure 4.1.

Symbols of national reconciliation and *convivencia* permeated the Spanish transition in a variety of ways. As we will see in the next chapter, virtually every major or minor party in the 1977 electoral campaign emphasized that "national reconciliation" was one of their most important goals, and sought to portray that they were the party best able to carry out national reconciliation. On the left, the communist poet and electoral candidate Rafael Alberti returned from exile saying, "I left with my fist closed because it was time of war, and I return with my hand open for fraternity";[9] on the right, a Catalan coalition called itself *"convivencia Catala."* Indeed, the call for "national reconciliation" was so pervasive that Spanish communist leader Santiago Carrillo lamented, "Now everyone talks of national reconciliation, of surpassing the division between the defeaters and the defeated, of burying the ax of the war . . . [but] we were the first to initiate [this]."[10]

In terms of the ritual process, living together with others *(convivencia)* and ending fraternal division (national reconciliation) epitomize the "communion of equal individuals" of the liminal state.[11] In this sense, the democratic transition itself came to reflect the sacred liminal state of homogeneity. As philosopher Julián Marías asserts, "Spain is being returned to herself, she moves with considerable liberty, they are erasing the differences between two Spanish classes, and many of us are beginning to feel that we are not going to be alien to our collective life."[12] This symbolic opposition between the "civil war" and both "national reconciliation" and "democracy" (as well as "a new beginning") is shown in Table 4.1, and illustrated in Figure 4.1.

Despite the sheer brutality of the war (and the Spanish Civil War *was* brutal), the notion of "national reconciliation" did not spring "naturally" from the "experience" of civil war itself. The "experience" of civil war can just as easily lead to revenge, as it so often has in Spanish as well as world history. Rather, "national reconciliation" emerged from individuals' perceptions and interpretation of the war. In terms of perception, one of the unique features of the Spanish Civil War is that it was the first war in twentieth-century Europe whose "horrors" were so thoroughly ensconced in the mass media. In sum, just as a special feature of the Vietnam War was that it was "played out" in American living rooms, the Spanish Civil War hit the European and Spanish consciousness so hard because so many people read about it, heard about it, and saw it on the newsreels.

This generalized perception of the Spanish Civil War led to a phenomenal surge of cultural and artistic interpretation. Since it ended in 1939, the Spanish Civil War has been one of the most studied events of the twentieth century. The Spanish Civil War has captured the national and international imagination, resulting in over 15,000 titles in the English language alone, and a tremendous surge of artistic creativity, of which *Guernica* is only the most famous example.[13] Put in another way, in the case of both Vietnam and the Spanish Civil War, the media provided the means for symbolic generalization. The collective "rethinking" of a national tragedy was abetted by modern means of symbolic generalization.

Pablo Picasso was basically apolitical before the Spanish Civil War. But, like many of his Spanish and European contemporaries, he was deeply affected by the media barrage about the war, and this is precisely what is reflected in his masterpiece, *Guernica* (see Plate 4.1). As Stephen Spender cogently observed upon viewing *Guernica* in London in 1938:

Guernica is a picture of horror reported in the newspapers, of which [one] has read accounts and perhaps seen photographs. This kind of second-hand experience, from the newspapers, the news-reel, the wireless, is one of the dominating realities of our time. The many people who are not in direct contact with the disasters falling on civilization live in a waking nightmare of second-hand experiences which in a way are more terrible than real experiences because the person overtaken by a disaster has at least a more limited vision than the camera's wide, cold, recording eye,

Plate 4.1. Picasso, *Guernica*. Reproduced by permission of the Centro Arte Reina Sofia, Madrid.

and at least has no opportunity to imagine horrors worse than what he is seeing and experiencing. The flickering black, white, and grey lights of Picasso's picture suggest a moving picture stretched across an elongated screen; the flatness of the shapes again suggest the photographic image, even the reported paper words. The center of this picture is like a painting of a *collage* in which strips of newspaper have been pasted across the canvas.[14]

As this passage reflects (and we see in Plate 4.1), it is the not so much the overtly political dimensions of the Spanish Civil War, but rather the horrors of the War that are captured in *Guernica*. It is the horrors of the Spanish Civil War that have captured the Spanish and international imagination.[15] Like Goya's earlier masterpiece *The Third of May, 1814, Guernica* high- lights the irrationality and furor of war.[16] However, *Guernica* also juxta- poses the gray coldness of modernity with innocence – the innocent suffering of women, children, and animals. This innocence and suffering is epitomized by the frantic horse in *Guernica*, an auxiliary animal not on either side, but simply caught up in the terror, helpless and panic-stricken. As Kaplan points out, the horse in *Guernica* recalls the most grisly moments in a bullfight, when the mounted picador tries to spear the bull with his pike, and the bull, crazed with pain, turns on the horse, the inno- cent bystander who lacks any heroic role in the fight.[17] The suffering of the innocent is also epitomized in the agony of the woman holding her dead baby, as well as in all the body parts (see Plate 4.1). All the heads are con- torted; all the mouths of the figures are more or less agape (except for the dead child), which connotes shrieks, cries, or groaning; and all the fingers on the hands are either splayed or lifeless.[18] As Fisch observes, "Earlier war pictures often gloried war and victory. In *Guernica* there is no victory. There is only suffering."[19] In sum, what is epitomized in *Guernica,* and what is true especially within Spain, is that the Spanish Civil War has become an alle- gory about man's ability to repudiate humanity.

Where did this allegory come from? All wars – and especially civil wars – are brutal.[20] Yet, one of the extraordinary features of the Spanish Civil War is the extent to which the horrors of both sides became public knowl- edge. This knowledge impeded the symbolic construction that "the good guys won"; the well-known brutality of both sides in the Spanish Civil War led many Spaniards (Picasso among them) to conclude that "we have met the enemy, and the enemy is us."[21]

Specifically, anti-clerical violence had occurred previously in Spain (most notably in 1822 and 1834). But never before in the history of Spain – and the history of the Christian Church – had the world seen such clerical bloodletting as in the early Civil War period. The stark facts (and, as Sánchez notes, they are the best recorded among the many deaths in the Spanish war and its associated terrors) are that nearly seven thousand clerics were killed, most of them within the six-month period from July to December 1936. These were not priests killed while serving as chaplains in the Nationalist army, nor those who died natural deaths while in hiding, but those who were killed purposely because they were clergy in Republican Spain. Of course, thousands of lay persons were also killed, churches were burned, and almost any and every conceivable anti-clerical act was brazenly committed.[22] This in a country in which, as Unamuno wryly noted, "We are all Catholic, even the atheists."

Yet, the frenzied clerical bloodletting on the part of the left was matched by the ruthless acceptance of the concept of "total war" on the part of the right. This is is precisely what is epitomized in the bombing of the Basque city of Guernica. The bombing of Guernica on April 26, 1937, shocked the world because Guernica had no strategic importance at all. It was the first total destruction of an undefended civilian target by aerial bombardment ever.[23] For three hours on a market day afternoon, junker 52Ss bombed and machine-gunned civilians, until some 1,600 people lay dead and more than 800 lay wounded. This, in the symbolic center of the Basque country, whose population had swelled by 3,000 because refugees had flocked to Guernica to escape the fighting in their own towns.[24]

The victors' rhetoric lost its impetus after the defeat of Germany and Italy in the Second World War. The rhetoric was desacralized, and this delegitimation, combined with repression and depolarization on the left, resulted in what philosopher Julián Marías has called a "momentary breathing space" within Spain. In other words, while many analysts describe political culture under Franco as "passive," "dealigned," and/or "repressed";[25] perhaps Spain was not "destroyed," "gloomy," and "inert" under Franco as most analysts profess – perhaps it was simply silent, freed from "manaical politicization":

The Republic had appeared as a promise, an incitement to freedom. That was why it aroused my enthusiasm, and the enthusiasm of so many Spaniards who judged freedom as worthy of being defended. But we must not conceal the fact that once the war had begun, freedom fell more and more into very illiberal hands, and the war's promise of freedom was seriously compromised . . . forced depoliticization was, in the last instance, a liberation from the maniacal politicization into which the country had fallen shortly before the war, and which led directly to it.[26]

What I am suggesting here is that it was within this extraordinary metaphysical environment – this "momentary breathing space" combined with the interpretive context of the Civil War – that the notion of "national reconciliation" was born.

Of course, the notion of "national reconciliation" did not breed itself. And interestingly, it was two of the most effervescent and controversial actors in the Civil War – the Catholic Church and the Spanish Communist Party – that were the two most important instigators of national reconciliation. Significantly, both were also influenced by two profound global trends: the liberalization of the Catholic Church and de-Stalinization.[27]

National reconciliation: the Spanish Communist Party and the Catholic Church

The Spanish Communist Party (PCE) had been a minor factor in Spanish politics before the Civil War. The official party, headquartered in Madrid, took most of its directives from Moscow, which was attempting to improve its diplomatic ties with the Western democracies through a policy of moderation. But the PCE became increasingly important after the start of the Civil War, for the Soviet Union heeded the Republicans' call for help, and supplied the Republicans with arms and money.[28]

Between the end of the war and the early 1950s, the Communist Party practiced guerrilla warfare against the Franco regime.[29] Yet, as early as 1948 the PCE called for a national front of all forces opposed to Franco, and undertook a non-violent strategy based on infiltration of legal institutions, such as the official unions (*sindicatos*). This non-violent strategy received new impetus after the death of Stalin and the Khrushchev second revolution in 1953. The Spanish Communist Party quickly de-Stalinized, and as early as 1954 began to readmit its expelled members.[30]

In 1956, the PCE adopted the "Policy of National Reconciliation," which formally committed the PCE to a strategy of "replacing Franco by peaceful means" (i.e. by legal methods rather than underground struggle). It also made it clear that the PCE was ready to enter into pacts, agreements, and alliances with all political groupings "wanting national reconciliation"; and it referred specifically to a reconciliation and alliance with Catholics. In the years that followed, Spanish communists and Catholic dissidents began to work side by side in the *sindicatos*, thereby bridging the previous civil war divisions. The PCE issued more and more statements friendly to the "middle strata," especially the "non-monopoly bourgeoisie," and they even went so far as to praise the police and the army.[31]

The brutal anti-clericalism of the Republic led many clerics to become nationalists; after the war, the clergy became involved in notorious reprisals and purges. There are many reports of clergy calling for death to the enemy (one priest reportedly stating that, "this is no time for scruples!"). Manuel Azaña claimed that he had not heard of anyone in authority in the Church speak words of peace, charity, or pardon.[32]

However, a few priests who had previously called for those who love the Church to "put themselves on the side of the Crusaders," later urged pardon and forgiveness of the enemy. Most importantly, in his first pastoral letter after the war, Cardinal Isidro Gomá y Tomás – who had vigorously defended the Nationalist uprising in his famous collective letter, "To the Bishops of the Whole World," published in July 1937 – counseled all Spaniards against the spirit of vengeance, and called for the pardon of all the enemies of the Church. Despite the timidity of his address, Gomá was censured for using the word "reconciliation" instead of "recuperation," and his letter was prohibited from being published outside of diocesan bulletins. Gomá died within a year, and was superseded by Enrique Plà y Deniel, the Bishop of Salamanca and one of the Nationalists' most fervent supporters, who occupied the position for the next twenty-seven years.

The formal re-evaluation of the Spanish Civil War and emergence of reconciliation in the Spanish Church did not come about until 1961. Significantly, it originated in the Vatican. In September 1961, Pope John XXIII sent a message to the Bishop of Barcelona, Modrego Casau, in which he lamented the deplorable and cruel Civil War; he did not use the term "Crusade." In his final encyclical, *Encyclical Pacem in Terris*, published in April 1963, Pope John advocated peaceful co-existence, freedom of speech, freedom of communication, freedom of association, and basic civil rights, including the right of a people to choose those who govern them.[33]

In 1968, the Vatican placed Mgr. Enrique y Tarancón as Primate and Archbishop of Toledo, and three years later the Vatican placed him in the even more powerful position of diocese of Madrid–Alcalá. In September 1971, Cardinal Tarancón introduced a resolution to the first Asamblea Conjunta de Obispos y Sacerdotes (Joint Assembly of Bishops and Priests), which rejected definitively the role of the Church as champion of the Crusade and redefined the Church's relationship to the the Civil War. It states: "We humbly recognize and ask forgiveness for not having been, when it was necessary, true ministers of reconciliation."[34] That such a resolution was put forth was important enough, but what really shook the regime was the result of the vote: 137 for, 78 against, with 19 abstentions. A two-thirds majority was required for policy decisions and this was not obtained, but there was a clear overall majority in favor. In fact, the Basque and Catalan clergy were not represented at the assembly. If they had been, the two-thirds majority would have been easily attained.[35]

Thus, just as de-Stalinization legitimized a moderate, reconciliatory path for the Spanish Communist Party, the Vatican Council II legitimized a moderate, reconciliatory path for Spanish clergy and laypersons. Of course, not everyone in either the Catholic Church or the Spanish Communist Party embraced these new democratic and reconciliatory paths. Three decades after the war, the theology of the war was still hotly debated, and those who called the Spanish conflict a "civil war" were still criticized by others for not calling it a "Crusade." Similarly, Mujal-León describes three different ideological positions within the Catalan communist organization alone.[36] And the Secretary General of the Spanish Communist Party, Dolores Ibárruri (La Pasionaria) – who was in exile not in France, like Carrillo, but in the Soviet Union – continued to resist communist moderation until the late 1970s. Nevertheless, these moderate and reconciliatory clerical and communist paths had simply not existed in Spain in the aftermath of the Civil War. But these new paths, linked to the "new generation," became hegemonic in Spain in the post-Franco period.

Democracy

The new beginning was not merely the debut of national reconciliation and *convivencia*, of course, but, most importantly, it was the debut of democracy (see Figure 4.1). "Democracy" was the "theme" of the transition; "democracy" was the new civil religion. Symbols of "democracy" invaded virtually all the major and minor parties of the left, right, and center during the 1977 electoral campaign. The Communist Party's principal slogan was, "To vote Communist is to vote democracy"; and the government party's (UCD) principal slogan was simply "The Center is democracy."

The sacrality of "democracy" was most often taken for granted, but at times it was noted by the press and the electoral candidates themselves. For example, in an article entitled "Democracy," Jaime García Anoveras, a candidate for UCD, stated:

The democratic furor has entered Spain . . . It is the new God that, just like the Transcendent God, enjoys not only a notable cohort of adorers and people who invoke him, but from some of those who most conspicuously don him . . . he is a cure-it-all that fixes everything. We're talking about a true religion . . . One of the forms of abusing democracy is to abuse the name . . . every day they hurl in our face that the school should be democratic . . . the theatre . . . the press . . . agriculture . . . Democracy is something very serious and breakable. So breakable that we cannot permit ourselves the luxury of wasting even the name.[37]

Here, García Anoveras explicitly points out that democracy is the new religion in Spain; at the same time, however, he reaffirms the sacrality of this new "religion." The sacred is separate from, apart and above, the normal workings of everyday life; by protesting the overutilization of "democracy" – and especially its overuse in the mundane, everyday world of "theatre," "press," "agriculture," etc. – García Anoveras is protesting the contamination, or pollution, of the sacred.

Still, the question remains: what did "democracy" mean in the Spanish transition?

Popular sovereignty, dialogue, compromise, and pacting

The single most important meaning of "democracy" in the Spanish transition was that of popular sovereignty, or "rule by the people." "Democracy" was the sacred symbolic opposite of (profane) authoritarianism or dictatorship (see Figure 4.2, which is a more detailed rendering of Figure 4.1). In the above-mentioned article, García Anoveras further explained:

Democracy is, for me, a way of political organization in which the people . . . elect their governors for a limited time . . . in which there are not political paths of going and not returning; respect for all the liberties . . . and all the fundamental rights.[38]

All the newly emerging political parties in the transition affirmed the sacred value of "rule of the people." In a special electoral supplement in *El País*, Socialist leader Felipe González noted that, while everyone espouses democracy in this sense, the Socialist Party was the only "genuine" democratic party because it had a long history of non-autocratic functioning. González stated:

The PSOE has 100 years of existence, of democratic existence; our militants are accustomed to debating problems in depth without taboos, to being in the minority . . . and to accepting the majority consensus. Not all of the forces that have fought for democratic liberties have mechanisms and structures of democratic functioning. Those that lack the democratic habits will find it difficult to avoid utilizing non-democratic methods to obtain the desired results.[39]

Those who "have fought for democratic liberties" but lack democratic "mechanisms and structures" undoubtedly refers to Spanish communists, while "those that lack the democratic habits" refers to the communist, conservative, and government parties – all of which tended to function autocratically.

As this statement also reflects, "democracy" was understood not only as a macro-level system of popular sovereignty, however, but as a micro-level system of open dialogue ("debating problems in depth without taboos") and consensus ("accepting the majority consensus"). Thus, just as (sacred) popular sovereignty symbolically opposes (profane) authoritarianism; (sacred) dialogue and compromise symbolically oppose (profane) confrontation and demagogy.

That democracy was perceived as both a macro-level process of popular sovereignty and public liberties and a micro-level process of dialogue and negotiation cannot be overemphasized – because this is precisely what links "democracy" and "national reconciliation." Only through dialogue and compromise could Spain avoid "another civil war"; only through dialogue and compromise could Spain achieve a system of popular sovereignty. As an electoral advertisement for UCD explicitly stated, "The Center is democracy. Because it impedes confrontation and establishes dialogue."[40] In the same vein, Joaquín Garrigues Walker maintained, "the only thing that is not negotiable in this [historic compromise] is precisely the public liberties which we are fighting for."[41]

Most interestingly, the reconciliatory and dialogical character of "democracy" served to differentiate "democracy" from "republic." In other words, part and parcel of the idea that Spain must never repeat the Civil War was the understanding that Spain must not reproduce the errors of the Second Republic either. Thus there was an almost superstitious avoidance of the term "republic," as well as an almost superstitious avoidance of key republican institutions. The new government would be a "parliamentary monarchy" rather than a "republic"; it would be a proportional electoral rather than a majoritarian system; it would be bicameral rather than unicameral; and the Constitution would articulate the unitary territory, rather than the three unique autonomies recognized by the Republic.[42]

Moderation/centrism/rationality/non-violence

Intertwined with "dialogue," "compromise," and "pact" in the Spanish transitional symbolic framework were understandings of "rationality" and "moderation." In an article entitled, "On Moderation and Other Excesses," Julián Marías stated:

The electoral campaign that is going to come to an end with the elections of June 15 is being strangely moderate . . .

All of this worries me a little. It has a clearly positive side: almost all the parties and coalitions understand that the Spanish people are moderate, or if you prefer, are being moderate. They guess that any extreme would meet with repulsion from the majority opinion, with very costly results at the polls. This appears to me very admirable: that for once demagogy is bad business. We have arrived at a historical situation in which far from triumphing he who shouts the loudest, aphonia is advisable . . . This immoderate moderation bothers me a little because it has an element of falsity; not all the parties are moderate . . .

Moderation has a positive meaning: that which derives from *being in touch with reality* . . . When one is in touch with reality, one must *moderate* every opinion and private preference in view of reality. Moderation equals then respect, civilization or simply intelligence. But one must not confuse moderation with gray lead weight. One can be moderate and at the same time brilliant, passionate, enthusiastic, ingenious, imaginative and inventive. Is it that one cannot feel enthusiasm except for the awkward, extreme, crude and simple? Is it that one has to limit enthusiasm to the hostile? Are we going to identify enthusiasm with fanaticism?[43]

Here, Marías explicitly links moderation with the new beginning: Spain has "arrived" at a new historical situation in which demagogy is bad business; the days of "triumphalism" (confrontation) are over, and they are being replaced by the new democratic means of rational ("being in touch with reality") moderation. And, parallel to García Anoveras' editorial regarding the overuse and thus profanation of "democracy" discussed above, here Marías laments that "everyone" is espousing "moderation," such that genuine "moderation" is losing its value (it is becoming confused with "gray lead weight").

In a similar vein, Suárez's centrist coalition, the Union of the Democratic Center (UCD), continually emphasized that it was *the* Center (i.e. moderate) party. As indicated previously, their principal advertising slogan in the 1977 electoral campaign was, "The Center is Democracy." Even more pointedly, the cover of the magazine *Gaceta Ilustrada* in May 1977 read, "Suárez: I am the Center." Without a political program, the UCD released a reduced document, which stated:

UCD has been constituted as an electoral coalition in order to offer a clear position in the Spanish political center, decided and moderate at the same time, neither Marxist nor authoritarian, with the true proposition – and not only verbal – of completing the profound reform that definitive and peaceful consolidation demands of the democracy in Spain. UCD is offered as a clear alternative of the center, as clear in its limits as respectful of the positions that are to its left and its right. Because only from a broad consensus . . . is it possible to elaborate the democratic Constitution that the country hopes for.[44]

Thus, "the center" is linked with moderation as well as tolerance ("respectful of the positions to its left and its right"), *convivencia* ("peaceful consolidation"), "consensus," and "democracy."

Yet, the UCD was not the only party to vie for the "center" position and symbol. Stated journalist Juan Cueto:

The centrist mania contaminates equally all electoral formations and in place of ideologies they offer us topographies and symbologies (every electoral block defines itself by its central *position* with respect to the two extremes that are most convenient, and by *opposition* to the rest).[45]

This critique of the overutilization of "center" parallels Garcia Anoveras' and Julián Marias' critiques about the overutilization (violation) of "democracy" and "moderation," discussed previously.

Finally, moderation was understood as a modern, rational attitude – the sacred symbolic opposite of "old" (profane) irrationality and extremism. As an editorial in *El País,* entitled "Against Provocations," stated:

There exists a correlation between a democratic mentality and the utilization of rational language. Given the clarity of objectives that democracy pursues – a society in which decisions are made by the majority, without prejudice against minorities . . . nothing pushes them [democrats] to enfold passions and emotions to defend their privileges. There is complete transparency in their programs and they propose goals really within reach, which lends itself to rational language . . .

Exacerbation of passions and emotional agitation are, however, the preferred instruments of the reduced minority sectors that, incapable of pursuing through rational processes the support of the majority, need other motivations to obtain it. The goals that these groups propose, such as the reestablishment of a totalitarian system that allows their power to perpetuate, are intrinsically unpopular, so they can't expose them as such.[46]

Of course, implicit in this symbolic dichotomy between rationality and irrationality is "violence"/"non-violence." Dialogue, moderation, and compromise are rational, non-violent democratic methods, which symbolically oppose irrationality, violence, authoritarianism, and civil war. Thus, anyone who even hinted at "violence" as a possible strategy during the transition violated both (sacred) "democracy" (and dialogue, compromise, etc.) and (sacred) "national reconciliation." For example, a statement by Blas Piñar, the president of the fascist group Fuerza Nueva ("New Force"), in which he said that he was prepared to "kill or be killed" for his beliefs, prompted harsh criticism from all sides. An editorial in the conservative daily *Ya* stated:

Even discounting a measure of demagogy and improvisation allowable in a political meeting, there are boundaries that one should never trespass. One of these is this tone that talks to us of death as a political solution . . . Spain and Spaniards need to live, not to die. This is an insensitive yelling that we wish we had never heard. Or, at least, not see repeated.[47]

Most significant here is the notion of an untrespassable boundary: death as a political solution – civil war – crosses the boundary that separates the sacred from the profane.[48] These oppositional links between sacred "democracy"/"rationality" and profane "Civil War"/"violence" and "irrationality" are illustrated in Figure 4.3. Again, note that Figure 4.3 is simply a more detailed rendering of the core symbols outlined in Figure 4.1.

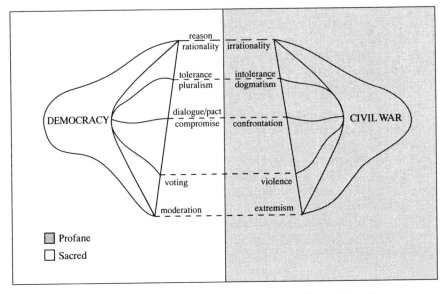

Figure 4.3. Symbolic opposition of "democracy" and "Civil War"

Modernization/Europeanization

Finally, one of the most important representations intertwined with "moderation," "rationality," and "democracy" in the Spanish transitional symbolic framework was "modernization." Spain's "place" in the western European cultural and intellectual community has been a volatile issue throughout Spanish history. Generation of '98 intellectuals, such as Miguel de Unamuno and Américo Castro sought to celebrate Spanish "intra-history," or the intimate character of the Spanish people as distinct from western Europeans; they did not anticipate perhaps that their notion that "Spain is different" would be integrated into the traditionalist position as meaning that Spain is incapable of self-government. For two centuries the notion that, as Spanish philosopher Ortega y Gasset succinctly stated, "Spain is the problem, Europe is the solution" had been a guiding idea of the liberal intelligencia.[49] This idea gained new impetus with the economic liberalization and "opening up" of the Franco regime in the late 1960s. As indicated previously, corporations such as El Corte Inglés reflected and reaffirmed Western standards. Similarly, the newly emerging media, most importantly *El País*, represented and reaffirmed Europeanization. Modeled after *Le Monde*, *El País* "revolutionized" the Spanish media with its modern layout and print technology.[50] Thus *El País* abetted the link between "modernization" and a "new beginning" of "national reconciliation" and "democracy" (see Figure 4.2).[51]

The transition from Francoism to democracy meant that Spain would be transformed into a modern western European nation, both in the sense of acceptance into the European Economic Community (EEC) and the North Atlantic Treaty Organization (NATO), and in the sense of attaining status within western European intellectual and cultural communities. Most of the party leaders in the first democratic electoral campaign not only affirmed the goal of European inclusion, but continually sought to project that European inclusion would be most achievable through their party. For example, one of UCD's advertisements stated: "Vote Center. The ideologies that make possible a democratic Europe. The people that will make possible a democratic Spain."[52] Similarly, one of PSOE's advertisements simply stated, "The key to Europe is in your hands. Vote PSOE."[53]

In addition, party leaders commonly sought legitimacy for their parties through foreign endorsement. The following editorial, titled "Foreign Support, an Obsession," criticizes party leaders of left and right for succumbing to the idea that external ideological support would be decisive for the success of their party:

> The PSOE brought the leaders of European socialism to its congress. Carrillo appeared with his companions of Eurocommunism, Berlinguer and Marchais . . . The Christian Democrats exhibited famous Italian and German colleagues at its congress . . . The Alianza [Popular] sent Mr. Fraga to Washington and Mr. Silva to Baveria to visit Strauss.
>
> It is imperative not to give the impression of a country town that needs pats on the back by socialists, liberals, conservatives or capitalists of other latitudes. Spaniards are those that have to make the decisions. It is here that you have to vote to resolve the many, grave and pressing problems of our country. External endorsement, if we are a strong and independent nation, will come to boot.[54]

Ironically, this article both condemns the party leaders for relying on foreign approval, and laments the negative "country cousin" effect that this "obsession" leaves abroad. The author argues that Spaniards must be like Europeans (independent and strong), rather than merely seek European approval; but if Spain is independent and strong, European approval will "come to boot."

Yet, international approval of Spanish transitional events did legitimize Spanish consensus and democracy. As an article entitled "European Parliament, Favorable to Spanish Democratization" stated:

> All of the European political currents represented in the European Parliament (socialist, christian-democrats, liberals, conservatives, "gaullists" and communists)

are favorable to the democratization of Spain. It is the first time in the history of the European Parliament that they take an attitude toward the Spanish government that excludes notes of criticism or condemnation. It must be that we are getting closer to democracy.[55]

That all European political currents agree as to Spain's democratic progress legitimizes the notion of inter-party consensus and agreeement; the implicit respect for the European Parliament carries over into an explicit affirmation of Spanish democratization. Moreover, that this is the "*first time*" that Spanish government has been approved of by the European Parliament lends credence to the notion that this *is* a new beginning of democracy.

Parliamentary monarchy and King Juan Carlos

As discussed in the previous chapter, King Juan Carlos played a critical role in the success of the Spanish transition. Yet, that King Juan Carlos was able to play this role was not merely a function of his structural position – it was a function of his multivarious links to the dominant transitional symbolic framework. Recall that, at the time of Franco's death, the monarchy was not especially popular. Monarchists were few in number (in large part due to Spain's history of bad monarchs); and monarchists were divided between those who supported Don Juan, those who supported Juan Carlos, and those who rejected the Bourbon dynasty.[56]

After Franco's death, however, Juan Carlos developed compelling links to the core transitional symbols. He became known as a young, modern, European monarch, rather than a backward authoritarian. First, not only by virtue of his age, but because his polemical father was "skipped" in the restoration of the monarchy, King Juan Carlos became a vital member of the "new generation." As an editorial in *Arriba* stated:

> The Count of Barcelona [Don Juan] represents the continuity of an Institution that dared difficult moments, but was maker of the unity of Spain . . . His son, the King, personifies a new talent, the reflection of a new generation, and he receives daily the adhesion of a people that see precisely in the Crown, the guarantor of their rights and an arbiter capable of guaranteeing a stable *convivencia*. Both realities are now unified in the persona of Juan Carlos.[57]

Here, Juan Carlos is linked to the communality embedded in the monarchy ("maker of the unity of Spain" – i.e. he is the "King of all Spaniards") as well as the communality of the "new generation": *convivencia*. In addition, as a parliamentary monarch (the "guarantor of rights"), Juan Carlos is linked to (sacred) "democracy."[58]

Interestingly, that Juan Carlos was a modern parliamentary monarch enabled even traditional opponents of monarchy – e.g. Spanish communists – to accept him in terms of, and while affirming, democratic values. Thus, for example, an official statement from the Spanish Communist Party maintained, "If in a freely celebrated referendum with all the people's rights, the peoples of Spain pronounce themselves for the monarchy, the PCE will accept the decision."[59] Significantly, this statement not only legitimized the King and reaffirmed popular sovereignty, but, because the communists accepted something that they had traditionally opposed, reaffirmed the spirit of compromise, pluralism and tolerance, reconciliation, and *convivencia* of the transition.

That Juan Carlos was Franco's own trainee was a symbolic problem for the young opposition: it contradicted the link between Juan Carlos and a new beginning. Moderate monarchists, especially, attempted to separate the monarchy from Francoism – and Juan Carlos from Franco – by evoking the traditional legitimacy of the monarchy: its transcendence. For example, Catalan monarchist Antonio de Senillosa stated:

Francoism and monarchy are two entirely distinct conceptions of the State . . . a Francoist monarchy is something inconceivable . . . Francoism looked for its origin and its legitimacy in a date and in the result of a civil war. The Monarchy doesn't have dates. It is present in thousands of years of our history . . . The Monarchy must support her legitimation in the popular consensus expressed by way of free universal suffrage, through elections and parties, not by designated procurators nor by non-existent organic channels. The Monarchy proclaims that sovereignty resides in the people, not in the State, as Francoism said in its Organic law. The Monarchy is based in the respect for liberties; in the extension of these liberties and not in their repression, nor in the restriction of human rights. The Monarchy will be constitutional and democratic if we want it to subsist.[60]

That Francoism finds its legitimacy in the "date and result" of the Civil War while the Monarchy "doesn't have dates," contrasts a (profane) false legitimacy (it is actually just force) with genuine (sacred) monarchical legitimacy. This traditionalist notion of monarchy, which emphasizes its transcendence, is epitomized in the comment that "Spain has a chief of State that is substantially different from her government. First, because he is the King, the King of all Spaniards, and second, because he is not compromised with the politics of things, and especially not governmental politics."[61]

Yet, this traditionalist conceptualization of monarchy is not democratic. Thus, de Senillosa converts to a democratic argument, contrasting the sacred democratic legitimacy of the (parliamentary) monarchy with the profane repression of authoritarianism. Here, that the monarchy is based on "free universal suffrage" (not "non-existent organic channels"), and "respect for liberties" (not "repression"), both links (sacred) "monarchy" and (sacred) "democracy" to (supersacred) parliamentary monarchy; and differentiates and separates (sacred) "parliamentary monarchy" from (profane) "Francoism."

The counter-discourse of the far right

The far right also oftentimes used symbols of a new temporality, "national reconciliation," and "democracy" during the Spanish transition. But, interestingly, the Francoist bunker tended to meld these symbols with old systems of meaning. For instance, the far right also perceived a new temporality in the Spanish transition, but they represented it as the "end of the course" rather than a "new beginning." As an editorial in *El Alcázar* (titled "End of the Course"), on the day of the 1977 democratic elections, stated:

On the 20 of November of 1975 Spain got ready to embark on the road of the future. With the baggage in customs, and the foreseen itinerary rejected, she began her journey. Today she arrives at her destination point. Now we can talk of another Spain. I am not saying better or worse. I am saying, simply, another Spain. The chronological border that separated us from the future – determined by the existence of one man – separates us now from the past.[62]

The temporal separation between the Spain of Franco and Spain since Franco's death is explicitly expressed here in terms of the "chronological border," "determined by the existence of one man." The metaphor of a "journey" (to a new land) expresses this separation as a new spatial beginning. But whereas in the dominant frame of the transition "journey" connotes hope and the future, here the journey leads not to the beginning, but to the end – of the order of Francoism. Moreover, "the foreseen itinerary rejected", reflects not only disdain for the new road Spain had embarked on, but disdain for the state of flux – lack of itinerary – of the transition. Similarly, "with baggage in customs" reflects the Francoist sense of disorder in not knowing what is ahead.

In a far more contradictory way, the far right at times utilized the reconciliatory rhetoric of the transition, but in so doing revealed its attachment to systems of meaning antithetical to (the dominant meaning of) *convivencia* and reconciliation. For instance, Luis Benitez de Lugo of the Confederación de Combatientes (Soldiers' Confederation), stated, "We represent a new generation and along with the new youth we must fight, even if it is only so that those who spilled their blood won't feel defrauded".[63] Of course, linking "the new generation" to fighting, and "those who have spilled their blood" is absolutely nonsensical in the dominant transitional symbolic framework: the "new generation" is, by definition, non-violent and not vengeful.

In a similar vein, *El Alcázar* columnist Torcuato Luca de Tena recognized and implicitly lauded the "reconciliatory" ideals of the transition, but nevertheless confirmed "non-reconciliatory" values. He stated:

The burning sincerity of trying to obtain the national reconciliation that we all desire: the noble yearning of the King to be King of all Spaniards: the Christian precept that tells us to forgive our trespassers, so that we ourselves be forgiven; obliges us, as Spaniards, to search for the better roads to reconciliation with good faith; as citizens, to facilitate the royal desire, and as Christians to beg for forgiveness. But neither good Christian faith, nor royal obedience, nor Christian forgiveness is tantamount to the amputation of our memory, nor the acceptance of the imposition of a collective amnesia . . .

Because in Spain there was a war. How I wish that it hadn't happened! How I wish that there weren't the causes that made it inevitable! But there were! And that victory that was reached is not what is in play, nor was it put in play by the referendum. This is what the Government must not forget . . . [64]

On the one hand, Torcuato Luca de Tena reaffirms "national reconciliation" ("Christian forgiveness"; "the national reconciliation that we all desire") and the homogeneity of the liminal state ("royal obedience" to the "King of all Spaniards"). At the same time, however, that the Civil War was "inevitable," and a sacred "victory" is absolutely antithetical to the transitional meaning of "reconciliation" (as well as "Civil War"). Moreover, that national reconciliation is tantamount to the "amputation of our memory" and "collective amnesia" reveals that for the far right "national reconciliation" is not sacred at all; on the contrary, it is a violation or profanation of (sacred) Francoism.

The Franco regime was based on an explicit rejection of mass suffrage. Franco believed that the self-serving elected officials of the Second Republic created the collapse of civil order in the Spain. Not surprisingly, then, the far right continued to see "democracy" as profane, rather than sacred during the transition. "Popular sovereignty" as well as "coalitions and alliances" meant (profane) disorder, rather than the (sacred) "will of the people." For example, one editorial in *El Alcázar* stated:

The 15 of June we aren't going to play "heads or tails" as to the existence of Spain . . . It is Spain, gentlemen, that is what we are playing for. Yes, Spain, with the weight of her history, with the weight of her destiny in the world, with the disturbing weight of her future. And before this there cannot be by virtue of minor distrust and bickering, coalitions and alliances in which one shrugs one's shoulders and plays heads or tails as to the destiny of a great country of Europe.[65]

Similarly, another editorial stated:

Democracy has made the fraudulent substitution from A Great, Dignified and Free Spain to an almoner, a dirty and vulgar Spain in which the monstrosity that a murderer, a drug addict, a prostitute can sit on the bench of Congress without embarrassment, is going to be possible. Never has a nation arrived to such degradation. And unfortunately, there isn't any Franco to save us from this chaos.[66]

Finally, that not only elections but "pacting" is a profanation for the far right is readily apparent in the following editorial, titled "We Don't Pact With The Enemies of Spain":

Despite those who try to scare us with the ghost of polarization . . . We don't pact with the enemies of Spain and the Spanish people. Nor do we pact with those who make politics a dangerous game of opportunism without concern as to the destiny of Spain, and her well-being that with so much sacrifice and effort was conquered for the Spaniards.[67]

The profane character of electoral politics for the far right was also reflected in the far right's perception of – literally – "pollution" in the 1977 electoral campaign. As *El Alcázar* columnist Alfonso Paso stated:

I don't believe in these elections; I don't believe in liberal democracy; I don't believe in the Regime of the parties . . .
    My city is dirty, filled with photocopies of Adolfo Suárez, or the portrait of Mr. González with his unkempt hair. Posters that matter less than that one for Coca Cola "coke is it." Children paid to put up posters have plastered Madrid so much that one can't breathe . . . [68]

In terms of the ritual process, clearly, the Francoist bunker did not embrace separation from the old social state (Francoism); they rejected the communal liminality embodied in "national reconciliation"; and they rejected reaggregation to the new social state of democracy. At the same time, however, that the far right felt compelled to utilize – or unwittingly utilized – the core transitional symbols at all, indicates the extent to which these symbols had in fact penetrated Spain. And ironically, while the far right continued to espouse anti-reconciliatory and anti-democratic rhetoric throughout the "period of consensus" (as we saw above in the case of Blas Piñar above, and we will see again in subsequent chapters), this "extremist" symbolization merely affirmed the symbolic opposition between (profane) "dictatorship" and (sacred) "democracy."

5

The curtain rises: the first democratic elections

The first democratic elections since 1931 were held in Spain on June 15, 1977.[1] The Union of the Democratic Center (Unión del Centro Democrático, UCD) and the Spanish Socialist Workers' Party (Partido Socialista Obrero Español, PSOE) received almost 63 percent of the votes cast, and over 80 percent of the seats in the lower house (Congress of Deputies) of the constituent Cortes. The center/center-right UCD secured 34 percent of the popular vote and controlled 165 seats in the Congress of Deputies, just 11 short of an absolute majority. The socialist PSOE emerged as the principal opposition party, with 28.9 percent of the vote and 118 seats. Two other political groups, the Spanish Communist Party (Partido Comunista Español, PCE) and the conservative Popular Alliance (Alianza Popular, AP) earned enough votes to ensure themselves a significant role in the new parliament. The remaining few seats were distributed among smaller parties, most importantly, the Catalan Democrats (Pacte Democràtic per Catalunya, PDC), which received 11 seats, and the Basque Nationalist Party (Partido Nacionalista Vasco, PNV), which received 8 seats.[2] Complete electoral results can be found in Table 5.1.

The 1977 election results were most surprising in the poor showing of both the Christian Democrats and Alianza Popular (AP). A poll conducted in January 1977 found that the Christian Democrats were by far the most favored political group in Spain.[3] According to a public opinion poll conducted merely two months before the elections, the AP led the electoral race with a twenty-point lead over the UCD.[4] The tides turned in the two-month electoral campaign, which lasted from April to June 1977. In this chapter I critically examine this electoral period. We will see that while all the major parties attempted to attach themselves to the core symbols of the transition, the UCD and PSOE were the most successful in this regard.

Table 5.1. *Returns of the 1977 election, Congress of Deputies (*Cortes Españolas*)*

Party	Number of votes	Percentage	Number of seats	Percentage
UCD	6,309,991	34.0	165	47.1
PSOE	5,371,466	28.9	118	33.7
PCE–PSUC	1,709,870	9.2	20	5.7
AP	1,488,001	8.0	16	4.6
PSP–US	816,582	4.4	6	1.7
PDC	514,647	2.8	11	3.1
PNV	314,272	1.7	8	2.3
UCDCC	172,791	0.9	2	0.6
EC	143,954	0.8	1	0.3
EE	64,039	0.3	1	0.3
DC	257,152	1.4	0	0.0
SD	206,238	1.1	0	0.0
Others	1,217,267	6.5	2[a]	0.6
Total	18,586,270		350	

Note:

[a] Two deputies representing "others" are of Candidatura Aragonés Independiente de Centro and Candidatura Independiente de Centro in Castellón.

Key:

UCD   Unión del Centro Democrático
PSOE   Partido Socialista Obrero Español and Socialistes de Catalunya
PCE–PSUC Partido Comunista Español and Partit Socialista Unificat de Catalunya
AP   Alianza Popular
PSP–US   Partido Socialista Popular – Unidad Socialista
PDC   Pacte Democràtic per Catalunya
PNV   Partido Nacionalista Vasco
UCDCC   Coalición Electoral Unió del Centre i la Democracia Cristiana de
           Catalunya
EC   Esquerra de Catalunya
EE   Euzkadiko Ezkerra (includes "Independent" slate #14 in Alava)
DC   Equipo de la Democracia Cristiana, Federación de la Democracia
           Cristiana, Democracia Cristiana Vasca–Euska Kristan Demokrasia,
           Equipo Democrata Cristiana e Social Democracia Galega, Partido
           Popular Gallego Unión Democrática Cristiana, Unión Democrática
           del País Valencia, Democracia Cristiana Aragonesa, Democracia
           Social Cristiana de Catalunya
SD   Alianza Socialista Democrática, Partido Socialista Democrático
           Español, Centro Izquierda de Albacete, ASD-Centro Izquierda,
           Reforma Social Española, PSOE(H), and (in Soria only) Independientes
Source: Gunther, Sani, and Shabad (1986: 38).

The center parties

As indicated previously, the appointment of Adolfo Suárez as President of Government by King Juan Carlos in July 1976 came as a surprise to most political observers. Suárez had not been a minister in the Franco government, and he had never held a high position in the administration of the State. He was simply a politician from the Movement (the only legal political party under Francoism), who rose through its hierarchy to minister secretary. In a 1976 survey of journalists as to expected "politicians of the future," in which Fraga placed first and González placed fifth, Suárez placed only nineteenth.[5] Significantly, Suárez's name was not even included in a public survey as to presidential preferences conducted in 1976, in which José María de Areilza, president of Partido Popular (Popular Party) and the expected successor to Arias Navarro, placed first. Most reformists – not to mention leftists – including Areilza, had grave doubts about Suárez's reformist intentions, and only Francoists, based on Suárez's success in the Movement, saw the appointment of the "outsider" Suárez as "excellent."[6]

On the other hand, unlike Arias Navarro, Suárez had the public support of the king, and there were virtually no explosive expectations and goals waiting for Suárez to achieve.[7] Moreover, as King Juan Carlos stated to Suárez in the speech announcing his appointment:

Your naming represents the arrival of a new generation to the responsibilities of Council of Ministers and to the head of the Ministerial Departments. You will form a governmental team with clear ideas, sincere propositions and decided will [to complete two objectives:] through the work of all Spaniards to surpass the present difficulties and make possible the clear and peaceful participation of all citizens in the determination of our political future.[8]

Here, Suárez is explicitly linked to the "new generation" and a new beginning of rationality ("clear ideas") and reconciliation. It seems his youth combined with his lack of prominence in the Franco regime meant that Suárez did not have the baggage of "the past" (as did the leading Francoist reformers, Fraga and Areilza); but at the same time, Suárez did not represent "rupture" to the more orthodox Francoists, as did the young socialist leader, Felipe González.

By 1977, Suárez was the most popular politician in Spain. In a poll conducted in 1978, shown in Figure 5.1, Suárez was perceived as the most "understanding," "honorable," "responsible," and "capable" of politicians. Whereas González was seen as sincere but inexperienced, Suárez rated very high in "political capacity" and "skill" as well as sincerity.

Merely a month before the 1977 elections, Suárez and his followers merged with the coalition Centro Democrático (CD), creating the Unión

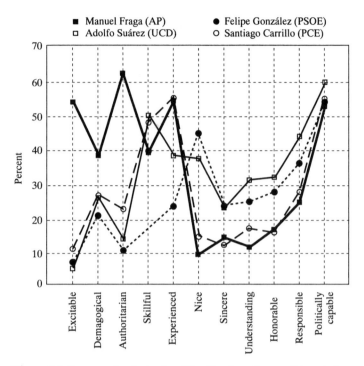

Figure 5.1. Images of principal political leaders. Source: Linz et al. (1981: 256)

del Centro Democrático (UCD). Moderate oppositional proto-parties had begun to emerge in 1956 with the first major anti-regime protest demonstrations. Although these groups were illegal, they were not persecuted, as were the Socialists and Communists, except when their leaders took part in highly visible protests against the regime.[9] The number of moderate oppositional groups increased as the death of Franco approached, especially between 1974 and 1976. These tiny proto-parties (which were called "taxi-parties" because they were so small their members were said to be able to fit inside a single taxi) began to coalesce within each political family, and a second phase of coalescence followed in which formal mergers were made among parties of different ideological families.[10] The first product of this process was the Partido Popular, created in December 1976. The two most prominent leaders of the Partido Popular, José María de Areilza and Pio Cabanillas, had held prominent positions in the Franco regime, but had fallen into disfavor. It was the Partido Popular (PP) that was the driving force behind the formation of the still broader coalition, the Centro Democrático (CD).[11] But as Gunther, Sani, and

Shabad state, while calling itself a party, Centro Democrático was really nothing more than "groups of notables with their respective personalistic followings, who happened to share certain basic notions about politics and wished to play important roles within the new democratic regime."[12] Centro Democrático lacked a national following and a core of militants, as well as financial means and organization.

The collaboration between Suárez and Centro Democrático was not initially sought by either Suárez or the CD: CD was formed as a political party independent of the government, and Suárez had originally intended to found his own party.[13] Furthermore, the coalition was not without problems. Areilza saw the merger as a cabal against his leadership and resigned from involvement in the 1977 campaign on April 24, 1977. The most problematic aspect of the merger itself was the formation of electoral lists. Suárez demanded and received full authority to draw up the various provincial lists of UCD candidates for the Congress of Deputies and the Senate, which caused much resentment and resulted in only about half the electoral candidates coming from the original CD.[14]

Nevertheless, the merger was certainly a strategy with advantages to both Suárez and the CD. Suárez augmented his image as a democrat by the alliance with liberals and social democrats; CD benefitted from the organizational and financial resources of the incumbent government as well as from Suárez's popularity and prestige. The UCD never attempted to formulate a precise ideology or program, preferring to stand as a vague coalition of the center, focused on "reform, moderation, democracy and liberty and, as the soul of all this, justice."[15] Thus, the youth and "outsider" status of Suárez linked the UCD with a "new beginning," while the "tolerance" and "moderation" of *the* center party linked the UCD with "national reconciliation" as well as "democracy" (see Figure 4.2).

Christian democracy vs. church neutrality

The victory of the UCD represents the failure of the Christian Democrats in Spain, among other things. This failure surprised many politicians, journalists, and social scientists alike, who predicted that Spain would adopt a strong Christian Democratic party, akin to that of Italy.[16] Indeed, the Christian Democrats had relatively long organizational histories and enjoyed considerable visibility and prestige, both domestically and internationally. As early as 1965 the two largest Christian Democratic parties in Spain, Izquierda Demócrata Cristiana (IDC, Democratic Christian Left) led by Ruiz Giménez and Federación Popular Democrática (FDP, Popular Democratic Federation) led by Gil Robles, had been recognized by the

Christian Democratic International, from whom they received funds and assistance.[17] Moreover, in a poll conducted in January 1977, Christian Democrats were judged the most appealing group, as compared with Continuists, Falangists, conservatives, Carlists, liberals, social democrats, socialists, communists, and revolutionaries, in Spain.[18]

But, though Ruiz Giménez's IDC and Gil Robles' FPD joined forces, creating the Federación de la Cristiana Democrática (FDC, Federation of Democratic Christians), they failed to heed the International's advice to seek out alliances with other moderate (non-Christian Democrat) political groups. Ruiz Giménez initially considered the Partido Popular too conservative to favor a coalition, though he reluctantly came to favor coalescing with the newly emerging UCD. Gil Robles preferred to keep his party independent, "to maintain the democratic purity and the Christian democratic identity of the party," and integration with the UCD was rejected by Gil Robles' wing of the FDC. The FDC did form an alliance with several regional Christian democratic parties (called Equipo Demócrata Cristiano del Estado Español, or EDC, Christian Democratic Team of the Spanish State), including the Partido Nacionalista Vasco (PNV), Unió Democràtica de Catalunya (Democratic Union of Catalonia), and the Unió Democràtica del País Valencia (Democratic Union of Valencia), but this did not strengthen the FDC in the majority of Spanish provinces.[19]

This lack of support for the Christian Democrats in the provinces was the fundamental reason for the failure of the Christian Democrats in the 1977 elections. Lack of support in the provinces was not only due to the Christian Democrats' failure to form a broader coalition, however, but also to their lack of support from the Church. While, like the rest of western Europe, the Church has traditionally been a major source of support for Christian Democrats in Spain, the Church maintained an official stance of neutrality in the 1977 Spanish elections. Gunther, Sani, and Shabad note that Church uninvolvement was shortlived, and thus they offer a "cynical interpretation of that [1977] policy": the existence of several parties purporting to defend the interests of the Church (UCD, AP, and FDC), and uncertainty as to which of them would have the best electoral prospects made it difficult for the Church to intervene on behalf of any one of them.[20] But whether or not this "cynical" interpretation of Church uninvolvement is "true," the "neutrality" of the Church coincided with the core representations and ritual processes of the transition. At the level of the sacred, neutrality was an endorsement by the Church of separation of Church and State (democracy), national reconciliation (liminality), and a new beginning (separation).

Specifically, as indicated previously, the Church was an explosive symbol and institution in the Second Republic and the Civil War. The fervent anti-clericalism of the Second Republic was a response to the ruthless economic and political privileges historically enjoyed by the Spanish Church; and the sacred "Crusade" to "save" Spain from the evils of secularization was a response to the left's mission to "save" Spain from right-wing tyranny. The official "neutral" position of the Church in the first democratic elections symbolized national reconciliation – the overcoming of not only the clerical/anti-clerical polarization of the Civil War, but of the Church's historical link with class, regional, and political divisions in Spain. In terms of the ritual process, "church neutrality" corresponds to both separation and the sacred homogeneity of the liminal state; it reflects religious tolerance, moderation and equality as well as reconciliation. In addition, church neutrality is explicitly tied to "democracy" and the ritual process of reaggregation, as it reflects the liberal democratic notion of separation of Church and State.

Interestingly, as Huneeus notes, the FDC would probably have been better off had they not used the word "Christian" in their name, had they – like Christian Democrats who joined Partido Popular – simply assumed the values of Christian humanitarianism.[21] In other words, Church neutrality did not mean simply the lack of endorsement for the Christian Democrats by the Church; it resulted in a contradiction between "Christian Democrat" and "Church" representations. Consider, for instance, a statement made by Cardinal Tarancón in November 1975:

The Christian faith is not a political ideology nor can it be identified with any of them, given that no social or political system can exhaust all the richness of Christianity. The Church does not support any political form or ideology, and if anyone utilizes its name to cover its flags they are blatantly usurping it.[22]

This suggestion by Tarancón that those using the name "Christian" in their party name are "blatantly usurping it" reflects the view that mixing politics and religion is a profanation which contradicts the ideals of the new democratic state, as well as as the transitional value of national reconciliation. Thus, regardless of the liberal ideological stance of the Christian Democrats, the name "Christian Democrats" conjures up the "using" of (sacred) religion, for (profane) political goals, which is linked to Francoism and the Civil War, and contradicts the images of democracy and the new beginning as well as national reconciliation.

Moreover, the FDC called up other images at odds with transitional processes and representations. As discussed previously, in the dominant symbolic framework of the transition, pacting and coalitions were linked to both national reconciliation and democracy, as well as the ritual processes of liminality and reaggregation. The hesitancy of the FDC to pact with others, and especially their refusal to pact with those lacking the "Christian democratic *purity*," then, contradicts transitional representations of compromise, moderation, and tolerance linked to national reconciliation and *convivencia*. While FDC propaganda focused on the fact that the FDC simply wanted to present "its own face, its own identity and its own program in the elections,"[23] this concern with "its own face" may have come to represent non-reconciliation which was far more salient than doctrinal purity during the transition.

Finally, the FDC embodied contradictory images which did not completely correspond to either conservative or left-wing constituencies. Anticlerical and anti-Catholic positions on the left had created a political "space" (clerical moderate-left) for the Christian Democrats during the Second Republic. But the dearth of leftist anti-clerical positions made the clerical moderate-left position virtually irrelevant in the 1977 democratic elections. Many of the more moderate members of the FDC joined the PSOE, and even the PCE. The FDC maintained a leftist ideological thrust in its 1977 campaign – but this thrust was at odds with the FDC's relatively conservative followers, who tended to focus on that which set the Christian Democrats apart from their social-democratic counterparts: "Christianity."

The Spanish Communist Party (PCE)

The Spanish Communist Party (PCE) was founded on April 15, 1920, out of a division within the PSOE and its affiliated organizations. It remained unimportant throughout the Second Republic, but following the outbreak of the Civil War grew enormously in size and political influence within the Republican camp.[24] The Spanish Communist Party was the principal force in the clandestine opposition to Franco, and by Franco's death it had become by far the largest political party organization in Spain. Because of its historic role, the PCE emerged from clandestinity in 1977 with considerable advantages: a large number of enthusiastic activists, an appreciable intellectual backing, a large union organization (the Comisiones Obreras, CCOO – Workers' Commissions), a fully funded organization, and continuity, experience, and discipline in its leadership.[25] Unlike other parties on the left, the PCE had some kind of organization in virtually all Spanish provinces, and PCE membership rose as the 1977 elections approached: the number of party members increased from 15–20,000 in 1975, to 90–100,000 in 1976–1977.[26]

Nevertheless, the PCE showing in the 1977 elections was poor, and its showing declined precipitously in the early 1980s.[27] There are several inter-twined reasons which account for the relative failure of the PCE, but all point to the fact that, despite Carrillo's adamant call for moderation, the PCE was plagued with representations at odds with the sacred transitional symbols of a new beginning of democracy and national reconciliation.

On the one hand, Carrillo unequivocally embraced the core transitional symbols of democracy and national reconciliation. In April 1977, he openly endorsed the compromises that enabled the legalization and participation of the Communist Party in the 1977 elections, stating that:

The politics of moderation were the best that PCE could follow, and their fruit is the legalization of the party . . . This reunion . . . is a great victory for the politics of national reconciliation and for the pact for liberty, and consequently, a confirma-tion of the line followed by the PCE.[28]

In addition, Carrillo set forth a moderate electoral program of five points that included, first, a call for a vote for democracy ("the democratic vote is the guarantee of the stability and the peaceful *convivencia* of Spaniards in the future"); secondly, that "to vote communist is a vote for democracy"; thirdly, the elements of the Constitutional Pact, including civil rights and liberties, democratization of politics, separation of Church and State, and autonomy for national communities; fourthly, that "in order to confront the economic crisis, the workers must occupy the space that corresponds to them"; and fifthly, "a plan to bring health to the economy and new forms of democratic economic development."[29] Most significantly, the PCE elec-toral program used the broad consensual phrase "democratic economic development" and did not mention nationalization; and the appeal for workers to occupy their due "space" is proclaimed in terms of the consen-sual goal of confronting the 1977 economic crisis, rather than in the Marxist-Leninist terms of "dictatorship of the proletariat."[30] Further-more, in the spirit of PCE's new moderation, the color red and the hammer and sickle were largely absent from the Communist Party's billboards and posters, and the national flag replaced the Republican tricolor flag at party rallies.[31]

On the other hand, however, the Spanish Communist Party often unwit-tingly called up images which conflicted with symbols of a "new begin-ning." Most obviously, many communist leaders, most importantly, Santiago Carrillo and Dolores Ibárruri (La Pasionaria), were not at all members of the "new generation." On the contrary, both Carrillo and Ibárruri played prominent and controversial roles in Francoism and/or the Civil War. Indeed, Ibárruri was a critical symbol of violent confrontation and republican resistance: she was accused of involvement in the killing of

José Calvo Sotelo, which was the catalyst for the July 18 military revolt; and, as her nickname "La Pasionaria" reflects, Ibárruri was well-known as a fiery orator, whose slogans, such as "It is better to die on your feet than to live on your knees"; and "*no pasarán!*" ("they will not pass") helped raise morale and mobilize Spanish citizens.[32]

Not surprisingly, this historic legacy and *raison d'être* was not shed easily. Thus, for example, the list of PCE candidates printed in *Mundo Obrero* contained the following data for each candidate: (1) place of birth, (2) occupation, (3) offices held in PCE, and (4) number of years in exile or prison.[33] The inclusion of the latter data in the mere listing of the candidates (i.e. the list provided minimal information) reflects the extent to which virulent opposition to Francoism was at the root of communist identity.

Interestingly, some communists explicitly confronted this affiliation with the "old" and the "past." For instance, the communist poet Rafael Alberti, who returned from exile at the age of seventy-five and stood as a candidate in the 1977 elections, read the following poem, called *Owing to This About Age*, as part of his electoral campaign (it was also reprinted in *Mundo Obrero*):

> I wanted in this moment,
> the youngest in my life,
> not to simply be a lost
> birth certificate.
>
> For like liberty
> man when he is alive
> in the light is ageless.
>
> And I am alive, though old
> and no one is going to tell me
> that I am now an empty skin.
>
> Nor see in me the pretentiousness
> of being a wise little boy
> in his first communion.
>
> To feel young is not to be
> young, it is only to feel
> the illusion of awakening.
>
> And like the light, I understand
> that when it is twilight
> day is almost breaking.
>
> And while the light shines,
> and whether hair is black or white,
> youth will shine on.[34]

This poem can be understood as Alberti's strategical (in terms of the electoral campaign) and/or personal reconciliation of his advanced chronological age to participation in "new-generation" Spanish politics. Alberti maintains that to "feel young is not to be young" (chronologically) but to "feel the illusion of awakening," which reflects not only that he is young "in spirit," but that he in fact embraces the "new beginning."

Thus, the Spanish Communist Party was faced with a "generational" problem: the "old generation" exuded a lack of separation from the old regime. This problem of separation was compounded by the problem of reaggregation, however, because the "old generation" continued to perpetuate non-democratic imagery. This problem became patently obvious in a dispute between "old" and "new" generation communists as to the "internal democratic functioning" of the PCE. Younger, "new-generation" communists (e.g. Ramón Tamames, Roberto Lertxundi, Antoni Gutiérrez Díaz, and Jaime Sartorius), who tended to have come to the Communist Party via involvement with the 1960s student movements, had an activist, participatory image of how the Communist Party should work. They suggested that centralized decision-making may have been necessary when the Communist Party existed "in clandestinity," but in this new democratic period, autocratic functioning was not only antiquated and unjust, but contrary to the new democratic goals of the PCE.[35] However, the older generation balked at the internal reorganization of the PCE, which called into question their commitment to a "new beginning" of "democracy."[36]

Interestingly, members of the PCE readily acknowledged the extent to which old, non-democratic, non-reconciliatory, images of the Communist Party contributed to their relative failure in the 1977 elections. An editorial entitled "Why They Didn't Vote For Us" in *Mundo Obrero* attempted to answer why Spaniards voted PSOE instead of PCE:

Because they want a leftist Government for Spain, and they imagine, erroneously, that a great majority of the elected communists will propagate a dictatorial regime, or at least a leftist authoritarian one. Because they don't like, they're scared of, the existing communist regimes, and according to their opinion, our Party is very much linked to them. Because "they see us" as very red, as very authoritarian, very know-it-all . . . For these reasons . . . they have voted for the socialists . . . But these ideas of theirs . . . are the ones which we communists have to make disappear with the tenacious, serene, friendly, non-aggressive exposition of our democratic positions, with our conduct, with our style, and with a tone, in more than a few respects distinct from the present one, that corresponds, in sum, to the democratic content of our politics. Exhibiting to all sides an image of our party that every day is more democratic and more humane from inside and outside our doors.[37]

Ironically, however, at the same time that Spanish communists acknowledged their problems of identity and image, the non-reconciliatory, non-democratic image of the PCE sometimes reared its head. For example, in an article entitled "On Signs of Identity," the prominent communist leader and economist Ramón Tamames stated:

They say that we are totalitarian. When the reality is that the only totalitarian State that has existed in the History of Spain has been that which these same accusers began to construct on the first of October of 1936 . . .

They say that we are not democrats. In spite of the fact that PCE bravely defended the constitutional legality of the Republic during the war, our Party never was implicated in a mono-party regime. In Spain the only party that has benefitted from exclusionist monopolies has been the Falange, transformed by Franco into the National Movement in 1937 . . .

They say . . . that we are against religion. In Spain, the communists have never been against the believers. And the features of anti-clericalism that they inserted in the Republican Constitution of 1931 are not in the least bit attributable to us, since our voice as a party, our first deputy, only arrived in Parliament in 1933. For us, religion is a problem of the individual person, a personal right in which nobody, and much less the State, can meddle . . . [38]

Here, Tamames refutes the non-democratic, totalitarian, and anti-clerical image of the PCE by explaining the role of the PCE in the Republic and the Civil War, and accuses the accusers (Francoists) of totalitarianism. But accusations as to the "totalitarianism" that "began on the first of October of 1936" and references to the Falange of 1937 merely recall the polarization of the communists and Francoists of the Civil War and contradict images of a new beginning and national reconciliation. And the factual rebuttal of anti-clericalism during the Second Republic reflects a failure to accept responsibilty for all the barbarities of the past, without which the communists cannot truly surpass the past and engage in national reconciliation. (Recall, for example, comments such as "who can throw the first stone," and remorse over "the barbarities committed by both bands of the Civil War," etc.)

The Spanish Socialist Workers' Party (PSOE)

Founded in 1879 by Pablo Iglesias, the Spanish Socialist Workers' Party (PSOE) is the oldest political party in Spain. It was the largest party of the left during the Second Republic; its affiliated trade union, UGT, claimed a membership of 1.4 million in 1933.[39] The PSOE organization, however, had been eliminated in many Spanish provinces by the end of the 1940s, in large part owing to PSOE's attempt to maintain a relatively open party structure, which made it especially vulnerable to the Franco regime. The frequent "falling" of its executive committee incited the PSOE to move its leadership into exile after 1945, which only further compounded PSOE's difficulties, as lack of contact and coordination, and lack of ideological and programmatic consensus between the exterior and interior plagued the PSOE. By the 1950s, the Socialists had been displaced by the communists as the principal leftist party organization in Spain.[40]

Interestingly, however, the fall of the PSOE under Franco may have aided the success of the PSOE in the transition to democracy. The PSOE emerged in the 1970s as "an old but new party" – a young party with a young leadership that presented a clean break from the Franco regime. PSOE's main attraction was its young leader, Felipe González, who at thirty-two years of age replaced Rodolfo Llopis as party secretary general in 1974. Following the change in leadership, PSOE membership increased significantly; it quadrupled between 1974 and 1976, and had reached 8,000 by December 1976.[41] Significantly, the former leaders in exile refused to recognize the new executive committee and formed a rival socialist party, the PSOE-Histórico. But the Socialist International rejected the claims of Llopis and his old guard, and voted to recognize the renovated PSOE as the genuine one.

In contrast to the PCE, which proclaimed its moderate and democratic nature but could not escape radical representations, the PSOE initially proclaimed its radical nature but attained a moderate and democratic image throughout the transition. The PSOE's first congress in Spain since the fall of the Republic was held in December 1976. The PSOE defined itself as "a class party, and therefore a mass party, Marxist and democratic," which, interestingly, was the first time the term "Marxist" had appeared in PSOE's self-description.[42] The principal objective of the PSOE was "the overcoming of the capitalist means of production through the seizure of economic and political power and socialization of the means of production, distribution and exchange by the working class"; the party rejected "any path of accommodation with capitalism or the simple reform of the system."[43] Like the PCE, the PSOE engaged in strikes and demonstrations (especially prior to PSOE's legalization), and called for a complete rupture with the Franco regime.[44]

Yet, despite its ideology, which was well to the left of the PCE, the PSOE enjoyed a moderate image in the 1977 electoral campaign. While nearly 20 percent of those surveyed classified the PCE as "extreme left," only 2 percent classified PSOE in that way.[45] As shown in Figure 5.2, the electorate considered the PSOE more "non-Marxist" than the PCE; and 67 percent of the electorate considered the PSOE "democratic," which was more than any other party, including the UCD. Far from being linked to the past and perceived as a threat to democracy, the PSOE came to reflect separation

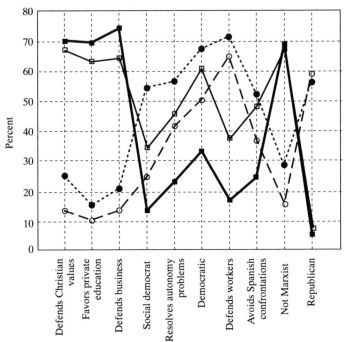

■ Alianza Popular (Popular Alliance, AP)
□ Unión del Centro Democrático (Union of the Democratic Center, UCD)
● Partido Socialista Obrero Español (Spanish Socialist Workers' Party, PSOE)
○ Partido Comunista Español (Spanish Communist Party, PCE)

Figure 5.2. Images of principal political parties. Source: Linz et al. (1981: 234)

from the Franco regime (a new beginning) and non-confrontation, which corresponds to the communal homogeneity of the state of liminality as well as to the new democratic norms of the state of reaggregation.

First, as suggested previously, the "PSOE was *reborn* as a socialist party of a radical character";[46] it did not represent the militancy and polarization characteristic of the Civil War and the Franco regime. In profound contrast to Ibárruri and Carrillo, who could not help but conjure up representations of the past, González himself represented the new beginning. Besides his youth, mentioned above, González was known for his informality: his "open shirts" were said to reflect his openness and tolerance as a person. As shown in Figure 5.1, González was perceived as an inexperienced politician – but without experience meant without participation in the (profane) politics of the Franco era – which corresponded to the new generation and a "new beginning." (Note the contrast between Suárez and González and

Fraga and Carrillo in the category "experience" in Figure 5.1.) As shown in Figure 5.1, González not only scored higher than all other political leaders in the category "nice," but lower than all others in the categories "authoritarian" and "demagogical"; and González (along with Suárez) scored very low in terms of "excitable." The categories "authoritarian," "demagogical," and "excitable" represent the old, profane standards of confrontation and irrationality in symbolic opposition to the new sacred democratic ideals of moderation and rationality. In correspondence with this evaluation of González, the PSOE headed by González was the party perceived most positively in terms of avoiding confrontations between Spaniards (see Figure 5.2). In sum, the non-authoritarian, non-confrontational, non-demagogical image of González and the PSOE represents a break from the past (separation), and its polarizations/confrontations, which corresponds to national reconciliation and the communal state of liminality, as well as to the norms of the new democracy: rationality, dialogue, and moderation, which reflect the liminal state of reaggregation.

In addition, while both the PCE and the PSOE presented moderate, democratic faces in the 1977 electoral campaigns, the Socialists also emphasized "modernization" and "Europeanization" (which was linked to González's own youth and the "new beginnning"). This link is epitomized in the PSOE campaign slogan, "The key to Europe is in your hands. Vote PSOE."[47]

Most importantly, the PSOE was indeed linked to Europe: unlike their rival socialist party, the Partido Socialista Popular (PSP), the PSOE was formally recognized by the Socialist International. This recognition by the Socialist International had important structural as well as symbolic advantages for the PSOE. Many Spanish emigrant workers joined PSOE because of its ties to socialist parties or trade unions in the countries in which they were working.[48] In addition, the PSOE received financial support and practical advice from the International, particularly the West German Social Democratic Party (SPD). According to Gunther, Sani and Shabad, while the exact amount of financial assistance from the SPD is unknown, the severe scarcity of funds at the disposal of its rivals on the left of the political spectrum meant that the PSOE gained a distinct advantage from such aid.[49] Finally, the PSOE became legitimized by its "great and intimate ties" to Europe. Ironically, this legitimation was enhanced when the PSP celebrated its "independentist," "Mediterranean" line, contrasting its "independence" with the "international" line of the PSOE.[50] While clearly the PSP sought to capitalize on the fact that it lacked the support of the International, this strategy of highlighting its "Mediterranean" line was patently out of sorts with the hegemonic transitional symbolization.

Moreover, this was a strategy from "the past": one of the critical schisms between leftists in the Civil War was the socialists' criticisms of Spanish communists' "blind" reliance on and adherence to the Soviet Union.

The Popular Alliance (AP)

The Popular Alliance (Alianza Popular – AP) was created in October 1976 as a coalition of several separate political and personalistic groupings: Reforma Democrática (Democratic Reform) headed by Manuel Fraga Iribarne, the Unión del Pueblo Español (Union of the Spanish People) of Cruz Martínez Esteruelas, Acción Democrática Española (Spanish Democratic Action) of Federico Silva Muñoz, Laureano López Rodó's Acción Regional (Regional Action), the Democracia Social (Social Democracy) under Licinio de la Fuente, the Unión Nacional Española (National Spanish Union) of Gonzalo Fernández de la Mora, and the Unión Social Popular (Popular Social Union) of Enrique Tomás de Carranza. These individuals, referred to as the "Magnificent Seven," had all served as high-ranking officials in various Francoist ministries. The AP was led by Manuel Fraga Iribarne, who acquired a "reformist" reputation as the author of the press liberalization law in his role as Minister of Information and Tourism in the Franco government.[51]

Fraga conceived of AP as an alternative of the "center," in contrast to the right and left extremes that "do not believe in democracy."[52] But, despite Fraga's vision of AP as "a conservative party in the American Republican tradition," AP attained the image of being a Francoist continuist party, which led to its poor showing in the 1977 elections. At the level of the sacred, Fraga and the AP had the same problem as the communists under Carrillo. Both leaders were "reformists" within their respective parties; but both had also been "participants" in confrontational politics under Franco.

First, despite his reformist tendencies, Fraga was nevertheless intimately linked to the Francoist bunker. Not only was Fraga Minister of the Interior in the first post-Franco government dismissed by King Juan Carlos owing to its lack of democratization, but the various police units under Fraga's authority were involved in incidents of excessive brutality. The most famous incident involving police brutality occurred on March 2, 1976, in Vitoria, in the Basque country. Three demonstrators were killed and over forty were injured in an altercation with the forces of public order, which led to massive protests in the Basque country not only by oppositional parties, but local Basque governments.[53] Needless to say, the association between Fraga and police brutality poignantly contradicted images of "democracy," "a new beginning," and "national reconciliation." As shown in Figure 5.1, in direct contrast to González, Fraga was perceived as the most "excitable," "demagogical," and "authoritarian," and the least "nice" and "understanding" leader of the transition. And, as indicated previously, the attributes "authoritarian," "demagogical," and "excitable" represent the "old generation" standards of irrationality, "triumphalism," and confrontation, which stand in stark contrast to the rational, non-confrontational, moderate, reconciliatory nature of the "new generation."

Secondly, other members of AP, such as Tomás de Carranza, López Rodó, and especially Gonzalo Fernández de la Mora, projected a decidedly Francoist image that contradicted notions of democracy and national reconciliation. For example, while Suárez maintained that the PCE was legalized out of "patriotism, because the service that in these moments we demand of Spain is to clarify the rules of the game, and number the participants," and that the legalization was necessary so "that there be not a single note of discord between the social reality and the legal reality of the country," Fernández de la Mora countered:

But if this were so, why not legalize all the parties? Why not legalize social realities like morphinism [drug use], abortion, theft, homosexuality, separatism, anarchism, etc.? If all social reality were to be legalized, the Law wouldn't exist, let alone penal law . . . Norms are not promulgated to recognize in writing what men do, but on the contrary, to arraign behavior and avoid their deviation. The thesis used to support the legalization of the PCE contains within it the liquidation of moral and judicial order, and consequently, the disappearance of the State. This argument has already been wielded in some meetings, but it's surprising that it can be subscribed to at the level of the sovereignty . . .

From the appearance of communism in 1848, this type of movement has acted with an almost monolithic faithfulness to Marxist thought and that of its epigoths Engels and Lenin . . . Its president and general secretary are the same as 40 years ago, and they have not renounced anything from their past, nor any of their writers. If anyone remains faithful to itself, it's the PCE . . . The PCE hasn't moved, who has been displaced is the president . . .

The arbitral function [of the State] consists precisely in permitting only certain players on the field, not every spontaneous one who wants to jump onto the court.[54]

The above passage contains several representations that pit AP on the profane side in the transitional (sacred) democracy vs. (profane) dictatorship dichotomy. First, Fernández de la Mora's argument pits AP on the "old" side of "order" rather than the "new" one of civil liberties: that the function of laws is to maintain "moral and judicial order," "arraign behavior," and "avoid deviation," stands in stark contrast to the "new" understanding of law as the embodiment of civil liberties. Similarly, the social "realities" cited, drug use, homosexuality, abortion, are cited as "evils" in the spirit typical of the Franco regime, rather than linked in the modern democratic sense to civil liberties. Ironically, the discussion of these "evils" in an article on the legalization of the Communist Party recalls also the Francoist notion that communism is to blame for all evil social realities. And, Fernández de la Mora's argument that government must regulate the rules of the game also reflects the notion that order takes precedence over pluralism. In addition, Fernández de la Mora's statement projects an image of AP which contradicts images of national reconciliation. Specifically, that the communists have not "renounced" their past reflects an understanding that the Civil War is "the communists' fault," and the idea that "the communists have not paid their dues" opposes the goal of national reconciliation, and the communal homogeneity of the state of liminality. Thus, while Fraga sought to cut his ties to Francoism and portray AP as a conservative but democratic party, not only AP positions, such as their stance against the legalization of the PCE, but the rhetoric used to justify these positions contradicted images of reconciliation, democracy, and a new beginning, and the corresponding ritual processes of liminality, reaggregation, and separation.

Finally, the nomination of Carlos Arias Navarro as an AP candidate for the Senate was "the point of no return."[55] Not only, as mentioned previously, was the government of Arias Navarro dismissed by King Juan Carlos for its lack of democratization, but Arias Navarro continued to proclaim his "dogged loyalty to the Caudillo." As Gunther, Sani, and Shabad state:

For the majority of the voters, the inclusion of Arias was decidedly negative. In spite of requests from the AP campaign committee and from Fraga himself that he "speak more of the future and less of the past," Arias frequently expressed his pride in the accomplishments of the old order, and provoked crowds at AP rallies to break out in chants of "Franco, Franco, Franco . . . "[56]

An appearance by Arias Navarro on nationwide television perhaps epitomized the Francoist image that he possessed. Arias Navarro explicitly mentioned the name of Franco seven times, and made fourteen additional allusions to him.[57] In one instance, he spoke of the "false, insidious and tolerated campaign against Franco" while a photograph of Franco dressed in his military uniform was projected.[58]

Poll data reflect also that AP was not at all associated with representations of democracy and national reconciliation. In Figure 5.2 we see that the AP was perceived as the least "democratic" of the four major parties, as well as the party least able to "avoid confrontation between Spaniards." Significantly, the AP was perceived as less democratic and more confrontational than even the PCE.

6

The 1977 Moncloa Pacts and the ritualization of communality

The Second Republic had coincided with the World Depression of 1929–1933, and following Franco's death Spain again experienced economic crisis and democracy simultaneously. This crisis was due largely to the unbalanced and dependent development from 1962 to 1975, uncontrolled inflation, the increase in the cost of raw materials, and the stabilization policies of western European countries.[1] Moreover, between 1973 and 1977, Spain had no anti-crisis economic policy. Since the assassination of Luis Carrero Blanco in 1973, Spanish governments had focused exclusively on the political transition, treating the economy with ad hoc palliatives rather than a coherent strategy.[2] The major problems were inflation and unemployment. While inflation never fell below 15 percent, unemployment increased by more than two and a half times between 1973 and 1977, from 3.8 percent of the active population in 1975 to 12.6 percent in 1980. Of this total number of unemployed, only 51.8 percent were entitled to unemployment benefits.[3] The number of strikes increased tenfold between 1973 and 1978. In 1976, Spain lost 156 million working hours through strikes, compared with 14.5 million in 1975, making it the Western country with the highest strike record.[4] And the balance of payments, which had been positive in the years up to 1974, showed a deficit of $4.3 billion in 1976.[5]

In early October 1977, Prime Minister Suárez finally began to address these concerns. He invited nine major party leaders to join him in a two-day meeting to discuss the country's economic problem. (These leaders are listed in Table 6.1.) On October 9, the leaders announced that they had reached a consensus on the broad outlines of an economic policy and of a program of political reform. By October 21, they had completed a forty-page text known as the *Pactos de la Moncloa* (Moncloa Pacts), named for the residence and office of the Prime Minister, where the meetings were held.

The Moncloa Pacts consisted of an economic and a political pact,

Table 6.1. *Party representatives, the Moncloa Pacts (October 1977)*

Party affiliation	Name of representative
UCD	Adolfo Suárez
	Leopoldo Calvo Sotelo
PSOE	Felipe González
	Joan Raventós
	Josep María Triginer
PCE	Santiago Carrillo
AP	Manuel Fraga Iribarne
PSP	Enrique Tierno Galván
PDC	Miquel Roca Junyent
PNV	Juan Ajuriaguerra

Key:
UCD *Unión del Centro Democrático*
PSOE *Partido Socialista Obrero Español* and
    Socialistes de Catalunya
PCE *Partido Comunista Español*
AP *Alianza Popular*
PSP *Partido Socialista Popular*
PDC *Pacte Democràtic per Catalunya*
PNV *Partido Nacionalista Vasco*

although the economic part of the Moncloa Pact was considered far more significant. The economic pact was essentially an austerity plan that offered social reforms and more parliamentary control over the economy in exchange for wage restraint. The government and the parties agreed to raise pensions 30 percent, increase unemployment benefits to the same level as the legal minimum wage, substitute progressive income taxes for indirect taxes, and undertake other fiscal reforms including new corporate taxes and a permanent tax on wealth. The social security system and government expenditures would be brought under closer parliamentary scrutiny and control. The government and parties agreed to the creation of new class-rooms for 700,000 more students as part of a move toward completely free education, and they promised to introduce the distinctive languages and culture of the various regions into the school curriculum. Programs of slum removal, control of urban land speculation, and construction of subsidized housing would be undertaken to help alleviate the housing shortage, as would an agrarian reform program designed to convert renters into land-owners and to put an end to sharecropping.[6]

In return for these reforms, workers were asked to accept a ceiling of 22 percent on wage increases in 1978. This would represent stagnation of real wages, but not a decline, since monetary and fiscal policy would be designed to keep inflation at or below 22 percent.[7]

The political agreements of the Moncloa Pacts were short-term legislative measures "to adapt the law to the demands of the new democratic reality" of Spain until the new Constitution was in place. Most important, perhaps, was the revision of the Law of Public Order. The government originally proposed a law of "Defense of the Democracy against Terrorism," but the left protested the "creation of a specific political unit with special prerogatives." The revised Law of Public Order did not include any special reference to terrorism. Rather, the new Law of Public Order redefined the concept of public order, basing it "on the free, peaceful and harmonious enjoyment of civil liberties and respect for human rights."[8] The Law of Public Order also included important legislation for reforming the police. The Civil Guard was placed under the Ministry of the Interior rather than the army; and the Armed Police was renamed the National Guard, although they remained a militarized unit.[9]

In sum, by 1977, grave politico-economic problems threatened the fledgling Spanish democracy, and the Moncloa Pacts were an agreement by which Suárez offered social reforms in return for the cooperation of the unions and left-wing parties. Regardless of the politico-economic effects of the Pacts (they were fruitful in some areas but less so in others), the drafting of the Moncloa Pacts was central to the Spanish transition in at least two ways. First, the drafting of the Moncloa Pacts ushered in a new type of political procedure in Spain. This procedure, called, significantly, the "politics of consensus," became the ground rules for the drafting of a far more potentially problematic and significant document: the 1978 Constitution. Secondly, at a more profound level, the drafting of the Moncloa Pacts reified and affirmed the core symbols and ritual process of the Spanish transition. Above all, the drafting of the Moncloa Pacts reaffirmed the communality of the liminal state – and that Spain was on the path toward democratic reaggregation.

Symbolization and the Moncloa Pacts

The meetings in the Moncloa were not designed for symbolic purposes; they were part of a serious effort to solve Spain's grave, institutional economic problems. Yet, from the very beginning, the Moncloa Pacts contained vital symbolic dimensions.

First, the very notion of an all-party meeting to resolve the economic crisis was not simply a "rational" response to the crisis itself. The June elections had produced a remarkable defeat of extreme parties on both the right and the left, and had given new impetus to the symbols of a "new beginning," "national reconciliation"/"*convivencia,*" and "democracy." It was this subjective momentum – the force of the new symbols – that created the very idea of an all-party meeting. This was the first time in Spanish history, that such a meeting – a gathering of former enemies in an effort to consensually solve serious politico-economic problems – had taken place. Specifically, among the major party leaders who attended the Moncloa conference were the General Secretary of the Spanish Communist Party, Santiago Carrillo, and the ex-Francoist minister who had had Carrillo imprisoned merely a year earlier, Manuel Fraga (see Table 6.1).

If the coming together of these former enemies was the result of former symbolic movements, the event itself had significant symbolic effects in turn. The Moncloa event both "opened" and "closed" with demonstrations of a "new beginning" of "reconciliation" and "democracy." On the morning of October 8, 1977, the first day of the Moncloa Pact meetings, ETA-militar (the terrorist wing of the separatist group "Basque Homeland and Freedom") assassinated the president of the Deputation of Vizcaya (in the Basque Country) and his two Civil Guard escorts. The Spanish public was outraged. The assassinations in the Basque country were dangerously linked to violent "Civil War." Thus the first meeting in the Moncloa was not begun with harsh political ideological debates about the economy. Rather, it began with a "unanimous public condemnation" of this "criminal act," signed by all the Moncloa conferees (except, significantly, for the Basque delegate, who had already left for Vizcaya). The Moncloa conferees' statement was "a unanimous expression of repulsion and indignation before this criminal act, that only serves as the most barbaric destabilization of the Spanish democratic process."[10] Thus the Moncloa conferees not only confirmed the symbolic opposition between (profane) violence/confrontation and (sacred) *convivencia*/democracy, but firmly placed themselves *together* on the sacred side of this equation. The Moncloa conferees pledged "to continue forward on the path that has already been taken, towards the full realization of collective freedoms . . . and the peace that we all desire for our country."[11]

Just as this stylized framework provided an opening to the Moncloa event, it provided a closing ceremony. The drafting of the Moncloa Pacts concluded with a highly formalized media event. Media events are opportunities to rearticulate and reform cultural categories; they are modern, unexpected rituals, which call up new as well as old meanings. The Moncloa event "closed" with a live telecast of the signing of the Moncloa Pacts by the Moncloa conferees. After the last signature was written (by Communist

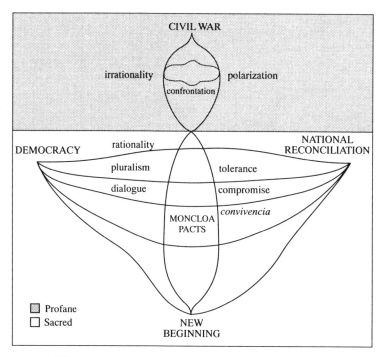

Figure 6.1. Legitimation of the Moncloa Pacts

leader Santiago Carrillo), the President declared, "I think, gentlemen, that we should all greet one another," upon which he stood up and embraced each leader.[12] Thus, the signing of the Moncloa Pacts was publicly finalized and affirmed as an act of tolerance and reconciliation as well as pluralism and democracy. As shown in Figure 6.1, the core transitional symbols legitimated the signing of the Moncloa Pacts, because the "Moncloa Pacts" were perceived and portrayed as being at the center of the core sacred transitional symbols. Note that, akin to Figure 4.2, Figure 6.1 is simply a more detailed rendering of the symbols of "a new beginning" of "democracy" and "national reconciliation" in symbolic opposition to "Civil War" (outlined in Figure 4.1). But, whereas Figure 4.2 shows the more intricate relations between core symbols, Figure 6.1 shows how the core symbols became intertwined in the perception and creation of a critical transitional event.

In between the ritual "opening" and "closing" of the Moncloa event, the sacred transitional representations were consistently maintained. The Moncloa Pacts were legitimated by the government (as well as much of the opposition) in terms of *convivencia*, rational dialogue, and democracy. Suárez confirmed the Moncloa "mission" as "the consolidation of a democratic state of law . . . through everyone in a state of harmony." The pacts were solutions found "in terms of civilized *convivencia* and not radical confrontation," a "convergence that is not of any one party but a coherent agreement among all."[13]

This statement can be unpacked to reveal several significant symbolic linkages. That the Pacts do not belong to any one party but are a convergence among parties links the Pacts with both *convivencia* and pluralism. "Coherent" agreements and "civilized" *convivencia* reflect the rationality of the Pacts, and directly contrast them with irrational, non-democratic political confrontation. Indeed, the joining of the words "civilized" and "*convivencia*" directly links rationality and reconciliation. This linkage is illustrated in Figure 6.1.

In Suárez's speech announcing the successful completion of the Pacts, we see not only the above symbolic linkages, but how the drafting of the Pacts reifies the ritual process of transition. Suárez stated:

In the preparation of this program and in its acceptance the biggest winner is the people who one day gave those of us who are seated on these benches, their confidence. Even though [the Pacts] are going to pre-suppose sacrifices from Spaniards, these sacrifices can and will be tolerable because there is no exclusion: because the burden will be shared equally: because we will know that the obliged hardship and difficulty of the present circumstances will serve to make healthy a country that still puts up with many irritating injustices and many inequalities of treatment.

Meanwhile that the Constitution is arriving, it appears clear that the democratic process is already irreversible. What has made it irreversible has been the spirit of the Crown, the maturity of our people, and the responsibility and the realism of our political parties.[14]

While, as indicated previously, the transition itself is a liminal state (journey from one social state to another), the drafting of the Moncloa Pacts epitomizes the state of liminality discussed by Turner.[15] Turner explains that in rites of transition initiates are homogenized and humiliated in acts (such as the stripping of clothes or shaving of hair) which serve to unite the initiates in a marginal state of lowliness in anticipation of the future (better) social state into which they will be reaggregated. In Suárez's statement above, the communal, homogenizing character of the transition is reflected in the "sacrifices" and "burdens" that will fall on all Spaniards (initiates) in anticipation of the future new social state ("democracy"). The arrival of the new social state will be marked by the new Constitution; but that this process is "irreversible" underscores that this hardship is worth it.

The new, desired social state will come; this is a genuine "new beginning."

In response to the apparent "sanctity" of the Pacts, columnists such as Manuel Vicent poked fun at – but ultimately affirmed – the link between the Pacts and (sacred) liminality. Vicent stated:

Before June 15 they talked of predemocracy. Now senators and deputies repeat a lot about [this] preconstitutional period. And in this traverse through the desert, the Moncloa Pacts have fallen like a vanilla-flavored manna.[16]

"Pre"-periods are liminal periods, periods of "betwixt and between." That the Moncloa Pacts were part of a "preconstitutional period" reflects not only liminality, but that it is with the new Constitution that democratic reaggregation will be achieved. The analogy of a "desert transverse" also contains a dual reference to liminality. The desert is a beige, homogeneous plain of "nothingness," which one crosses only in order to get to a (much-desired) destination. That the Moncloa Pacts "have fallen like a vanilla-flavored *manna*" (manna being the food miraculously supplied by God to the Israelites in their journey through the desert) confirms (albeit sarcastically) that the pacts are perceived as a temporary, vital, sacred sustenance for this (difficult, liminal) journey. That the manna is "vanilla-flavored" challenges the supposed sanctity of the pacts, by implying that they are superficial and commercial (although still a very popular flavor).

Finally, the sacrality of the Pacts was reflected in that being against the pacts was equated with being against democracy, and on the side of dictatorship or single-party demagogy. For example, Minister of Labor Jiménez de Parga severely condemned an amendment presented by the Alianza Popular, arguing that perhaps the AP *wanted* "chaos and the disgovernment of Parliament with this amendment to the totality."[17]

Of course, the rhetoric of the far right and far left, who were against the pacts, only confirmed the equation of being against the pacts with being against democracy. On the left, the Revolutionary Workers' Organization (ORT, Organización Revolucionaria de Trabajadores) organized a series of public acts against the Moncloa Pacts with the intent of "knocking down" ["*echar abajo*"] the Moncloa Pacts through the fight of a "common front of workers."[18] "Knocking down" or "destroying" the pacts through a "fight" reflects confrontation and divisiveness, at odds with reconciliation and democracy.[19]

The President of Fuerza Nueva, Blas Piñar, took a different tack. He trivialized (and thereby desacralized) the Pacts, calling the Moncloa meetings "circus games" and "card games," and insisting that "the people are letting themselves be fooled like children." Interestingly, the far right also attempted to desacralize the Pacts by calling Suárez "dictatorial," which calls up the hegemonic (profane) "dictatorship" vs. (sacred) "democracy" symbolic equation. For example, an editorial in *El Alcázar* stated:

Neither the laws still in force nor the institutions of democracy have been taken in account in pacting. Dictatorial, Suárez has signed an agreement with the astute representative of an International. If the people chose democratic reform and put it in the hands of the UCD, now they find the spectacular and tragic advance of a totalitarian party, for whom barely a minority voted.[20]

This statement reflects the traditional far right-view that the Communist Party is "totalitarian" and controlled by the International (read Soviet Union). It also may reflect that pacting by ex-Movimiento leader Suárez and Communist leader Santiago Carrillo was found particularly profane, or polluting. Yet, in criticizing Suárez for being "dictatorial," and suggesting that the people voted for democratic reform and the UCD, and that is what and who should prevail, even this far-right editorial can be seen as reaffirming the core transitional dichotomy of (profane) "dictatorship" (and totalitarianism) vs. (sacred) "democracy."

The Popular Alliance (AP)

On the one hand, Alianza Popular leader Manuel Fraga lauded the Moncloa negotiations and signed the economic pacts, and tried to link AP with the sacred themes of "democracy" and "national reconciliation." Thus, for instance, Fraga introduced his former enemy, communist leader Santiago Carrillo, when Carrillo gave a speech at Club Siglo XXI – which publicly affirmed his commitment to (sacred) "national reconciliation."[21]

On the other hand, however, AP rejected the political pact, and Fraga's criticisms of the pact linked AP to the side of authoritarianism in the sacred transitional symbolic equation of "democracy" vs. "dictatorship." For example, Fraga stated:

We have not believed that this pact was either opportune or effective. Moreover, it seems immoral to us that two parties come to an agreement on themes about which they have maintained very distinct positions in their programs . . . it would be a hoax for the country if every subject were to arrive already pacted to the Parliament.[22]

That Fraga found the pacts neither "opportune" nor "effective" is a critique at the mundane level of politics; at the deepest level, it reflected, perhaps, rational differences in the spirit of democratic negotiation. But that Fraga found the pacting of the parties of Suárez and González/ Carrillo "immoral" calls up the far-right view that *all* liberal politicking is somehow dirty (see chapter 4). This is quite the opposite of the hegemonic

transitional view – that "pacting" was linked with (sacred) "national reconciliation," "compromise," "tolerance," "pluralism," and moral "dialogue" (see Figure 6.1).

Fraga's ambivalence toward not only the Moncloa Pacts, but the "new
beginning" of "national reconciliation" is readily apparent in most of his
statements during this period. For instance, in one statement, Fraga explicitly acknowledged a "new beginning" by maintaining that the AP is
"plainly conscious that we are in the irreversible mode of post-francoism";
and he explicitly called up "moderation," "modernity," "tolerance," and
"rationality" by stating that AP has "no relation whatsoever" to the far
right, and that the AP is a great party of the center-right, "at the same time
conservative, reformist, modern, open, and well organized."[23] Nevertheless,
Fraga goes on to project a traditional, Francoist conceptualization of
public order and morality, asserting that "a crisis of public morality, and
degradation in the public order exists," and that the AP will "never be part
of this anti-francoism, that for some is revenge, and others treason, and in
many simply ingratitude and bad taste." Obviously, accusations of "ingratitude" toward Franco, "revenge," and "bad taste" contradict the sacred
transitional notion of a "new beginning" of "national reconciliation."

Yet, while Fraga's statements and behavior were contradictory and
ambiguous, other members of the AP seemed to link the AP directly with
Francoism. Consider, for instance, the following statement by Ramón
Hermosilla:

The most obvious characteristic in the politics of don Adolfo Suárez has been
acceleration . . . If one calls a complete turn a revolution, it is apparent that we have
already completed one . . . Why has he forced the normal tempo necessary to accom-
modate the political changes to the exigencies of a distinct society? In life, from a
trip, to a pregnancy, to a concerto, to a lecture, everything is subjected to the time
naturally required for its realization; to force this does not produce acceptable
results, rather on the contrary: in some way acceleration is rejected and it breeds dis-
turbances, because of the difficulty experienced by our physical, mental and moral
organisms in directing and assimilating the abnormal transitions more quickly than
that of the reasonably expected space of time . . .
    The Spanish political tempo has been so unnecessarily disturbed by the imposi-
tion of this acceleration that it has produced, among other things equally strange,
the disconcerting phenomenon that a man who four days ago walked in Madrid disguised with a wig [Carrillo], is today deposited in the political conferences of the
president of the Government . . . [24]

That the transition is not only too fast but "revolutionary" and not
"natural" calls up the Francoist notion of an "organic" social order, in symbolic opposition to any social change. That Carrillo's presence in the

Moncloa is "strange" and "disconcerting" (profane), rather than sacred (linked with a "new beginning" of "democracy" and "national reconciliation"), explicitly places the AP on the side of Francoism in the (sacred) "democracy" vs. (profane) "dictatorship" transitional symbolic equation. Yet despite Hermosilla's rancorous renewal of old, Francoist categories, Hermosilla nevertheless confirms the liminal character of the post-Francoist state, i.e. there *is* a new temporality and an on-going "journey" (the problem is that it is going "more quickly than that of the reasonably expected space of time"). In sum, while Suárez and the center-left anxiously anticipated the new social state of democracy (reaggregation), AP lagged in this ritual process, as they only reluctantly separated themselves from Francoism.

The Spanish Communist Party (PCE)

Of the opposition, the communists were the participants most in favor of the Moncloa Pacts, and most instrumental in their formulation. The communists eagerly embraced the Pacts, thereby demonstrating their zeal for "a new beginning" of "national reconciliation" and "democracy."[25] In turn, Suárez eagerly obliged the communists in the Moncloa discussions, which helped combat the more aggressive socialist campaign and dispel charges of Francoist continuation.

Consequently, the communists' statements about the Pacts paralleled those of the government (discussed above): they both emphasized "a new beginning" of "national reconciliation" and "democracy." For example, an editorial in *Mundo Obrero* stated:

Santiago Carrillo has been maintaining that "we must all lend a hand [*"arrimar el hombro"*], in the parliamentary as well as public tribunals." And in order for the people and the workers to do that, he stated, they must be represented by the organs of decision, as a guarantee that power will be shared. In the Moncloa, everyone has lent a hand and the parties representative of the working people have had decision-making capacity . . .

The parties present in the Moncloa have contributed to putting an end to the tradition of two Spains and its dramatic consequences. Each one representing what he represents, without renunciations or pacts regarding what is not pactable, they have negotiated and begun to find emergency solutions for the serious economic crisis, that open the way for major reforms in order to agree upon a common denominator of rules for the democratic game as the cement of a modern Spain.[26]

That everyone must "lend a hand" in this special moment celebrates the communality of the liminal state. That the party representatives have put "an end to the tradition of two Spains and its dramatic consequences" clearly reflects "national reconciliation." With "each one representing what he represents," and that the "rules for the democratic game" become "the cement of the modern Spain" reaffirms a new beginning of "democracy" and democratic reaggregation.

The communist-affiliated Workers' Commissions (CCOO) also backed the Moncloa Pacts, and affirmed their association with democracy. In an interview in *Mundo Obrero*, the leader of the CCOO, Marcelino Camacho, stated:

I value the agreements very positively, I consider them historic . . . The CCOO has defended the idea that the economic crisis and the political crisis can only be resolved in the frame of a global negotiation of all the political forces. And this has occurred in the Moncloa.[27]

In sum, Camacho affirms that the pacting in the Moncloa is a rational, pluralistic process of communal, democratic negotiation (see Figure 6.1).

Yet, despite their fervent embrace of the Moncloa Pacts, as in the case of the 1977 electoral campaign, the communists oftentimes continued to exude contradictory, non-reconciliatory, non-democratic representations. For example, an article in *Mundo Obrero* stated:

Observe that, unlike what has happened in other European countries at the end of periods of fascist dictatorship, here from the elections of June 15 has emerged a hegemonic political force – or alliance of forces. No one alternative can say legitimately, this is the program, these the solutions, these the methods. What prevailed in the [electoral] consultation was the option for democracy . . .

The agreements of the government and the political parties of the parliamentary arc constitute an important democratic triumph, a solid base with which to clear the rubble of the ruins that even now are found on the ground and so that the economic crisis does not culminate in new political tragedies.[28]

On the one hand, that the Pacts are a result of an "alliance of forces" such that no one can say "this is the program," etc. clearly links the Moncloa pacting with tolerance, pluralism, and moderation. That what "prevailed" and "triumphed" was "democracy" underscores the symbolic opposition of (sacred) "democracy" and (profane) "dicatorship." On the other hand, however, in calling up other European periods of "fascist dictatorship," the author rekindles Franco's (profane) association with Mussolini and Hitler, which symbolically opposes national reconciliation. Moreover, that the end of the period of fascist dictatorship left a "rubble of . . . ruins" still on the ground, implies not that the on-going economic crisis is a "liminal" burden to be shared, but a crisis engendered by the fascist state.

Similarly, contradictory images abound in the following editorial in *Mundo Obrero*, titled, significantly, "On the Footpath of the Constitution":

We are in a constituent period. The fascists . . . talk of "parliamentary dictatorship." [But] it is childish slander. What occurs is the contrary. What we are talking about is that the whole country – the Government, the people, the bankers, the workers, the military and the monks – from now on walk on the footpath toward the Constitution.

. . . In the Moncloa they have drawn a political path, and a kind of government of concentration in the shadows so as to not hamper the Constitutional march. Now we all must go on the footpath of the Moncloa Pacts in order to go later on the footpath to the Constitution.[29]

Once again, on the one hand, that the Moncloa Pacts are the "footpath" to the Constitution reflects the liminal or transitional character of the Moncloa Pacts: the Pacts are part of the (sacred) "journey" to democratic reaggregation. The communality of this liminal state is reflected in the notion that everyone – the rich (bankers), the poor (workers), the conservative (military), the religious (monks) – walk together on the "footpath to the Constitution."

On the other hand, the communist use of the term "government of concentration" was unfortunate in terms of the dominant symbolic framework of the transition. The PCE equated a "government of concentration" with a "government of democratic consensus" – but in the dominant symbolic framework "government of concentration" evoked images of extremism, confrontation, demagogy, and authoritarianism, because it recalled the liberal "government of concentration" of 1922 – which was the last gasp of a chaotic six-year parliamentary monarchy that ended with the revolt of General Primo de Rivera. As Joaquín Garrigues Walker (UCD) bluntly stated, history shows that it was a government of concentration that "took us to the penultimate dictatorship of 1923."[30] Similarly, AP representative Laureano López Rodó warned that a government of concentration "automatically means the disappearance of parliamentary opposition, and this is anti-democratic."[31]

While conservatives tended simply to reject the term "concentration" outright, Suárez quickly and adamantly rejected the term "government of "concentration," while confirming the notion of genuine (sacred) "consensus" and "democracy" (which "saved" the Moncloa pacting from pollution).[32] Similarly, Jordi Pujol (Convergencia Democrática de Catalunya, Democratic Convergence of Catalonia) denounced the idea of a government of concentration, while confirming the idea of a "programmatic agreement."[33] The damage had already been done to the Spanish Communist Party, however. That the Communists could even think to equate the new (sacred) consensual strategy with the old (profane) "government of concentration" merely underscored the inability of the PCE to embark on a genuine "new beginning" of "national reconciliation" and "democracy."

The Spanish Socialist Workers' Party (PSOE)

Of course, the Moncloa Pacts did not exist only in the symbolic world, and the socialists, especially, had important reasons to be critical of them. Unlike the PCE (who simply sought to play a role in the transition, "no matter how small"), the difference between UCD and PSOE in the June elections was less than 5 percent, and the PSOE felt that – if they played their cards right – they could win the next election. The PSOE was reluctant to support a plan which, if successful, would be of electoral benefit to the government. What the government was asking, in effect, was that the socialists accept responsibility without power.[34]

But the PSOE eventually accepted the pacts. According to Gilmour, "that the socialists did sign the agreement in spite of its disadvantages is a measure of *their* sense of responsibility."[35] Yet perhaps there were reasons at the level of the sacred for the socialists to accept the pacts which outweighed or counteracted the "strategic" reasons for rejecting them. Specifically, the Moncloa Pacts were becoming firmly linked to national reconciliation and democracy; they symbolized liminality on the path toward democratic reaggregation. Once this linkage had been firmly made, the socialists could not reject the pacts without linking themselves to the (profane) anti-democratic side of the symbolic equation.

The socialists' debate for and against the Moncloa Pacts clearly reflects this struggle at the level of the sacred. Like right-wing critics of the pacts, the socialists tried to disassociate the Pacts with (sacred) "democracy" and link them with (profane) irrational, elitist, closed, demagogy (see Figure 6.2). For example, an editorial in *El Socialista* entitled "Govern without Parliament: Destroy the Democracy," stated:

The coup that the newly born democracy has suffered is already a reality. Ex-francoists and communists, who have just discovered democracy, still seem not to have learned the principal lesson: a democracy is only consolidated through democratic means . . . If the problems of the country are better resolved outside of Parliament, or if we stumble upon democratic institutions more efficient and representative than the parliamentary ones, we must take account of that and take the pertinent measures; but let us not relegate the Parliament to a battlefield, where they agree in public to what they pacted in private. This way not only does not build democracy: this is how one begins to destroy it.[36]

That extra-parliamentary procedures are a "coup" against democracy reaffirms the sacred symbolic opposition of rational, pluralistic dialogue

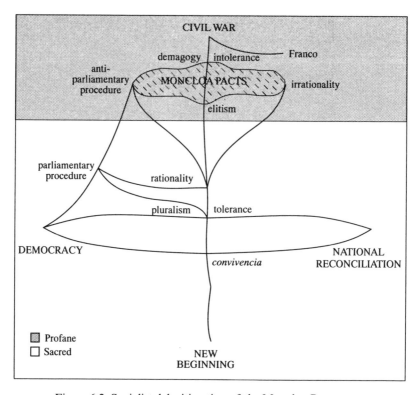

Figure 6.2. Socialist delegitimation of the Moncloa Pacts

and demagogical force (or violence), and the sanctity of democracy ("democracy is only consolidated through democratic means") (see Figure 6.2). That ex-Francoists (i.e. Fraga) and communists (i.e. Carrillo) "have just discovered democracy" implies that the socialists are the "real" democrats (recall their 1977 electoral campaign).

A similar symbolic equation is readily apparent in an editorial by Carlos Luis Alvarez in *Hoja de Lunes*:

The behavior [in the Moncloa] has not been what is called transparent, and furthermore, the completed negotiations depend on the ambiguous nature of the moral responsibility of the businessmen and the workers, even though this responsibility does not come from the norms and compromises that they themselves have negotiated. The economic pact is, more than anything, ideological, this is the other [hidden] side of the moon . . . It is curious that the businessmen and the workers, that have to save Spain at the expense of their interests, have not been represented in the Moncloa. It seems, that it is this same democratic ideology that has been excluded.[37]

That the pacts have not been "transparent," and that they are like the "other side of the moon" links the Pacts with secrecy and evil; they lack the openness, transparency, and accountability of genuine democracy (see Figure 6.2).

Even more harshly, Manuel Villar Arregui, a spokesperson of the group Senadores Progresistas y Socialistas (PSI – Progressive and Socialist Senators), called the meetings in the Moncloa a "cenacle for initiates."[38] The notion of "initiates" reflects an exclusivity quite the opposite of (democratic) inclusivity. A cenacle is the room where Christ and His apostles had the Last Supper. Hence, "cenacle" suggests an elitist group, so closed (or closed because) they perceive their "mission" as sacred. This suggests a religious fervor bordering on irrationality.

In addition, Gregorio Peces-Barba of the Grupo Parliamentario Socialista del Congreso (Parliamentary Socialists) admonished Minister of Labor Jiménez de Parga (who had criticized Alianza Popular's proposed amendments to the pacts) for suggesting that "when someone presents an amendment to the totality he is an enemy of democracy"; and Peces-Barba chastized Jiménez de Parga for his "frankly demagogical tone" and for substituting an "authentic," "juridical-constitutional based argument" with "emotional digression and demagogical embroidery."[39] Thus, interestingly, though Peces-Barba links the Moncloa conferees with the non-democratic side, the symbolic equation remains the same: the sacred is the side of rational, pluralistic dialogue; and the (profane) symbolic opposite is irrational, non-democratic demagogy and intolerance (see Figure 6.2). Moreover, that Peces-Barba defends the right not of the socialists but of the conservatives (their "former enemy") to propose amendments, affirms not only genuine "democracy" but "national reconciliation."

The most serious criticisms of the pacts, however, came from the socialist-affiliated trade union UGT. Indeed, unlike the PSOE, the UGT ended up rejecting the pacts, stating that "we understand the critical situation that we face in this country and we refuse any type of demagogy, which in these moments can be criminal."[40] Yet, once again, the UGT couches its rejection of the pacts not in a narrow, pragmatic concern for union members, but in the sacred transitional symbols of the transition: (genuine) democracy as opposed to (evil) demagogy (see Figure 6.2).

Similarly, UGT leader Nicolas Redondo affirmed "national reconciliation" in his condemnation of the Pacts. Redondo stated:

The pact for UGT is not really a pact, but rather some *bases for discussion*, since in the view of the Socialist central committee one cannot talk of a pact when the unions and businessmen, the authentic protagonists of working life, have been marginalized from the negotiations.[41]

Here, Redondo disparages not simply the absence of the unions – but of businessmen – from the Moncloa reunion. Thus he affirms the ultimate transitional goal: rational, inclusive, pluralistic dialogue between historical enemies (e.g. workers/bourgeoisie).

On the other hand, the socialists' criticism did not carry much weight against the pacts. Most importantly, the UGT's argument that the pacting was exclusive and anti-democratic was weakened by the fact that the communist-affiliated union (CCOO) proclaimed itself not at all hurt by their lack of participation. CCOO leader, Marcelino Camacho, stated:

> If the central committees have not been in the Moncloa, the meetings are in good measure a result of the pressures of the campaign . . . and the demonstrations that we have organized. But moreover, I think that it was not obligatory that we be in the first meeting. Now, a second round of negotiations with the participation of the central committees is necessary, that is fundamental to put the finishing touches on the agreements. And that is where we have to fulfill our role.[42]

Camacho goes on to explain that the CCOO's role will be in enacting the pacts, which portrays the pacts in terms of negotiational and reconciliatory and not exclusionist representations.

Moreover, even within the socialist camp, the pacts were intimately linked with democracy. In direct opposition to UGT's portrayal of the Moncloa discussions as demagogical, the PSOE accepted the invitation to the Moncloa, stating that, "the PSOE has decided to attend the [Moncloa] meeting because it considers positive all debate in reference to the political, economic and social situation of the country,"[43] which links the pacting to the democratic values of dialogue and negotiation, rather than demagogy (see Figure 6.1).

More pointedly, Joaquín Navarro of PSI expressed "absolute disagreement" with the statement by Manuel Villar Arregui (also of PSI), that the conversations in the Moncloa were "a cenacle for initiates." Far from being a cenacle for initiates, Navarro maintained, the Moncloa conferees were "representatives of political parties with sufficient parliamentary entity that the planting of these themes does not hurt the Parliament, since the resulting texts of the conversations will be debated at length in both Houses."[44] That the conferees are "representatives" means that the pacting is pluralistic and democratic (rather than demagogical); that "the resulting texts . . . will be debated at length in both Houses" suggests that the process is not only democratic but rational.

As indicated previously, the socialists ultimately accepted the pacts. The socialists portrayed their criticism, and then acceptance, of the pacts as constructive and pluralistic (rather than oppositional): "We socialists have debated the program presented by the Government, we have made it better and we have returned it to the Government, under the ineludible control of the parliament, to administer its execution."[45] Perhaps in response to Santiago Carrillo's earlier assertion that "the PSOE acts as if the democracy were stabilized, as if it were possible to develop a normal parliamentary game,"[46] the socialists acknowledged that they could have "pursued the points that have been forgotten" in the pacts, but that they were "not going to do so" because of their "zeal for the consolidation of the democracy."[47]

In sum, while the socialists voiced important criticism of the pacts, these criticisms reaffirmed the dominant transitional framework. And, in the end, the PSOE's acceptance of the pacts affirmed the communal, reconciliatory, and democratic nature of the pacts, which corresponded to the transitional process of liminality on the path toward reaggregation.

Most importantly, the victory of the "moderate" socialists was not only critical to the successful drafting of the Pacts, but to the eventual consolidation of moderation in the Socialist Party. The victory of the moderates in the drafting of the Moncloa Pacts in no way ended the internal Socialist Party debate. This debate was not officially resolved until 1979, when "Marxism" was officially removed from the Socialist Party program.[48] But the moderation shown in the Moncloa meetings brought the Socialist Party into the center; and if the Socialist Party had not been brought into the center, the transition might have broken down into harsh class conflict.

PART III

Conflict and consensus in the institutionalization of Spanish democracy

7

Democratic reaggregation and the 1978 Constitution

In the previous chapter we saw that there was a critical symbolic dimension to the drafting of the Moncloa Pacts. The Moncloa pacting reaffirmed a (sacred) "new beginning" of "*convivencia*"/"national reconciliation," and "democracy" in symbolic opposition to (profane) "Civil War" (see Figure 6.1); and it ritualized the communal state of liminality in the process of transition (see Table 4.1). We also saw that the drafting of the Moncloa Pacts engendered a specific strategy of elite negotiation, called the "politics of consensus." This strategy was evoked again in the drafting of the Spanish Constitution. In both cases, party leaders confronted and worked through potentially explosive issues by wittingly and unwittingly calling up the core transitional symbols of "a new beginning" of "democracy" and "national reconciliation." The drafting of the 1978 Constitution was a far more lengthy, complicated and consequential process than the drafting of the Moncloa Pacts, however.

Constitutionalism and symbolization

In the industrialized nations of the West, constitutionalism represents the claim that the people possess the authority to regulate the relations among all members of the political community, including those who govern. While in the older states, the constitution typically was drafted by a group of revolutionaries united in their opposition to political autocracy, in the new nations of the twentieth century the constitution is not so much a revolutionary document of liberation as an effort by the ruling elite to integrate a diverse, already mobilized, national population. The twentieth-century constitution subordinates political interests to a higher, more integrative order, in which partisan division, however intense, accepts the ultimate authority of the political institution to resolve conflict.[1]

Thus, constitutionalism is an attempt by political elites to forge political order, by expressing the shared value of democracy, i.e. the right of the people to govern, rather than the partisan interests of the elites of the political community. In addition, however, constitutionalism is an attempt to forge political order by expressing a shared national identity. Just as partisan political interests are subordinated to a more abstract level of consensus regarding democracy, the constitution also seeks to subordinate particular religious, regional or other cleavages to a more abstract understanding of national community. The constitution frequently does this by celebrating those differences and diversity in the name of pluralism. It also incorporates specific references to the community's shared memories, traditions and history, and common political destiny.

In order to draft a new constitution successfully, then, Spanish elites had to forge a transcendent understanding of democracy and communality. Significantly, these representations were not plucked from thin air; they were found in the symbols that had been emerging throughout the transition. The 1978 Spanish Constitution symbolizes – it *is* – a "new beginning" of "democracy" and "*convivencia*"/"national reconciliation." Moreover, the successful ratification of the Constitution marks reaggregation, or the closing of the ritual process of transition, since these core symbols became institutionalized (see Table 4.1).

In this chapter, I focus not on the constitutional document itself, but on symbolization and the process of drafting the 1978 Constitution.[2] This analysis of the meaning attended to the Constitution reveals how the Constitution helped close the ritual process of transition. In the second half of this chapter, I focus on the two most volatile issues in the drafting of the Constitution: the separation of Church and State, and "regional nationalism."[3] We will see that volatile Church–State and regional issues were overcome by evoking the transcendent values of democracy, *convivencia,* and national reconciliation. The exception in this "politics of consensus" is the volatility surrounding Basque nationalism, which will be discussed in the subsequent chapter. Before we delve into symbolization and the 1978 Constitution, however, a brief outline of the constitutional process is in order.

The Drafting of the 1978 Spanish Constitution

The drafting of the 1978 Spanish Constitution involved four stages.[4] The first and most decisive stage began in August 1977 with the appointment of seven prominent party members (listed in Table 7.1) to a subcommittee (*Ponencia*) to produce a draft constitution. These seven came to be known, significantly, as the "consensus coalition." As shown in Table 7.1, three of

Table 7. 1. *Members of the Congressional*
Subcommittee on Constitutional Affairs
("Consensus Coalition")

Party affiliation	Name of representative
UCD	Gabriel Cisneros
	José Pedro Pérez Llorca
	Miguel Herrero de Miñon
PSOE	Gregorio Peces-Barba
PCE/PSUC	Jordi Solé Tura
AP	Manuel Fraga Iribarne
MC	Miquel Roca Junyent

Key:
UCD   *Unión del Centro Democrático*
PSOE   *Partido Socialista Obrero Español* and
           Socialistes de Catalunya
PCE/PSUC *Partido Comunista Español* and *Partit*
           Socialista Unificat de Catalunya
AP   *Alianza Popular*
MC   *Minoría Catalana*
Source: Bonime-Blanc (1987: 38).

the seven were members of the UCD; the remaining four represented
PSOE, PCE–PSUC, AP, and MC (*Minoría Catalana*—a Catalan coalition)
respectively. According to analysts such as Bonime- Blanc, "no other coali-
tional force could have carried as much legitimacy."[5] Significantly, there
were no Basque representatives on this subcommittee.

By early January 1978, the *Ponencia* had completed a preliminary draft
that provided the basic framework for the Constitution, and set forth an
agenda of urgent issues. The "consensus coalition" then examined 1,333
amendments that had been proposed by the deputies. Consensus among
the seven began to break down over the amendments on regional autonomy, education, and the Church. On March 7, 1978, the PSOE angrily
withdrew its representative, Gregorio Peces-Barba, from the subcommittee.
Catalan representative Miquel Roca reported that "the only consensus that
exists is that we must finish the work."[6] Despite the absence of the socialists, the remaining committee members hammered out a revised draft.
Under protest, Peces-Barba signed this draft together with the other six
subcommittee members on April 10, 1978.

The second stage of the constitutional drafting process began on May 5, 1978, with the opening of talks by the thirty-six-member Committee of Constitutional Affairs. The commitee's task was to amend the consensus coalition's rough draft of the Constitution. With some notable exceptions, the tenuous consensus of UCD, PSOE, PCE, and MC prevailed, though negotiations were always intense and often on the verge of breakdown. The AP and the Basques became increasingly marginalized in this phase, largely owing to their stances on Church/education and regional issues. After 148 hours of congressional debate and 1,342 speeches, the congressional committee finalized its work on June 20, 1978.[7]

The third stage of the drafting of the Constitution began in July 1978, a year after the formation of the original "consensus coalition." In this phase, the text finally reached the *Congreso* (Congress), where it was passed with only two negative votes and fourteen abstentions (most of them from *Alianza Popular*). It then went to the *Senado* (Senate), where further amendments were suggested, and the text approved. Yet, since the text approved by the *Senado* contained important differences from the one passed by the *Congreso*, it was left to yet another committee to reconcile the two. On October 31, 1978, the amended text was at last approved overwhelmingly by both chambers. The distribution of the vote reflected the consensual coalition: except for one UCD deputy, all UCD, PSOE, MC, and PCE members voted affirmatively; but five AP and three Basque representatives voted against the constitution, and three AP members and twelve Basques abstained.[8]

The fourth and final stage of the drafting of the Constitution was its public approval and royal sanctioning. The campaign for the national referendum was, not surprisingly, dominated by pro-constitutional forces, and on December 6, 1978, the Constitution was approved by a vast majority. As shown in Table 7.2, nearly 68 percent of all eligible voters participated in the referendum, and only 7.8 percent rejected the Constitution.[9] The entire process came to a close on December 27, 1978, when King Juan Carlos signed the Spanish Constitution.

Symbolization and the 1978 Spanish Constitution

Separation: a new beginning

The ratification of the Constitution in December 1978 was celebrated in the media in precisely the same way as the first democratic elections had been – it was "a new beginning" of "democracy" and "national reconciliation." Parallel to the June 15, 1977, headline in *El País* proclaiming the "debut"

Table 7.2. *Results of the 1978 Referendum on the Constitution: the Basque Country, Catalonia, and Spain as a whole*

Region	Turnout (%)	Yes (% of those who voted)	No (% of those who voted)	Abstention (%)
The Basque Country	45.5	68.2	23.8	51.7
Catalonia	68.3	90.4	4.6	31.7
Spain	67.7	87.8	7.8	32.3

Source: Compiled from Bonime-Blanc (1987: 42, 63); and Ysàs (1994: 101–102).

of democracy (discussed previously), *El País* announced the results of the referendum with the headline, "The Dawn of a New Day." The article stated that "the Constitution . . . proposes to officially close the period of violence from those in power, and open the doors to *convivencia*, dialogue and respect for other persons." [10] Similarly, an article in *El Socialista* stated that people voted "yes" in the constitutional referendum "in order to come out of so many years of dictatorship and its aftermath" and because "one cannot live in the past." [11]

In the first democratic elections, the "dictatorship vs. democracy" dichotomy had helped separate the "new" from the "old" social state. This same dichotomy, illustrated in Figure 7.1, was expressed even more pointedly in the campaign for the Constitutional referendum. As one *El País* reporter noted, the slogan "Constitution or Dictatorship" was used by "practically all the Government, the entire executive of PSOE, the principle directors of the PCE, and the general secretaries of PTE [*Partido del Trabajo de España*], and ORT [*Organización Revolucionaria de Trabajadores*] among others." [12] For example, Socialist leader Felipe González stated:

The choice today is Constitution or dictatorship; any other exposition is false, since the Constitution is the only path to democracy.

The enemies of democracy have made the Constitution the symbol of their ferocious attacks.

We in favor of democracy have the duty to make the Constitution the symbol of our fight for liberty. [13]

In sum, to be against the Constitution was to be against democracy. And to be against either the "Constitution" or "democracy" was a profanation (see Figure 7.1).

The "Constitution vs. Dictatorship" dichotomy was also expressed as

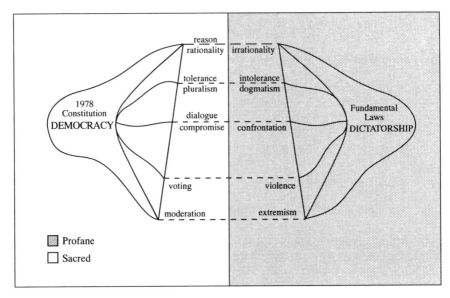

Figure 7.1. Symbolic opposition of "Constitution"/"democracy" and "Fundamental Laws"/"dictatorship"

a choice between "Franco's Fundamental Laws" and "The 1978 Constitution" (see Figure 7.1). An article in *El País* described the differences between the 1978 Constitution and Franco's seven Fundamental Laws, and provided a concise full-page chart summarizing those differences.[14] Another article in *El País* stated:

> What is in play this coming December 6 is not the approval of an ideal text, but rather the abolition of the Fundamental Laws and the Principles of the Movement of Francoism, and the settling of the life of a country on some bases that sufficiently guarantee social *convivencia*, political and ideological pluralism, the rights and liberties of citizens, the election of governors by popular sovereignty . . . It is evident that the Constitution of 1978 sufficiently covers these necessary minimums.[15]

Similarly, communist leader Santiago Carrillo maintained:

> If the 6th [of December] does not result in the approval of the Constitution, the Fundamental Laws of Francoism will remain in place, and this is one of the reasons why the Communist Party will vote "yes" [in the national referendum].[16]

That the far right was in fact against the Constitution only affirmed the (profane) dictatorship/Franco's Fundamental Laws vs. (sacred) democracy/1978 Constitution dichotomy shown in Figure 7.1. The president of

Fuerza Nueva, Blas Piñar, called for "a flat *yes* for Spain, and with that end, a strong and flat *no* for the Constitution."[17] In response, columnist Ricardo Lezcano stated:

That they [the far right] order us to vote "no" [in the Constitutional referendum] is natural. To them, it is not that this Constitution disgusts them, but all Constitutions. They favor military orders to political laws; they prefer macho dictatorships ["*viriles caudillajes*"] to prosaic voting booths ["*las prosaicas urnas*"] . . .

[As an aunt of mine said], "To vote for this Constitution I don't even need to read it. It was made by the politicians that we elected with our votes. If it has defects, they will be corrected, and if those that made it defraud us, then we will vote for others. What I am voting 'yes' for is to have a Constitution, as we have been lacking one for forty years."[18]

That this Constitution (and all constitutions) "disgusts" the far right reflects the perception that "democracy" is "profane" for the far right; it also demonstrates that for the moderate right, center, and left, the very idea that "democracy" is "bad" is in itself a profanation. This parallels González's statement (above) that only "enemies of democracy" ferociously attack the Constitution, i.e. violate (sacred) democracy.

Communal liminality: convivencia *and national reconciliation*

In addition to marking a "new beginning" of "democracy," the 1978 Constitution marked a new beginning of "national reconciliation." The choice between dictatorship/Franco's Fundamental Laws and democracy/the 1978 Constitution was the choice between ideological intolerance and dogmatism, and dialogue, consensus, and *convivencia*/national reconciliation (see Figure 7.1). As indicated previously, the Constitutional drafting committee was called the "consensus coalition." The 1978 Constitution itself was hailed as the "Constitution of Consensus and Harmony."[19] Political leaders all praised the Constitution by speaking about it in these terms. For example, government representative Landelino Lavilla emphasized that "it is a Constitution of consensus . . . not of a single party, which allows it to belong to everyone."[20] Similarly, the spokesman for the UCD, Jiménez Blanco, stated, "Satisfactory for everyone . . . it permits that from now on there are not two Spains."[21] On the left, the general secretary of the PSOE, Felipe González, maintained:

We don't ask for a "yes" to our party, but to the participation of all citizens in the construction of a text that is for everyone, including those that do not like it, but this is the greatness of democracy, that it defends even those who attack it.[22]

And an editorial in *Arriba* maintains:

The Spanish Constitution of 1978 is evidently not a Communist Constitution, and nevertheless the communists will vote yes. The Spanish Constitution is not a conservative text, and nevertheless, the most reasonable and realistic conservatives will vote yes. The Constitution is not a socialist text, nor is it of UCD, but rather a frame which enables us to find a valid formula for a minimum agreement of *convivencia*.[23]

In sum, that the Constitution is "for everyone" and that all are equal under the Constitution reaffirms the communality of liminality as well as *convivencia* and national reconciliation. That "the most reasonable and realistic conservatives will vote yes" on the Constitution links this communality and *convivencia* with rationality.

Of course, the symbolic opposite to this rational, communal *convivencia* is irrational, non-democratic violence. As Carlos Hugo de Borbón stated, the 1978 Constitution was "the best path with which to construct a democracy that evades the dialogue of fists and pistols."[24]

Ironically, the far right also affirmed the link between "pacting," "consensus," and "the Constitution," though their intent was obviously to criticize the Constitution. For instance, Jesús Pascal of *Fuerza Nueva* stated:

We refuse a Constitution that is a consensus between all the enemies of Spain and those politicians who have converted lying and disloyalty into a professional career.[25]

Thus, even though Pascal perceives that the consensus "between all the enemies of Spain" is evil, he nevertheless confirms that the Constitution is the result of "professional" elite negotiation, pacting, and "consensus."

Democracy and reaggregation

Finally, the successful drafting of the Constitution symbolized reaggregation, and an end to the liminal phase of transition (see Table 4.1). The front-page headline in *El País* on the day of the national referendum read, "The Popular Vote Ends the Post-Francoist Transition Today."[26] And, an article in *El País* stated:

The period of transition initiated with the death of Franco and the proclamation of Juan Carlos as King of Spain in November 1975 will close this coming week with the constitutional referendum. The approval of the *Carta Magna* will mean the definitive interment of the Francoist regime, the beginning of a new period of modernization, approximation with the occidental countries and fundamentally the constitutional consolidation of the Monarchy.

It will end the process of transition to democracy that has lasted three years and has been extremely intense.[27]

Interestingly, this article also notes that the transition to democracy has lasted three years and required three governments: the first failed government of Arias Navarro, and the two governments – the pre-electoral and elected governments—of Adolfo Suárez. This distinction of three governments symbolizes the three phases of the ritual process of transition. The first (Arias Navarro) government (November 1975–July 1976) symbolized the stage of separation from the past. Arias Navarro held onto Francoism, and the ousting of Arias Navarro symbolized the ousting of Francoist leadership. The first Suárez government (July 1976–June 1977) "opened the doors of dialogue with the opposition," which represents the liminality and *communitas* of the second stage of transition. Yet, because Suárez was not elected, his government had only a provisional (marginal) democratic legitimacy. On the other hand, the third (present) government, which began with Suárez's electoral victory in June 1977, is seen by the author as an entirely distinct period. The elected Suárez – and his accomplishments – reflect reaggregation in the ritual process of transition. The second Suárez government "carried out its position supported by consensus, and has as its principal reflection the Constitutional debate and the signing of the Moncloa Pacts."

Volatile issues: clericalism and regional nationalism

Of course, the drafting of the 1978 Constitution was a long and complicated process, and constitutional negotiations could not remain at this generalized level of abstraction. The consensus coalition had to delve into polemical political issues in order to redact a viable Constitution. Not surprisingly, then, many constitutional articles were the source of harsh political ideological debates. The most serious of these were the historically sensitive issues of clericalism and regional nationalism.[28]

The issues of clericalism and regional nationalism have distinct histories and dynamics, but they share certain characteristics that prescribed their volatility in the drafting of the 1978 Constitution. Clericalism and regional nationalism were two of the fundamental axes of polarization in the Spanish Civil War; and, in their pure forms, both regional nationalism and clericalism assert loyalties which supersede the communal and democratic loyalties of the Spanish Constitution. The very notion of "divine law" contradicts constitutionalism; and regional "nationalism" challenges the very idea of *a* "national" constitution.[29]

Church and state

Perhaps the most polarizing issue in the history of Spain has been that of Church and State. In the nineteenth and early twentieth centuries, Spain was increasingly characterized by drastic pendular swings between clericalism and anti-clericalism. With hindsight, we can see that the harsh and vengeful anti-clericalism of the Republicans – albeit a direct and perhaps understandable response to the integrist (reactionary) tradition of Spanish Catholicism – helped consolidate the ultra-right in their "Crusade." As many analysts have pointed out, the origins of the Civil War can, to some extent, be seen in the Constitution of the Second Republic, in which militant anti-clericalism served to "poison the atmosphere" of the early and mid-1930s.[30]

After the Civil War, Franco declared Catholicism to be the official religion of the State again. Protestants lost the right to hold office, worship publicly, and to proselytize, and a certificate of baptism was required for admission to schools. Most importantly, the Church regained control of the education process. Religious instruction became mandatory in both Church and State schools, and the Church selected and censored textbooks. In return for restoring the Church's privileges, Franco was given a key role in the appointment of Spanish bishops.[31]

The possibility of renewed religious polarization loomed as the constitutional committees broached the articles involving the Church in the 1978 Constitution: article 16 on disestablishment, article 27 on public versus private (religious) education; and articles 15 and 32, which involved abortion and divorce, respectively. There were numerous anti-clericals among the Spanish Socialist Workers' Party (PSOE), and the PSOE initially adopted an unequivocally anti-clerical stance. At the opposite end of the spectrum, most members of *Alianza Popular* (AP) were staunch defenders of the Church. Indeed, some members of AP took clerical stands much more extreme than those of the church hierarchy itself.[32] The UCD, which was initially formed as a coalition of Christian Democrats, liberals, social democrats, and independents, was heterogeneous, though they tended to side with the Church. Most interestingly, while the PCE maintained an almost neutral stance throughout these debates, siding with the PSOE on divorce and abortion, but voting in favor of continued state subsidies to religious schools and special mention of the Catholic Church in the constitutional text, the Communist Party was still perceived as anti-clerical. The result was a party system in which two parties were clearly identified with Church interests (the UCD and the AP) and two parties (the PSOE and the PCE) were identified as antagonists of the Church.[33]

The threat to consensus

Polarization came to a head on March 6, 1978, when socialist representative Gregorio Peces-Barba walked out of – and did not return to – the meetings of the *Ponencia*. Simultaneously, a large section of Suárez's cabinet resigned and was replaced by a notably more conservative group of ministers.[34] Yet, a few days after the socialist walkout, Suárez and Felipe González held a summit, which began a series of secret talks between the socialists and the government. These talks culminated in a private dinner meeting at a Madrid restaurant on the evening of May 22, 1978. On this night, which came to be known as "the night of José Luis" (the name of the restaurant where the negotiations took place), the socialists and the government reached the specific compromises for the Church/State articles of the Constitution.

The UCD and the socialists had previously met with the leaders of other parties, seeking approval for the private government–socialist meetings. The Catalans and communists agreed to be excluded, but the private, interparty bargaining infuriated the AP. Though his decision was later reversed by Manuel Fraga, AP representative Federico Silva Muñoz even withdrew the AP from the constitutional committee.[35] AP representatives all pointed out that "constitutional matters should be decided in parliamentary committees and not in restaurants."[36] And Fraga went on to state:

It is without a doubt that the Constitution has positive aspects. The first is the spirit of compromise that has inspired all the political forces in its preparation. This compromise dominated in the works of the *Ponencia*, but it was broken by the unanticipated and unjustifiable retirement of the socialist delegate. It is convenient to remember this, when now they talk of those who accept and those who reject this so-called "consensus." The compromise was real, and the solution to the questions in which a conclusion was not reached was only logical: vote by the majority, in correspondence with the programs of each one, and after hearing the arguments of each one. The consensus has been another thing: concessions done in the dark and without stenographers, of a partisan ["*partitocrático*"] character. The majority of the shadows ["*sombras*"] of the final text came from there.

   The Constitution is, of course, democratic . . . but . . . it only functions well if it avoids the two corruptions of the system: "partyitis" and partisanship. Both are consecrated, unfortunately, in the constitutional text.[37]

Interestingly, here Fraga criticizes the undemocratic character of the "strategy of consensus" which parallels the socialists' criticism of the Moncloa pacting discussed previously (and illustrated in Figure 6.2). In both cases, the critics contrast genuine, inclusive, rational (sacred) democracy with elitist, irrational (profane) extra-parliamentary procedure. Yet, in this passage Fraga attempts to do something else: he tries to separate and polarize "compromise" and "consensus" – two representations which in the dominant transitional symbolic framework are linked. Fraga equates "compromise" with (sacred) rationality and democracy (it is "real" and "logical," and a function of "vote by the majority . . . after hearing [program] arguments") – which accords with the dominant symbolization. But Fraga contrasts this (sacred) "compromise" with (evil) "consensus" – irrational, anti-democratic politicking (something "done in the dark and without stenographers").

Yet "consensus" was a sacred transitional symbol, intimately intertwined with "democracy" and "national reconciliation." Thus, despite Fraga's careful redefinition of the term, Fraga's criticism of "consensus" pitted him on the "profane" side of the "democracy" vs. "dictatorship" symbolic equation. Indeed, the mere attempt to separate "compromise" and "consensus" was a *faux pas* that recalls Santiago Carrillo's blunder in equating "consensus" and a "government of concentration," discussed previously. Both Carrillo and Fraga attempted to operationalize core transitional symbols in a new way, but they "misused" them; thus they merely ended up calling into question their ability to *really* embrace a genuine "new beginning."

In addition, Fraga heightened his symbolic linkage with "the past" and the "old generation" (rather than the "new") by asserting that "in the midst of easy consensuses, AP has the difficult role of acting as the conscience of Spain."[38] Clearly, that the AP serves as "the conscience of Spain" recalls the far right's *Cruzada* ("Crusade") mentality ("saving" Spain), which led to civil war. Furthermore, that the role of "conscience of Spain" is pitted against "easy consensuses" pits the AP on the far right against democracy.

The socialists criticized the anti-democratic "extra-parliamentary" character of the "strategy of consensus" too. But, as in the case of the Moncloa pacting, and in contrast to Fraga, the socialists never attacked the notion of "consensus." Moreover, the socialists rationalized their participation in these seemingly undemocratic processes by implying that they were necessary in this special (liminal) period – a period that would end with the Spanish Constitution. As the prominent socialist Raúl Morodo stated:

The strategy of *consensus* has facilitated a difficult political change, and as such, has had to consciously hide differences . . . with the approval of the Constitution a first period is over: from now on, consensus has no meaning.[39]

That the special period of consensus involved focusing on commonalities rather than differences reflects the communality of liminality. That this "first period is over" means that with the approval of the Constitution genuine democratic pluralism – involving dissensus – can now begin. To this end, Alfonso Guerra of the PSOE maintained that while "consensus . . . has avoided our coming up with a Constitution useless to the majority of Spaniards," after the Constitution "we socialists will practice the politics of the opposition, of pressure on the government."[40]

The night of José Luis

Most analysts think of "the night of José Luis" in terms of stragetical political bargaining. For example, Gunther, Sani, and Shabad describe the use of a specific "decision-making style" that facilitated the making of concessions in private meetings.[41] But of course, the very idea of the "night of José Luis" – i.e. private negotiations whose goal was to find compromise and consensus – was a function of the transitional notion that the "mission" of the coalition was to redact a Constitution that was not the agenda of any one political group or party, but simply one to which "everyone could agree."

The immutable transcendence of this goal is evident in that the socialists and the government each accused each other of "breaking the consensus," i.e. of (profane) intransigency. For example, on the side of the government UCD representative Javier Solana argued that the PSOE's "breaking" of the consensus amounted to "a gala disdain for parliamentary democracy, which is now threatened."[42] The term "gala disdain" reflects not only the perception that breaking the consensus was profane (a violation of democracy), but that the socialists reveled in it (i.e. as something analogous to stomping on a flag). The socialists, on the other hand, defended their walk-out by saying that it was the UCD that in fact "broke" the consensus, by positioning itself so close to the AP (a profanation in itself). Thus, Felipe González maintained that the notion "that the PSOE has broken the consensus is literally false"; the PSOE would return to the *Ponencia* if the UCD would "return to the initial consensus."[43]

Significantly, the compromises worked out on "the night of José Luis" ambiguously – even contradictorily – reflected both sides of the disestablishment, education, abortion, and divorce debates, although, as in the case of the Moncloa Pacts, the socialists were under more pressure to "agree." In the case of article 27, the socialists had initially staked out a markedly anti-clerical position, calling for the creation of a unified system of "public education, which signifies the progressive disappearance of private education, as well as the elimination of subsidies or state aid to private education."[44] The PSOE also proposed "self-management" prescriptions, in which "teachers, pupils, parents and popular organizers would have total power of decision."[45] AP and UCD officials, on the other hand, proposed the continued flow of state financial aid to private education (either directly or indirectly through a voucher system), minimal involvement of the state in the private educational sector, and exclusive control of the schools, against demands for "self-management."[46] Nevertheless, both sides agreed to a vague, contradictory text, which encompassed some of each party's demands, but did not wholly satisfy any one religious or political group. In conjunction with conservative demands, state financial support for religious education was guaranteed (although the extent of support remained an open question). In accordance with socialist proposals, the state was granted authority to inspect and license educational centers, and private schools were democratized in general conformity with self-management principles (although the exact nature of democratization was not determined). Thus, article 27 states:

(7) Teachers, parents and, when appropriate, pupils shall participate in the control and management of all the centers maintained by the administration with public funds, under the terms to be laid down by the law.
(8) The public authorities shall inspect and standardize the education system in order to guarantee compliance with the law.[47]

Similarly, ambiguity solved (or deferred) the abortion and divorce debates. Both the PSOE and the PCE initially advocated the inclusion of language in the text of the Constitution that, in itself, would legalize divorce and abortion. Not surprisingly, most AP deputies and some important Catholic bishops not only vigorously opposed these proposals, but wanted the Constitution to include an explicit prohibition against abortion and divorce. The UCD favored a constitutional text that would make possible the legalization of divorce at some point after the constitutional referendum; on the issue of abortion, they sided with the Church. Yet, despite the volatility of these issues, compromise was reached. The right agreed to terminology which would allow prompt enactment of divorce legislation; in return, the PCE and the PSOE abandoned all attempts to push for legalization of divorce and abortion in the constitutional text itself. Article 32.2 of the Constitution states that, "the law will regulate the forms of matrimony . . . [and] the causes of separation and dissolution."[48]

More ambiguously, the final draft of article 15 states that "all have the right to life" ("*Todos tienen derecho a la vida*"). Interestingly, the UCD and the AP inserted the term "all" ("*todos*") in place of "the person" ("*la persona*") in the final draft of this article, so as to leave open the possibility that this right might also apply to fetuses. Indeed, Fraga maintains that the right interpreted this article to mean that abortion was unconstitutional.[49] For communists and socialists – and at least one Spanish constitutional expert – however, this language was so vague it could not be regarded as the legal prohibition of abortion.[50]

The case of article 16 on disestablishment was somewhat more complex. The first draft of article 16 flatly disestablished the Catholic Church, stating "no confession will have a state character." This abruptness incensed Church officials, and UCD and AP representatives of the subcommittee proposed the addition of the following statement:

The public powers will take into account the religious beliefs of Spanish society and will maintain the consequent relations of cooperation with the Catholic Church and other confessions.[51]

For the UCD and the AP, this statement acknowledged the institution of the Catholic Church, but nevertheless reflected religious tolerance and pluralism by including "other confessions." That the government would maintain "relations of cooperation" with the Church reflected the spirit of negotiation, compromise, and consensus.

The communist, socialist and Catalan members of the subcommittee, however, were all against the explicit mention of the Catholic Church. The socialists were most outraged; socialist representative Gregorio Peces-Barba stated:

We are against that unjustified mention [of the Catholic Church] because . . . it has broken the attempt that has been made to establish a consensus . . . Nobody has told us why, contrary to Vatican Council II, it is necessary to include the words "Catholic Church" . . . in contradiction to the principle of secularization of the modern world.[52]

Here, Peces-Barba argued that article 16 contradicts the (sacred) values of consensus, modernization, and secularization integral to the new democratic state. He also legitimized his claims, and sacralized his position, by asserting that the Vatican Council II itself supports this position (modernization, secularization, and complete separation of Church and State). While in the subsequent full committee hearings that followed communist and Catalan delegations voted in favor of the clause mentioning the Catholic Church, the PSOE delegation voted as a bloc against article 16. Nevertheless, on the historic night of May 22, "in exchange for concessions on other things," the PSOE accepted article 16.[53]

Regional nationalism

Regional autonomy is another historically volatile issue that had to be broached in the drafting of the 1978 Constitution. Recall that the Second Republic granted a limited Statute of Autonomy to Catalonia, which further incited the right to "save" the "destruction" of Spain. "Impose on them unity, unity above all," had been the cry of traditionalist leader Pradera to the military rebels of July 18, 1936.[54] After the Civil War, Franco immediately revoked the Catalan and Basque Statutes, banned the use of Catalan and Basque in schools, and suppressed media in minority languages as well as all manifestations of regional culture.[55]

While it was apparent that the distinct Spanish regions must be recognized in the new Constitution, the four major parties, as well as the regional nationalist parties, held varying positions as to the magnitude of autonomy the regions ought to take. At one end of the spectrum, the AP proposed a strictly unitarian state in which regions would be recognized but only nominally, within a context largely unchanged from Franco's. At the other end of the spectrum, nationalistic groups and parties, including the moderate Partido Nacionalista Vasco (PNV) and less moderate groups such as Euzkadiko Ezkerra (EE, Basque Left), proposed allowing regions the right to self-determination (with the concomitant possibility of separation and independence). In between these extremes, the UCD wanted Spain to remain basically unitarian, with greater regional self-management; and most liberal and leftist parties and moderate regional groups backed some form of federalism, in which regions would have substantial powers of self-government.[56]

Catalonia in transition

It is commonly said that they ran out of champagne in Catalonia on the day Franco died. Certainly, Franco had been no friend of the Catalans.[57] While Franco had had the support of Navarre and certain of the Basque industrial elite, the Catalan upper and middle classes had not supported Franco. Thus, thousands of Catalan prisoners were executed between 1939 and 1943, including the President of the Generalitat, Lluis Companys.

Yet, despite the severe repression, a modernistic, progressive type of nationalism emerged in Catalonia in the post-Franco period. As early as the 1960s, "a norm of accommodation and moderation emerged . . . transcending the cleavages of class and ethnicity and standing above residual acrimony from the Civil War."[58] In point of fact, whereas coalition opposition groups, such as the Junta Democrática de España (Democratic Board of Spain) set up by Santiago Carrillo and Rafael Calvo Serer, and its rival organization, the Plataforma de Convergencia Democrática (Platform of Democratic Convergence), were not formed until 1974 and 1975, respectively (and did not merge until 1976); a united democratic opposition group, called the Assemblea de Catalunya (Catalan Assembly), was created in Barcelona as early as 1971. Composed of a diversity of organizations, including the CCOO (Workers' Commissions), the Grup Cristià de Defensa dels Drets Humans (Christian Group for the Defense of Human Rights), the Assemblea Permanent d'Intelectuals (Permanent Assembly of Intellectuals), Comunitats Cristianes de Base (Basic Christian Communities), Assemblea Permanent de Capellans (Permanent Assembly of Priests), certain professional associations, and later on, neighborhood associations from the industrial working-class suburbs; the Assemblea was, according to one of its leading personalities, Agustí de Semir, an organization based on "compromise," with four basic demands: freedom, amnesty, a statute of self-government, and the coordination of the Hispanic peoples against the dictatorship.[59]

Of course, this moderate, democratic nationalist approach did not emerge out of thin air. On the contrary, rationality, *pactisme*, democracy and western Europeanism have been central Catalan nationalist symbols for centuries. Specifically, though both the Basque Country (to be discussed shortly) and Catalonia governed themselves throughout the Middle Ages, Catalonia has long celebrated her early liberal democratic institutions. The Catalan parliament (Corts) was inaugurated at the time of the Magna Carta, and the constitutional system of the Crown of Aragon (today the regions of Catalonia, Aragon, and Valencia) is said to have been the most advanced constitutional system in fourteenth-century Europe.[60] Moreover, Catalans are known for their modernism, pragmatism, rationality, and business acumen, which is negatively stereotyped as stinginess and coldness, but heralded by Catalans as *seny*, which refers to a sense of perspective, level-headedness, and common sense. There is an extensive native literature extolling *seny* as a core element of the Catalan national character; as there is to *pactisme*, the Catalan tradition of negotiation and compromise.[61]

These modernist, democratic values are projected in the Catalan national dance, the *sardana,* which according to Stanley Brandes, is a "metaphor of Catalan identity."[62] The *sardana* is said to reflect *harmonia* (harmony), *germanor* (companionship), and *democracia* (democracy), and especially the achieved rather than ascribed status of being "Catalan" (since the *sardana* is a circle dance, and anyone who knows the simple steps can join in). As Josép Miracle stated in 1948:

the *sardana* is living democracy . . . the realization of . . . Liberty, Equality, Fraternity . . . the *sardana* is not formed by a portion of the [population] but rather by the totality; the people. The people with all their social classes, with all their differences, in all their forms. The *sardana* in Catalonia is everybody's just as the sun that gives us light each day is everybody's.[63]

Similarly, the legal definition of "Catalan" according to the Statute of Autonomy of 1932, and reinstated in the Statute of Autonomy of 1979 (article 6), is notably inclusive rather than exclusive: a Catalan is anyone who has administrative residence in any municipality in Catalonia.[64]

In sum, core symbols at the heart of Catalan nationalist identity – pragmatism, democratic inclusion, and Europeanization – were not merely contiguous with the core symbols emerging in the post-Franco period;

Catalanism itself helped define the new modernist, transitional symbolic framework. Put in another way, Catalonia has long been said to "face Europe" (rather than Spain); and in the transition everyone wanted to "face Europe."[65]

Most importantly, because core Catalan nationalist symbols overlapped with the core symbols of the transitional "period of consensus," Catalan nationalist elites could embrace the core transitional symbols without calling into question their commitment to Catalanism. As we will see in the following chapter, this situation contrasts tremendously with the situation of the Basque nationalist elites, who oftentimes had to choose between Basque nationalist and "transitional" symbolization.

Regional nationalism and the 1978 Constitution

On September 29, 1977, a decree was issued establishing a provisional Catalan autonomous government through an adaptation of the 1932 Statute. On October 23, 1977, the seventy-seven-year-old Josép Tarradellas returned to Barcelona after an absence of thirty-eight years; and on the following day, Suárez presided over an event in which Taradellas was installed as president of the Generalitat. Tarradellas was certainly not trusted by everyone, but nevertheless he was overwhelmingly perceived as the legitimate Catalan leader. Tarradellas was the son-in-law of the legendary Colonel Macià, the first president of the Catalan government, and he had proudly borne the standard of the Generalitat during a lonely and austere exile.[66] Taradellas did not participate in the anti-Francoist opposition; he considered himself to be above parties, and to be the "spiritual leader" of Catalonia. In return for the re-establishment of the Generalitat, Tarradellas pledged Catalan loyalty to the monarchy, acceptance of the unity of Spain, and respect for the armed forces.[67]

Thus, the restoration of the Generalitat at the height of the "period of consensus" affirmed the link between Catalan autonomy and the "new beginning" of "democracy" and "national reconciliation." Tarradellas symbolized both the Catalan autonomous past, and a "new beginning" of autonomy. Most importantly, this same symbolization – the linking of Catalan nationalist and the dominant transitional symbols – emerged once again in the drafting of the 1978 Constitution. Catalan nationalist elites, most importantly Miquel Roca Junyent, portrayed "autonomy" and "democracy" not simply as parallel developments, but as indivisible components of the same process. The Generalitat approved the Constitutional text and campaigned in favor of the Constitution, insisting that an affirmative vote "will mean a vote for democracy, and liberty and the autonomy of Catalonia."[68] As shown in Table 7.2, over 90 percent of Catalans who voted in the Constitutional referendum voted in favor of the Constitution – which was a higher percentage than in Spain as a whole. Moreover, in none of the four Catalan provinces did the negative vote reach 5 percent, and the Catalan abstention rate was lower than the national average.[69]

This does not mean that there were not fundamental disagreements between Catalan nationalist and non-nationalist elites over the drafting of the Constitution. On the contrary (as indicated previously), there were harsh debates about the extent and meaning of "autonomy"; and there were significant discrepancies simply about whether or not Catalonia was a "nation." Yet, the point is that throughout the constitutional debates, Catalan nationalist elites consistently linked autonomy (as understood by Catalans) with the core symbols of the transition. For instance, regarding inclusion of the term "nation," Catalan Senator Alexander Cirici stated:

We know that the majority of our fellow citizens of our State consider with surprise the fact that practically all of us Catalans consider that our nation is Catalonia. Without direct knowledge of our country, and educated by official teachings that conveniently identifies nation with state, it appears to them strange, and even false. But there is no doubt whatsoever that any really democratic system is obligated to pay attention to the thinking of the rest, to respect it and try to understand the reason for its existence . . .

There is no doubt that all of us are wrapped up in constructing a State in which we all can feel at home. In order to do this it is imperative that no nationality, including the Castilian majority, perpetrate a situation of power over another . . .

The purely geographical, and not political, name of "region" came into being only due to the attempt to depersonalize us politically. Because of that . . . we must know that Catalonia can be called nation, nationality, country, people or whatever, but that all of us Catalans take the word "region" as an insult that means: you all are not a community with political rights, but rather only a portion of territory . . .

If we want to be just, equitable and democratic, it will be imperative to respect [the national conscience of the Catalans]. It is the only way to live together.[70]

Here, Cirici links the notion of "nationalities" to minority rights, which is linked to pluralism and democracy. He also implies that it is Catalans who should decide what their region will be called, which is a form of respect and tolerance requisite to *convivencia* ("the only way to live together"), and a form of "democracy."

By contrast, the *Alianza Popular* found the term "nationalities" particularly distasteful, and protested at the inclusion of this term in the constitutional text. Stated Manuel Fraga, "the expression 'region' or 'autonomic region' is perfectly sufficient to describe the geographic and historic base of the autonomies . . . [the word] 'nationalities' [is] mistaken and full of possible complications . . . [complications that] are full of difficulties for the future and would be desirable to avoid . . . in order to service the sacred and indestructible unity of Spain."[71] Elsewhere, Fraga stated:

Alongside the positive aspects, the constitutional text contains some very profound and very obscure shadows . . . the most grave, without a doubt, is the ambiguous writing of Article 2 . . . that regulates the autonomies. To accept the concept of "nationalities" is, without a doubt, a time bomb for the national unity and strength of the State. Nobody can fool himself on this point: each day flags are burned, vociferous demonstrations, open interpretations [*"interpretaciones sin tapujos"*] by Basque and Catalan nationalists show us the real measure of what will be the future concessions, based on the indicated texts. And if Spain breaks up, even more will follow.[72]

This statement by Fraga clearly calls up the past: that the term "nationalities" is a "time bomb" for the "national unity and strength of the State" recalls Pradera's cry of July 18, 1936, to "impose on them unity, unity above all." The idea that "flags are burned," etc., reflects the profanation inherent in regionalism for the right, which, needless to say, contradicts the notion of national reconciliation.

In addition, the notion that the use of the term "nationalities" will cause more radical nationalist violations reveals a typically Francoist understanding of the relation between the issue of regional autonomy and more radical nationalist violations, such as terrorism. Whereas Catalan nationalists such as Cirici link the issue of regional autonomy with "democracy" and *convivencia* (which opposes both Francoism and terrorism), Fraga lumps the radical nationalists' violations of democracy with the constitutional article on regional autonomy – as did Franco in his repression of regional culture in the name of the war against terrorism.

Led by Miquel Roca Junyent (who subsequently acquired a reputation for "moderation"), the Catalan nationalists promptly agreed to a compromise, whereby the word "nationalities" is used but preceded by a statement as to the indissolubility of the Spanish nation. Article 2 states:

The Constitution is founded on the indissoluble unity of the Spanish Nation, the common and indivisible fatherland of all Spaniards, and it recognizes and guarantees the right of autonomy of the nationalities and regions that comprise it, and the solidarity among all of them.

Fraga also reluctantly accepted this redaction of article 2; and Fraga agreed to endorse the Constitution. However, two prominent members of the AP, Federico Silva Muñoz and Gonzalo Fernández de la Mora, actively spoke out against ratification of the Constitution, largely because of articles 2, 16, and 27. The clash between Fraga and Silva and Fernández de la Mora resulted in Silva and Fernández de la Mora withdrawing their respective organizations from the AP federation. This withdrawal failed significantly to influence the outcome of the national constitutional referendum, but seriously weakened the political right. While the groups of Silva and Fernández de la Mora faded into obscurity, AP reformed itself into the *Coalición Democrática* (Democratic Coalition) – and was devastated in the March 1979 elections.

Basque nationalists, on the other hand, rejected the new redaction of article 2, just as they rejected the 1978 Constitution. In the following chapter, we explore this crucial exception both in terms of the successful ratification of the 1978 Constitution, and in terms of the historic Spanish "politics of consensus" in general.

8

The Basque exception: questions of communality and democracy

The crucial exception in terms of Spain's "consensual" transition is the Basque Country. In contrast to communist, socialist, and Catalan leaders, who became more moderate and consensual as the transition progressed, Basque nationalist leaders became more estranged from "consensus" throughout the transition. The Basque Nationalist representative, Juan Ajuriaguerra, signed the Moncloa Pacts in October 1977 "with reservations"; but there were no Basque representatives on the Congressional Subcommittee on Constitutional Affairs (*Ponencia*), the subcommittee formed to draft the Spanish Constitution. As shown in Table 7.2, over half the Basques abstained in the 1978 Referendum on the Constitution, as compared with 31.7 percent in Spain as a whole. Moreover, of Basques who did vote, nearly 24 percent cast negative votes, in comparison with only 4.6 percent of Catalans, and 7.8 percent of Spaniards (see Table 7.2). Most alarmingly, as Basque participation in the "period of consensus" declined, violence by the Basque insurgent group *Euzkadi ta Azkatasuna* (Basque Homeland and Freedom – ETA) increased. As shown in Table 8.1, between 1968 and 1975, ETA was responsible for thirty-four deaths; but, despite an important lull in 1977, ETA was responsible for sixty-seven or more deaths each year in 1978, 1979 and 1980.

Historical background

The Basque Country lies in northern Spain and southwestern France, where the Pyrenees meet the Bay of Biscay (see Map of Spain). The Basque Country is composed of four provinces in Spain – Alava, Guipúzcoa, Navarre and Vizcaya – and three in France (Labourde, Basse Navarre, and Soule).[1] The Basques may be one of the most ancient ethnic groups in

Table 8.1. *ETA victims 1968–1980*

Year	Killed	Wounded
1968	2	0
1969	1	0
1970	0	0
1971	0	0
1972	1	1
1973	3	1
1974	11	58
1975	16	5
1976	17	0
1977	9	7
1978	67	91
1979	72	141
1980	88	81

Source: Clark (1984: 133).

Europe, but they have never been a single "people." By Roman times, the Basque Country was divided into the "Saltus Vasconum" (the "thicket of the Basques"), in the moist and heavily forested Atlantic Zone, which gave the name for Basque rural people "*Baserritarrak*" ("*basa*" + "*erri*" = woodsmen); and the more southern Mediterranean climate and culture, known as the "Ager," or agricultural land. The "Ager" became more important than the "Saltus," leaving many more archeological remains, and reaching a higher level of progress and development.[2]

The Basques are purported to be the only European people not to have suffered under the feudal system.[3] Basques owned their own land or worked for a wage or share (not as serfs). When Basques fought, they did so freely, for a share of the spoils, rather than as mercenary soldiers. Basques paid only those taxes which they imposed on themselves.

The ancient political system of the Basques is called the *Fueros* (foral laws), which means the right and capacity of organization from within the community. The tradition was oral until the *Fuero Navarro* was written in 1237. Over the following decades, the process that began in Navarre was extended to Alava, Guipúzcoa, and Vizcaya. The basic component of the *Fueros* was the house (*caserío*). The *caserío* was a workplace and a place of rest, but also a temple and a tomb, controlled by the *Ahaide Nagusiak*, or "Elder Parents." A grouping of houses formed the "Valley," which formed the *Batzarre* or "General Assembly," and the union of the *Batzarre* formed the Kingdom. Political issues were brought up and discussed at each level.[4]

By the time of the formation of the Spanish State, in the sixteenth century, the provinces of Alava, Guipúzcoa, and Vizcaya had belonged to the Crown of Castile for several centuries; Navarre was annexed by Ferdinand II in 1512. Throughout the sixteenth, seventeenth, and eighteenth centuries, the four Basque provinces retained some of their historic rights under the *Fueros*. Taxes were apportioned and collected by provincial assemblies, and local questions were decided locally. Though linked by geographic proximity and to some extent the Basque language, the four Basque provinces had no common institutions and little sense of common identity.[5] The Basque language was used domestically, while Castilian continued to be the language of public culture and government, as it had been since the Middle Ages.[6]

Serious contention over Basque rights began in the nineteenth century and culminated in two civil wars (the Carlist Wars). The first Carlist War (1833–1839) started as a dynastic dispute between Carlos de Borbón and his infant niece Isabel. The war pitted liberal supporters of Isabel, who controlled the government in Madrid and were trying to centralize Spanish administration along the lines established earlier in France, against Basque peasants, who supported Carlos (hence they became known as "Carlists") and who defended the region's traditional local liberties.[7] The war ended with a negotiated settlement and the Carlists' surrender. Basques were promised that their *Fueros* would be "respected and preserved."[8] In fact, the *Fueros* were annulled in 1841, although the Basque provinces were left with considerable autonomy in matters of administration and taxation. The second Carlist War broke out in 1873, and ended in 1876, again with the Carlists' defeat. Basques lost their administrative autonomy, but retained the right to negotiate and collect taxes for the central government through an agreement called the *Conciertos Económicos*.

Throughout the nineteenth century, the use of the Basque language *(Euskera)* declined, especially in the cities. Three of the greatest literary figures of the early twentieth century, Miguel de Unamuno, Pío Baroja, and María de Maetzu, were Basque, but wrote exclusively in Castilian.

Over the same course of time, the Basque country changed from being one of Spain's poorest to being one of Spain's wealthiest regions. This change was to a large extent, due to the discovery of the Bessemer process for the production of steel in 1856, which resulted in a dramatic increase in demand for Basque iron ore. By the 1890s, the Basque Country, especially Vizcaya, had become the center of Spanish heavy industry and mining, and iron-ore exports.[9]

The emergence of Basque nationalism

Basque nationalism arose in the late nineteenth century. Its undisputed ideologue and founder was Sabino de Arana y Goiri (1865–1903), a highly charismatic, conservative, devoutly Catholic son of a Basque entrepreneur and Carlist supporter. Sabino de Arana had been living in Barcelona while the Catalan nationalist movement was gaining ground, and he was deeply influenced by the Catalans' integration of linguistic revival and political separatism. When he returned to Vizcaya, Sabino de Arana pointedly sought to revive the Basque language (*Euskera*). He invented the name *Euzkadi* to refer to the Basque Country (since no independent Basque nation had ever existed); and in 1898 he founded the *Partido Nacionalista Vasco* (PNV). The PNV linked religiously inspired urbanites (like Arana) with former members of the defunct Euskalerría Society, a private club of businessmen who wanted political decentralization in order to industrialize the Basque Country. As many authors have pointed out, the Basque capitalist elite were not nationalist; they enjoyed protectionism from the Spanish state, and supported the monarchist and liberal parties.[10] Arana died in 1903, leaving an uneasy coalition of theocrats, led by his older brother, Luis Arana, and capitalists led by Ramón de la Sota.

Yet, in contrast to the modernist nationalism dominant in Catalonia, the type of nationalism developed by Arana was highly traditionalist – a defensive reaction against what he saw as the evils of liberalism. Arana presented the struggle for Basque independence as a struggle for the religious salvation of the Basque race through complete isolation from other peoples, especially Spaniards. He hated Spanish immigrants because of their secular and socialistic (rather than Catholic and paternalistic) views, and because they were important agents of change in the traditions and culture of the Basque country. Arana believed that efforts needed to be made to preserve and strengthen the Basque race, and that political independence was both a right and the objective for the Basque people. This type of nationalism dominated Basque nationalist discourse until the Civil War.[11]

The Basque Nationalist Party was of little political significance in the early twentieth century. During the five years between the declaration of the Republic in 1931 and the outbreak of the Civil War in 1936, however, Basque nationalism grew rapidly, as Basque nationalists became important defenders of the Church against the notorious anti-clericalism of the Republic.

Carlists (whose stronghold was still Navarre), too, were important defenders of the Church. Yet, despite their ideological and political similarities (Catholicism and the goal of local self-rule), Basque nationalists and

Carlists never achieved a successful political alliance in the Republican era. Carlists and Nationalists drafted a statute for autonomy (called the Estella Statute), but it was rejected by the Spanish Parliament in 1931. The tenuous alliance between Basque nationalists and Carlists subsequently broke down. By the last months of the Republic, Navarrese Carlist leaders had dedicated themselves to cooperating with the organizers of a rightist revolt against the Republican regime. Meanwhile, Basque nationalists drafted a more moderate and somewhat vague Autonomy Statute, which was finally accepted by the Republic. This secured the loyalty of Basque Nationalists to the Republican side – but by this time the Civil War had already begun.

The Basque Country in Civil War

The Spanish Civil War (1936–1939) is notorious for its brutality, and this was exemplified in the Basque region. The bombing of the city of Guernica on April 26, 1937, by German allies of the Nationalists was the destruction of one of the oldest and most sacred of Basque cities and symbols: the tree of Guernica symbolizes the Basque *Fueros*, or liberty for all the Basque people, the place where the heads of families, the *Batzarre* ("General Assembly") met to discuss important communal issues. To add insult to injury, Franco denied responsibility for the attack, claiming that Guernica had been dynamited by the Basques themselves in order to fabricate an atrocity for propaganda purposes.

The notorious fraternal division of the Civil War is also exemplified in the Basque region. The subsequent military conquest of Guipúzcoa and Vizcaya in the summer of 1937 was carried out largely with Carlist troops from Navarre and Alava. Not only provinces and towns, but even families, were split between Carlist supporters of Franco, and Basque nationalist defenders of the Republic.[12]

The Basque Country under Franco

Divisions and tension in the Basque country continued long after the victory of Franco. Franco revoked the Basque Autonomy Statute, but, in recognition for their support during the Civil War, he allowed the provinces of Alava and Navarre to retain special fiscal dispensations and limited powers of local administration (called *Conciertos Económicos*). Franco also appointed Basque elites to important political positions. Of the eighty-nine ministers who served in Franco's cabinets between 1938 and 1969, six were from Navarre and six more from other Basque provinces. The percentage of ministers from the Basque country was almost two-and-a-half times as great as the percentage of Basques among the population. Needless to say, the men who served in Franco's cabinet had no ties to Basque nationalism. Over half of them were Carlists, and the others were closely identified with Franco and his policies.[13]

In the first two decades of the Franco regime, Basque nationalism was concentrated in the very limited activities of the PNV, which staffed the Basque government in exile, and the activities of rural Basque clergy. The church hierarchy did not persecute Basque priests for using *Euskera*, and the Basque clergy took advantage of the limits of Francoist repression by founding clandestine Basque-language schools (called *Ikastolas*), which would eventually involve thousands of people. The Basque rural clergy also founded Catholic organizations, such as *Baserri Gaztedi* (Basque Youth), based on the ecclesiastical movement *Acción Católica* (Catholic Action). These organizations provided a new activist Catholic mentality: they replaced the traditional peasant maxim *"ver, oír, callar"* ("see, listen, be silent") with the slogan *"ver, juzgar, actuar"* ("see, judge, act").[14]

In the later years of the Franco regime, some of the schisms that had plagued Basque nationalism earlier (such as the issue of Basque racial distinctiveness) began to fade away, but other issues became more salient. The two most important sources of division were: class vs. ethnicity and *ekintza* ("direct action," i.e. insurgent violence) vs. non-violent mass mobilization.

In 1959, some of the younger, more militant members of the PNV broke off and founded the insurgent organization *Euzkadi ta Azkatasuna* (ETA). From the beginning, ETA was a heterogeneous organization, made up of an uncomfortable mix of nationalists and socialists, students and labor activists, and rural Catholic youth. By the late 1960s, ETA was being pulled in at least three ideological directions: (1) toward a new left, proletarian tradition; (2) a guerrilla national front tradition; and (3) non-violent, ethically oriented, cultural tradition. This heterogeneity resulted in a series of splits. In 1966–1967, ETA split into ETA-Berri (New ETA) and ETA-Zarra (Old ETA); in 1970, it split into ETA-V (followers of the program of the Fifth Assembly) and ETA-VI (Sixth Assembly).[15]

Despite its external image as a "terrorist" organization, ETA enjoyed significant popular support under Francoism (and, indeed, well until the 1980s) in the Basque provinces. Most Basques felt more threatened by Spanish security forces than by ETA. Whereas ETA killed 6 people in the 12 months prior to Franco's death, Spanish police and civil guards killed 22, and injured 105.[16] ETA was viewed in terms of "patriotic action" (*ekintza*), rather than of (irrational) terrorism. ETA militants (called *etarras*) were admired for "giving up everything for their country," and for "acting" rather than merely "talking." According to a poll conducted in

1979, over half the Basques surveyed thought that *etarras* were "patriots" or "idealists" and only 14 percent considered them "madmen" or "criminals." Of those whose self-identification was "Basque" (rather than "Spanish," "both Basque and Spanish," etc.), 71 percent considered *etarras* to be "patriots" or "idealists," and only 13 percent considered them to be "madmen" or "criminals."[17]

The link between Basque identity, *ekintza,* and ETA was confirmed by the infamous Burgos trial of December 1970. In August 1968, Melitón Manzanas, a hated police commissioner, was killed by a single gunman outside his apartment. The Spanish government imposed a state of emergency, and more than two thousand Basque residents were arrested. Sixteen *etarras* and ETA sympathizers were finally charged with complicity in the killing, though they pleaded innocent.[18]

The military trial of the *etarras* in the old Castilian city of Burgos turned into a public-relations nightmare for Franco. European journalists published the defendants' detailed accounts of torture and condemned the Franco regime for the violation of internationally recognized principles of due process. When six of the defendants were sentenced to death, European workers struck, and intellectuals such as Jean-Paul Sartre issued statements in support of ETA. Of even more importance, especially within Spain, was the fact that even the Pope appealed to Franco for clemency. In the end, Franco relented and signed reprieves for the six death sentences.

Within the Basque region, the "Burgos 16," as they came to be known, became heros. Young children could recite the names of the "Burgos 16," and over half of all industrial workers in the Basque provinces purportedly struck to protest against the trial.[19] While ETA had been decimated organizationally by the arrests and flight of its members in the wake of the Manzanas killing, ETA gained new members, popular support, and legitimacy as a result of the trial.[20]

Bolstered by its increased visibility and the militancy of new young recruits, ETA unleashed a critical wave of violence in the early 1970s. In March 1973, ETA committed its most serious act – the killing of Franco's apparent successor, Luis Carrero Blanco. While even today some analysts consider the assassination of Carrero Blanco the only thing ETA has ever done to "further the cause of Spanish democracy,"[21] it is imperative to realize that the intent of ETA was not to eliminate Carrero Blanco in order to force a more moderate, reform-oriented democratic transition. On the contrary, the killing of both Manzanas and Carrero Blanco were part of ETA's action–repression spiral theory. According to this theory, attacks on the Francoist state would lead to a blatant, universal repression, which would lead to greater popular anger, which would spiral into mass rebellion, and eventually civil war and Basque secession.[22]

The Spanish government responded to the assassination of Carrero Blanco as it had to the Manzanas killing: it swiftly rounded up all known labor and political dissidents, and instituted a new series of states of emergency. Nevertheless, many Basque nationalists (including some of ETA's own leaders) began to doubt the potential for mass revolution. Following a particularly brutal bombing of a Madrid cafe in 1974, which killed nine and wounded fifty-six people (most of whose political preferences and loyalties remain either unknown or unclear), ETA split into "political-military" (ETA-pm) and "military" (ETA-m) factions. ETA-pm openly declared itself a Marxist organization, aligned itself with other Marxist groups (e.g. MCE and ORT), and pushed for mass mobilization. ETA-m, aligned with the *abertzale* (patriotic), rather than the Spanish left (e.g. the *Branka* group), and continued the armed struggle. ETA-m did not want or expect any liberal-democratic reforms, and it saw no reason to change its strategy of violence for the post-Franco period.[23]

Under Franco, then, there were strands of shared meaning as to what it means to be "Basque." There was (1) a myth, a shared understanding of an ancient Basque past (including the *Fueros*), (2) an awareness of the structural pressures for the extinction of the Basque culture, which increased the participative function of Basque language, music, games, etc., and its capacity for symbolizing solidarity and differentiability,[24] and (3) anti-state violence, as an expression of Basque *ekintza* (action). Yet, the symbols perceived to be "Basque" – including the *Fueros* as well as the Basque language – were defined largely by their transgression from and rejection of the centralist regime. There was no consensus as to the nature of the new Basque post-Franco state, or even how to define Basque identity.[25]

Basque representations and the transition

Separation and a new beginning

Analysis of the Basque media during the "period of consensus" reveals that the core representations discussed previously – a "new beginning" of "national reconciliation" and "democracy" – certainly pervaded the Basque country in the post-Franco period. For instance, akin to *El País,* *Deia* celebrated the "debut" of democracy on the day of the first democratic elections (which reflects a "new beginning" and the ritual process of separation).[26] On the day after the elections, *Deia's* back-page photos showed "everyone" – celebrities, old people, hospitalized people, cloistered nuns – going out to vote, thereby celebrating not only pluralistic democracy, but the communality of the voting experience (i.e. liminality and reaggregation). Titled "Making Tracks to Vote" ("*Se hace camino al votar*"), this article stated:

In one day forty years have been erased. Erase, and start again. By instinct, more than experience, Spaniards have gone to the voting booth. With the anxiety of the debut that has cost blood, sweat and tears. Yesterday, the day that democracy was born, when fortunately, we quit being "different." Yesterday, a day to remember to our children, to our grandchildren, those people that will be born and will live in democracy.[27]

This statement coincides with the dominant symbolic framework discussed previously: the "new beginning" is reflected in the "debut" and "birth" of democracy. The lack of voting "experience" and references to "our children and grandchildren" reflect the innocence and optimism of the new generation, and the hope that this democracy will not be a mere "parenthesis" in Spanish history.

However, at the same time, there was oftentimes a different emphasis regarding the new temporality in the Basque Country – an emphasis on the past, the death of Franco, rather than on the "new beginning." For instance, on the day of the first democratic elections, an editorial in *Deia* entitled "Franco dies today" repeatedly states that, "No matter the outcome of the elections today, one thing is clear: Franco dies today, definitively."[28] While obviously symbols of "death" and "rebirth" are intimately linked, this emphasis literally on "death" (rather than "rebirth") recalls the far right focus on the "end of the course" discussed previously (see chapter four). In both cases, the emphasis is on the "old" (whether it be sacred or profane), rather than on the "new beginning".

This emphasis on the "past" rather than the "future" is even more apparent in an interview with PNV representative Xabier Arzallus published on the eve of the June 1977 elections.[29] In response to the question, "What feeling do you think describes your life in Euzkadi?," Arzallus said: "Wrath [*ira*]. The same anger of the child when he is harassed and punished." And in response to the question, "How much rancor and how much hope do you find interwoven in Euzkadi today?" Arzallus stated:

Much rancor, because [Basques] have suffered a lot, and unjustly. The Basque is conscious of the fact that he has behaved well, even during the Civil War . . . older Basques . . . have suffered the persecution of the Dictatorship more intensely [than the young]. The young have also suffered, but they have not experienced the gradual persecution by the little things: to be thrown out of your job, to not be able to speak Euskera, the shots to the head, the embarrassing returns to jail, the systematic arbitrariness [of repression]. Persecution has been much less in the last ten years . . .

The interviewer's questions clearly give Arzallus an opportunity to focus on "hope," reconciliation, and the future. Indeed, the dichotomy posed – do you feel (old) "rancor" or (new) "hope" – is typical of the dichotomous symbolic framework of the transition. Yet, Arzallus sacralizes the "old" and "the past" (i.e. older Basques suffering under Franco), rather than the "young" and the "new"; and his statement that Basques have suffered "a lot, and unjustly," and that they "behaved well, even during the Civil War" contradicts the notion of national reconciliation.

The ambiguity of the new temporality in the Basque nationalist transitional discourse is also evident in the "forty year frame" discussed previously. Recall that, in the dominant symbolic framework, Spain had not been "herself" for the past forty years: Francoism was like a false "cover" that could be "removed", "excised" or "erased", in order to let the new Spain "bloom". This "forty year frame" is readily apparent in the *Deia* article, "Making Tracks to Vote," ("In one day forty years have been erased" – see page 130).

But at the same time, the "forty year" frame did not completely make sense in the Basque Country. As the following editorial in *Deia* maintains:

If for many Spaniards, the democracy that is inaugurated today was suspended only forty years ago, for the majority of the citizens of the Basque country it [democracy] didn't perish only forty years ago, nor even with the sad infamous decree of 1937 that punished Vizcaya and Guipúzcoa. For the Basques, democracy succumbed more than one hundred years ago, first in 1839, and it died definitively in 1876 . . . those are the dates in which *the power* of the people was snatched away.[30]

In other words, the "forty year" frame presumes that there is a concrete, idealized "natural" state to be returned to. Here the author suggests that for Basques this moment/state is not 1936 (i.e. before the start of the Civil War); this moment/state is before the first and second Carlist wars (the first Carlist War ended in 1839, the second in 1876). Yet, these "dates" are not particularly effervescent moments in Basque history; in fact, the exact moment and state to which the Basque Country should be "returned" (in order to be "returned to herself") is tremendously ambiguous. In sum, in contrast to Catalan nationalists, who could – and did – "excise" the past and focus on the "new beginning" by celebrating the restoration the Generalitat, the restoration of the 1931 Catalan Statute of Autonomy, and the restoration of the Catalan symbolic leader (the President of the Generalitat, Tarradellas); there was no specifically Basque modern form of government (akin to either the thirteenth-century imperialist Catalan nation-state or the more recent Generalitat) to be "restored" (only the ancient *Fueros*); there was no sacred Statute of Autonomy to be returned (since the Basque Statute of Autonomy was instituted only during the Civil War and in the midst of division); and there was no universally accepted and "legitimate" Basque leader (parallel to Tarradellas) to "come home."

Violence, non-violence, and ekintza: *communality and national reconciliation*

In addition, "death" as well as "violence" had multifarious linkages in the Basque nationalist transitional symbolic framework, and oftentimes these linkages conflicted with the hegemonic transitional symbolic system. Specifically, on the one hand, akin to Catalan nationalists, moderate Basque nationalist leaders sometimes linked the issues of autonomy and amnesty (the complete exoneration and liberation of all political prisoners, the majority of which were Basque nationalists) with the core transitional symbols of a "new beginning" of "national reconciliation"/*convivencia.* For instance, one representative of the PNV called for political amnesty by stating:

We need a great solemn act that pardons and forgets all the crimes and barbarities committed by both sides of the Civil War, before it, in it, and after it, until our days. This great pardon and forgetting can only be done by the King, the Chief of State, who had not participated in either of the two sides of the Civil War, nor in its consequences. Done in the name of peace and reconciliation, it would be the first title of honor and glory of the beginning of a reign . . .

The pardoning and amnesty of a period so dramatic demands that everyone swallow thousands of angry words, but the pity, the peace and the *convivencia* of the new generations demands it.[31]

Clearly, a great "pardon and forgetting" represents national reconciliation and *convivencia.* And that "this great pardon and forgetting only can by done by the King, the Chief of State, who had not participated in either of the two sides of the Civil War, nor in its consequences" links the "new beginning" and "national reconciliation." In short, in order to truly bury the Civil War, Spain must be turned over to leaders who had no part of it (the new generation).[32]

However at the same time, an entirely different configuration of amnesty was readily apparent in Basque nationalist transitional discourse. In this symbolization (put forth especially by ETA militants*)*, amnesty was not linked to peace, harmony, and *convivencia*; rather, amnesty was a "non-negotiable minimum condition," which if not granted would compel a return to armed fighting. Stated one ETA representative, "we call to the Basque people and especially her working class to actively abstain from the elections, while there exists a single prisoner in the Fascist jails."[33]

Obviously, the notion of "non-negotiable" conditions contradicts the notion of dialogue and consensus; the notion that the "new" government is "fascist" contradicts the notion of a "new beginning" of "democracy"; and the notion of a return to armed fighting contradicts both the sacred new standards of the new social state (democracy, non-violence) and "national reconciliation."

Yet, it was not simply that Basque nationalist transitional symbolization was divided into "radical" (ETA) and "moderate" (PNV) sectors. Rather, the point is that there were distinct, multiple configurations of "death" and "violence" in the Basque Country, as "violence" and "non-violence," and communality and *convivencia* were particularly ambiguous transitional issues in the Basque Country. Specifically, for most Spaniards the non-violent, reconciliatory character of the new democracy was taken for granted and celebrated. Indeed, this non-violent, reconciliatory nature of the "new beginning" was at times celebrated also in the Basque media. Thus, for instance, parallel to the dichotomization of (sacred) "voting" and (profane) "violence" discussed previously (and illustrated in Figure 7.1), Joseba Elosegui, a candidate for the PNV stated in his electoral campaign that, "Now we want democracy through a voting coup, not at gunpoint" ("*Ahora queremos la democracia a golpe de voto, no a punta de pistola*").[34]

At the same time, however, the supposed "tranquility" and "peacefulness" of the "new" post-Francoist period was oftentimes challenged in the Basque Country. For example, an article in *Deia,* entitled "The 74 Deaths of the Reform," explicitly subverted the notion that Franco's death led to a "new beginning" of tolerance, democracy, and reconciliation, by pointing out that since November 20, 1975, there had been seventy-four political deaths in Spain, and that a "disproportionate" number of these deaths involved Basques, and a disproportionate number of these deaths occurred in the Basque country. In sum, in writing about these seventy-four deaths, the article both affirms the symbolic opposition between (genuine) "democracy" and (evil) "violence," and challenges the notion of a (genuine) "new beginning" (as these deaths occurred in this purportedly "new" period).

Even more importantly, the symbol "violence" was also linked to the Basque action frame, *ekintza,* in which ETA violence is legitimized by state repression. Both the Basque action frame (*ekintza*) and the more universal "voting vs. violence" frame are evident in an interesting interview with Manuel de Irujo, published in *Deia.*[35] Manuel de Irujo was a prominent leader of the PNV during the Second Republic and later a political exile; his father was the good friend and lawyer of PNV founder Sabino de Arana. When asked, "What do you think of violence," the eighty-six-year-old Irujo stated:

I understand them when they take to the streets. I don't share their violent methods, but I understand them. I prefer to go to the elections and obtain seats to permanently influence the Government . . . I don't favor violence, but I understand when an eighteen year old boy who loves his country puts a pistol against the pistols.[36]

On the one hand, here Irujo juxtaposes "going to the elections" with "violence" in a manner typical of the dominant transitional symbolic system (see Figures 4.3 and 7.1). On the other hand, however, Irujo explicitly links insurgent violence to the idealism of youth, Basque patriotism, and even Basque democratic self-rule. This contradicts not only the symbolic opposition between "violence" and "democracy," but between "violence" and the "new generation."

Democracy and the Fueros

Perhaps the most interesting core transitional symbol in the Basque Country, however, was "democracy," for "democracy" was linked both to the dominant transitional notion of modern, representative government, and to the specifically Basque notion of local, communal self-rule, i.e. the *Fueros*. Specifically, on the one hand, in correspondence to the hegemonic transitional symbolization, an editorial titled "Last Minute Democrats" pointed to the overutilization (pollution) of the term "democracy" by "last minute democrats";[37] and a column titled, "Do You Want to Assassinate the Democracy?" by García Olano stated:

The democracy that is just beginning to appear has many enemies. Some are those that really don't want to change anything, even though in the [electoral] arena they portray themselves as being democrats all of their lives . . . [In addition] fanaticism, intransigence, dogmatism, incapacity to listen, the lack of respect for one's rival, these are the little knives that assassinate democracy daily.[38]

Akin to the dominant symbolic framework discussed previously (and illustrated in Figure 7.1), the (evil) threat to (sacred) democracy ("assassination" of democracy) is both false democrats, and non-democratic, non-reconciliatory, non-moderate behavior, e.g. (profane) irrational "fanaticism, intransigence, dogmatism, incapacity to listen, the lack of respect for one's rival."

Yet, juxtaposed with this core transitional meaning of "democracy" was the traditional Basque meaning of "democracy" as Basque local self-rule, i.e. the *Fueros*.[39] Most importantly, in this latter frame, the *Fueros* is the *genuine* (sacred) "democracy," symbolically opposed to the (evil) false centralist "democracy" of the Constitution/transition. For example, in an article entitled "Foral Democracy," Adrian Celaya maintained:

[The *Fueros*] are not something imposed from above, but something thought about and felt by the society, the base . . . [*Fueros*] do not hold that a king, an authority, tries to impose his own criteria, making his subjective vision of things the only valuable one. Laws must not be an imposition, but rather the clamor of the people . . .

I am not convinced that democracy can only be condensed into that aphorism "one man, one vote" . . . The star of political life must be the people [*"el pueblo"*], and not the big personalities. I think that a happy society is one in which the administrators barely shine. Who has heard of Swiss politicians? And nobody doubts that Switzerland is well governed. On the other hand, who has not heard of Stalin, Hitler or Pinochet?

To talk of the *Fueros* today, is not to return to the past, nor even to put on certain old laws. It is, on the contrary, to concede to our people [*"nuestro pueblo"*] their role as protagonist in social life.[40]

On the one hand, here Celaya affirms the sacred transitional symbols of modernization and Europeanization: he juxtaposes (sacred) democracy ("Switzerland") with (profane) dictatorship (whether of the left [Stalin] or right [Hitler, Pinochet]) – which corresponds to the core "dictatorship" vs. "democracy" dichotomy of the transition (see Figure 7.1). In addition, Celaya explicitly acknowledges the link between the *Fueros* and the ancient past, and rectifies this with an explicit call for modernity.

At the same time, however, Celaya criticizes the individualistic Western emphasis on "one man, one vote" and "big personalities" by juxtaposing it with the more genuinely democratic, communal system of governance embodied in the ancient *Fueros*. In addition, Celaya implicitly links the elite process of pacting (truly a case of "big personalities") with dictatorship (rules "imposed from above"). Thus, as shown in Figure 8.1, Celaya juxtaposes genuine (sacred) democracy/the *Fueros* with (profane) "democracy" (read centralism) of the 1978 Constitution.

This link between (genuine) democracy, (genuine) autonomy and the ancient *Fueros* in the Basque nationalist framework cannot be overemphasized. It corresponds to the lack of separation evident in the Basque Country (democracy without autonomy is not democracy, therefore the "new" social state is not new at all). It also helps explain Basque skepticism about the new post-Franco regime. From a Basque nationalist perspective, there *is* no such thing as a "democratic" centralist state, because to govern from the center is to dictate to the periphery. As an article entitled "Autonomy is Not a Privilege" stated, democracy without autonomy is not only "incomplete," it is "to roll out once again the wheel of the dictatorship of silence, the dictatorship of repression, the dictatorship that is even worse than the military vendetta. It is everything but democracy."[41]

In precisely the same way, "King Juan Carlos" was an ambiguous symbol

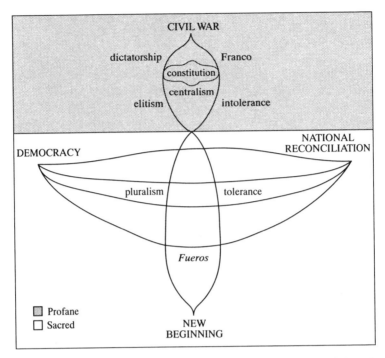

Figure 8.1. Basque nationalist delegitimation of the 1978 Constitution

in the Basque nationalist symbolic framework. This is readily apparent in the interview with PNV representative Manuel de Irujo in *Deia*, discussed previously. On the one hand, the interviewer paints a favorable picture of King Juan Carlos, which coincides with the linkage of the King with a "new beginning" of *convivencia* and democracy (discussed above); and the interviewer asks Irujo a leading question, "Do you think that thanks in part to Juan Carlos, the people of this country will recuperate the liberty that belongs to them?" On the other hand, consider Irujo's response. Rather than unilaterally laud the King, he states:

I think the King has a great will to preserve his throne. He knows how his grandfather lost it, and he knows how his brother-in-law Constantino lost it, and he will do everything possible to not commit those errors . . . The monarchy does not enthuse me much; it is not that I am going to take to the streets with a sub-machine gun, but it does not enthuse me.

Thus Irujo pointedly desacralizes King Juan Carlos. He equates Juan Carlos with the self-serving monarchs who came before him, which explicitly links Juan Carlos to the past and disconnects him from the "new beginning" and the "new generation." In addition, in suggesting that Juan Carlos just wants to "preserve his throne," Irujo reduces Juan Carlos to the mundane level of politics as usual, which contradicts the notion that King Juan Carlos is the (sacred) "King of all Spaniards."[42]

The drafting of the 1978 Constitution

These volatile symbolic linkages became manifest during the drafting of the 1978 Spanish Constitution. The central problem was article 2, which stated that "respect for the historic rights of the foral territories will be accomplished . . . *within* the framework of the Constitution and of the statutes of autonomy" (emphasis added).[43] Basque nationalist leaders were incensed by this positioning of the *Fueros* "within" the Constitution. As a PNV poster calling for abstention in the referendum explicitly stated, "The *Fueros* are our Constitution."[44]

That the *Fueros* "are" the Basque Constitution desacralizes the "Spanish" Constitution for Basques. This desacralization is readily apparent in the following comment by Basque representative Xabier Arzallus:

Ancient Basques lived within an ensemble of kingdoms that were later called Spain . . . and as a guarantee that its way of life would be respected, the right of secession was always reserved. We also reserve [that right], *be it or be it not in the Constitution* [emphasis added].[45]

In conjunction with this desacralization, Basque nationalists reversed the symbolic dichotomy of "dictatorship vs. democracy" discussed previously. Basque representatives linked the 1978 Constitution with "dictatorship" (i.e. centralist domination) in symbolic opposition to the (sacred) democratic *Fueros* (see Figure 8.1). As an editorial entitled "The Dictatorship of the Constitution," by Navarran Francisco Berrete, explicitly stated:

According to the explanations of the politicians, the Constitution recognizes [the *Fueros*]. We say this is a lie. What necessity does one have . . . that someone recognizes that you are son of your mother? Whether they recognize it or not, you will always be the son of your mother. For many people, the Constitution says that it loves and respects our mother *Fueros*. But it is not like that . . . It is the tricking and cynicism, and exploition of the innocent doña democracy. Navarros, don't pay any attention to those that talk like that because they are looking out for votes for their party, not for Navarre.[46]

In sum, in contrast to the Catalans, who linked autonomy, democracy, *convivencia,* and the 1978 Constitution, here the *Fueros* are linked to (sacred) love and eternal (genuine) democracy; and the Constitution is linked to the symbolic opposite: manipulation and dictatorship, and the violation of democracy. These symbolic linkages are illustrated in Figure 8.1.

Negotiations between the government and Basque nationalists over the Constitution completely broke down, as Basque nationalists rejected the government proposal that the *Fueros* be recognized "within" the Constitution, and the government rejected the PNV's proposal for explicit recognition of the right of self-determination.[47] The PNV delegation walked out of the Congress of Deputies just before it approved the existing text of the Constitution and abstained from the final Cortes vote on the Constitution. The PNV also campaigned for abstention in the Constitutional referendum. Euzkadiko Ezkerra voted against the Constitution and campaigned against its ratification in the national referendum. As a result, less than half the Basque electorate participated in the national referendum (46 percent, compared with a turnout of 68 percent throughout Spain); and only 68.2 percent of those who voted cast favorable ballots – some 20 percent less than the national average. By comparison, in Catalonia, the turnout was 68 percent and the affirmative votes 90.4 percent, which exceeded the national average.[48] (These results are shown in Table 7.2.)

9

Conclusion and epilogue

The recent transition from Francoism to democracy in Spain is remarkable for historical, political, as well as cultural reasons. Historically, the Spanish transition is noteworthy because it is the first time in Spanish history that parliamentary democracy has worked, or been self-sustaining. Politically, the Spanish transition is exemplary, because, while a plethora of countries have recently undergone or are currently undergoing democratic transition, few countries have so successfully transformed themselves from the inside out using consensual strategies. Culturally, the Spanish transition is extraordinary because an effervescent system of shared symbols emerged and became transcendent in a critical historical moment fraught with possibilities of division and conflict.

This emphasis on the phenomenon of the Spanish transition has not been particularly prevalent in the substantive area of democratization. Modernization perspectives minimize the achievement of Spanish democracy by viewing it as "easy" or inevitable, i.e. as simply a process of updating political procedures to fit economic and social "reality."[1] Rational choice and elite perspectives also minimize the extraordinary nature of the Spanish transition by chalking up the success of the transition to the strategic choices of a few pivotal elites.

As Przeworksi points out, the empirical problem with the modernization perspective is that the liberalization or breakdown of an authoritarian regime does not ensure democracy.[2] History is replete with moments – most recently, in China – in which democratic or capitalistic openings have been abruptly reversed. And even if the outcome is not the old or a new dictatorship, transitions can get stuck somewhere along the way, in non-competitive regimes that limit contestation or suffer from an organized threat of military intervention. While rational choice and elite theorists (e.g. Przeworski) quite rightly challenge these macro-level accounts by focusing on the actual micro-level processes of elite transitional transaction, these analysts ignore the complex plethora of factors which circumscribe elite decision-making.

The process of "consensual" transition is far more complex and delicate than either functionalist/modernization or elite/rational choice approaches allow. Politico-historical transitions are embedded in intricate metaphysical, symbolic worlds, and the contents of these worlds shape the transitional process. In this book, I have shown that behind and within the so-called Spanish "period of consensus" were four core, intertwined symbols: "a new beginning," "Civil War," "national reconciliation"/"*convivencia*" and "democracy." In Parts II and III of this book, I have argued that the transcendence of these four core symbolic categories enabled the successful institutionalization of Spanish democracy.

To recapitulate: the 1977 elections were enabled by shared meanings as to the democratic ground rules of voting and pluralism; and the elections reaffirmed separation from the Franco regime. The electoral success of Suárez (and González) affirmed a "new beginning" of "national reconciliation"/"*convivencia*" and "democracy" led by members of a "new generation." In the effervescent aftermath of the first democratic elections, Spanish leaders engendered a new political mechanism, called the "politics of consensus." This mechanism was first used in the drafting of the Moncloa Pacts in October 1977, a set of agreements between the opposition and the government regarding the potentially explosive issue of the Spanish economy. These meetings in the Moncloa Palace were extraordinary not only because they involved former enemies (including communist leader Santiago Carrillo and ex-Francoist minister Manuel Fraga), but because elites sidestepped divisive ideological currents inherent in issues such as inflation, unemployment, and development and came up with specific economic and political policies. The Moncloa representatives did this by evoking the core representations of the transition. They defined their task as combatting the "mutual enemy" of world-wide inflation and economic crisis; they declared that this "burden" be faced collectively, the mutual goal being, again, the institutionalization of "democracy." The process of pacting itself, as well as the notion of a collectively faced burden, symbolized the communality and homogeneity of the liminal state: the Moncloa Pacts symbolized liminality on the path toward democratic reaggregation – a reaggregation which would be achieved with the drafting of the 1978 Constitution.

Despite the successful elections and drafting of the Moncloa Pacts, however, the transition was far from over. The drafting of the 1978 Constitution was a long, complex process, which necessitated delving into historically volatile issues, including regional nationalism and separation of Church and State. These explosive issues were superseded (or deferred) by evoking the shared cultural symbols of the transition. Indeed, the new Constitution celebrated and institutionalized a "new beginning" of "*convivencia*" and "democracy." The new Constitution replaced the Fundamental Laws (and Civil War/post-Civil War divisions) with the ground rules of democratic pluralism, and *convivencia*/national reconciliation.

Yet, this is a highly contingent process: just as democratic openings could have been reversed, the ritual process could have lapsed or reverted. A shared cultural framework can easily unravel, as even shared symbols are also attached to other, oftentimes oppositional, ideological currents and systems of meaning. This is precisely what is revealed in the case of the Basque nationalists – the "exception" in terms of Spain's historic "consensus." Overall, Basque nationalists did not embrace consensus; unlike the Catalan nationalists, they conceptualized the recuperation of autonomy in the Basque Country (e.g. the *Fueros*) as antithetical to the institutionalization of the new *Spanish* Constitution. Nevertheless, the Basque "exception" underscores the hegemony of the dominant (Spanish) symbolic system. Though Basque nationalists did not legitimize many elements of the new "democracy," Basque nationalist symbolization remained peripheral. It did not undermine or paralyze the ritual process of the transition. Even more importantly, Basque nationalist symbolization was not entirely anti-thetical or columnized in relation to the dominant symbolic framework. Though they were complicated by a cross-cutting symbols, a "new beginning" of "*convivencia*" and "democracy" penetrated even the Basque Country.

Epilogue: after the Constitution

On the same day that Spain's new Constitution entered into effect, Suárez announced in a televised speech that the now constitutional monarch, King Juan Carlos I, would dissolve the Cortes and convoke new elections. A new Senate and Congress of Deputies would be chosen on March 1, 1979, and municipal elections would be held on April 3. Suárez claimed that holding early elections would give "popular legitimacy" to the country's political institutions and clear the way for a new government to address many unresolved problems, "without the conditions and limitations inherent in a period of transition."[3] Of course, the UCD would also benefit from the atmosphere of good will and accomplishment produced by the recent ratification of a consensual constitution, and the short-term organizational difficulties that early elections would cause the PSOE and newly created Coalición Democrática (CD – Democratic Coalition).[4]

Thus, held less than three months after the ratification of the Constitution, the 1979 elections were still a transitional event, arranged by a handful of Spanish leaders because of the "special" conditions of the transition. Accordingly, the symbols of "democracy," "*convivencia*" and "national reconciliation" were again central in the 1979 electoral campaign, though, significantly, this symbolization was starting to become taken for granted, and lose its symbolic effervescence.

The results of the 1979 elections were predictable. None of the main national parties received a significant increase in support, except for the Communists, who won three extra seats, though they had hoped for a much greater improvement on their 1977 result.[5] Interestingly, however, the reign of Suárez and the UCD peaked with their victory in the 1979 elections. After that, internal conflict became so severe that by the next national elections, in 1982, the UCD had split into no less than five parties.[6]

One of the most serious sources of internal and external conflict for the UCD was the unremitting issue of regional nationalism. The UCD was split between "*pactistas,*" who were willing to negotiate an autonomy agreement, and more conservative "*constitucionalistas,*" who believed in the "letter of the constitution," which, according to them, precluded autonomy.[7] This governmental ambiguity and indecision, coupled with the virtually paralyzing fear of alienating the military,[8] meant that even minor victories for regional nationalists were offset by a painfully slow process of negotiation. For instance, although the Basque nationalist leaders had agreed on a "Pre-Autonomy Statute" in December 1977 and approved a draft regional autonomy statute in December 1978, the Autonomy Statute was not brought to the Basque electorate until nearly a year later, and the Basques did not elect their first government until March 1980.

Both symptom and cause of UCD division and paralysis was the fact that Suárez was becoming more and more reclusive. In the year following the 1979 elections, Suárez stayed in the Moncloa Palace, refusing to talk to journalists and meeting fewer and fewer people. He failed to attend the funerals of leaders murdered in the Basque country; he missed over three-quarters of the parliamentary votes, and only rarely visited the Congreso.[9] Despite Suárez's popularity in previous years, by 1980, even people from Suárez's own party were demanding his replacement. As a leading Spanish journalist, José Oneto, told Suárez in October 1980, "The political class seems convinced that you were the right man for the transition, but that you are not the right man for democracy."[10]

Meanwhile, ETA had divided into three aggressive factions, not only raising the level of absolute violence, but adding new targets to the list of ETA victims. As shown in Table 8.1, the number of ETA killings jumped from 9 in 1977 to 67 in 1978; and between 1978 and 1980 ETA groups killed 227 people. Clark estimates that between 1977 and 1980 there were at least half a dozen attempts to negotiate a cease-fire between ETA and the Spanish government. These negotiations failed, however, and the Spanish government responded to heightened ETA violence with a counteroffensive marked by new anti-terrorist laws and police measures that reminded many Basques of some of the worst features of Francoism.[11]

Although Suárez had successfully fought off a vote of no confidence in May 1980 and won a vote of confidence in September, in January 1981, he resigned his position as prime minister.[12] Interestingly, in his resignation broadcast Suárez again called up the core transitional symbols, saying that he was stepping down because he did not wish "the democratic system . . . to be once again a parenthesis in the history of Spain."[13] Recall that the notion of "parenthesis" reaffirms that the new democracy must be a genuine new beginning: it must not be a temporary imposition on the "true" Spanish character, like the "forty years of Francoism."

Shortly after Suárez's resignation, however, a group of Civil Guards (*Guardia Civil*) led by Colonel Antonio Tejero tried to do just this: circumscribe the new democracy, and make it merely a "parenthesis" in Spanish history.

23–F

As we have seen, the Spanish army has a long tradition of internal political meddling. Between the Constitution of Cádiz (1812) and the uprising of 1936, parts of the army rebelled, with the intention of changing Spain's form of government, on more than fifty occasions.[14] During the dictatorship, Franco showered the army with parades and decorations, and fortified its sense of political responsibility. The armed forces provided 40 of Franco's 114 ministers and nearly a thousand members of the Cortes.[15]

Under the direction of the Vice-President of Defense, General Gutiérrez Mellado, the Suárez government tried to depoliticize the Spanish armed forces. They banned the army from taking part in political activities, from joining political parties and trade unions, and from expressing political views in public. The victory parade held to commemorate the end of the Civil War was changed to "the Day of the Armed Forces." Gutiérrez Mellado promoted a number of liberal-minded generals to positions such as captain-general of Madrid and commander of the *Guardia Civil*.[16]

Yet, these changes oftentimes infuriated the more conservative sectors of the army. The circumvention of strict seniority practices in order to promote more liberal generals especially enraged the passed-up officers. As the democratic reforms progressed – and ETA violence increased – reactionary sectors of the armed forces grew more volatile. In addition to increasing skirmishes between regional nationalists and the police and the army in the Basque country, between 1978 and 1982, five different plans for a coup d'état against the democratic regime were uncovered.[17]

The only one of these plans actualized was hastened by Suarez's unexpected resignation. On February 23, 1981, a ballot roll call on whether to accept the new administration of Leopoldo Calvo Sotelo was underway when Colonel Antonio Tejero and a group of Civil Guards burst into the Cortes.[18] Within a short time Tejero was in full control, and the entire parliament was held hostage. Meanwhile the captain-general of Valencia, Jaime Milans del Bosch, declared martial law in Valencia, issued a manifesto in the name of the king, and began telephoning his fellow captain-generals.[19] At the same time that Milans was asking for the captains' support "in the name of the king," however, Juan Carlos was on the phone telling the captains that he was on the other side. By the early hours of February 24, Juan Carlos had won the loyalty of the fence-sitting generals. Milans withdrew his troops from the streets at 4:00 a.m.; shortly thereafter, Tejero negotiated his surrender. Merely six hours later, Leopoldo Calvo Sotelo was elected Prime Minister by a vast majority.

Irrespective of its intentions, "23–F," as the aborted coup came to be called (after the date), turned into a crisis that reactivated, reformulated, and reaffirmed the core symbols of the transition. First, 23–F dramatically reaffirmed the symbolic opposition between democratic parliamentarianism and violence/confrontation. Tejero and his accomplices literally enacted this symbolic dichotomy, as they violently halted the (slow and tedious, but democratic) process of parliamentary voting. Most importantly, since the parliamentary session was being televised live, the "Tejerazo" (Tejero incident) also was televised live – and replayed over and over again on Spanish television. The Spanish public saw parliamentary democracy being aborted by violence. In the tape, there was a few minutes of the ballot roll call, then Tejero emerged and fired two shots into the ceiling of the Cortes, yelling "*todos al suelo!*" ("everyone to the floor!"); then Tejero tussled with the uncooperative Gutiérrez Mellado, and there was some scrambling and fumbling of the camera before the picture went dark.[20]

In his parliamentary address the next day – also televised and replayed repeatedly throughout Spain – King Juan Carlos explicitly confirmed the core transitional symbols, as well as the symbolic opposition between (irrational) violence and (rational) democracy. The king stated that the parliament must maintain the same "serenity and prudence" that he himself had shown on the evening of 23–F; it must surpass its secondary differences and peacefully, rationally, and pluralistically resolve the grave problems facing Spain.[21] In addition, since the coup was inspired by leftist insurgent violence, the extremist left and right were joined in symbolic opposition to the non-violent, democratic process.

Even more significantly, however, the coup dramatically re-evoked the condition of liminality: from 6:20 p.m. (when Tejero burst into the Cortes) to 1:15 a.m. (when Juan Carlos appeared on television to announce the putting down of the coup), the Spanish democratic state was literally in suspension. The party representatives of left and right – liberals, conservatives, socialists, communists, Basques, and Catalans – were all seized from their parliamentary seats and reduced to the lowly, humiliating (but communal) status of "hostage." One could even argue that the entire nation was being held hostage, as Spaniards dared not leave their homes, and merely waited and watched for the end of whatever was happening. In accordance with the communality of the liminal state, when the coup was over, three million Spaniards – of all political persuasions – took part in (communal, effervescent) "demonstrations for democracy" throughout Spain. The communal, reconciliatory spirit of the moment was epitomized in that Manuel Fraga, Felipe González, and Santiago Carrillo, as well as leaders of the UCD and national labor organizations, jointly carried the lead banner in the massive demonstration in Madrid.[22]

In the aftermath of the reawakening of the sacred transitional symbols as a result of the coup, the government introduced the strategy of "cooperation" (*concertación*).[23] This meant that, despite his previous program of retrenchment, Calvo Sotelo started to consult regularly with the leaders of the other parties and with senior generals. In response, Felipe González, Manuel Fraga, and Santiago Carrillo all agreed to support the government in the Cortes. Even more significantly, ETA-pm released three kidnapped foreign consuls and announced an indefinite cease-fire.[24]

The 1982 elections

On October 28, 1982, national elections were held in Spain. The PSOE demolished the reigning UCD. Gunther, Sani, and Shabad describe the UCD defeat as "perhaps the single greatest electoral disaster ever to befall a contemporary Western European party."[25] As shown in Table 9.1, the PSOE garnered nearly 50 percent of the valid electoral votes. And, despite its near disappearance in 1979, the AP (renamed CD) won a quarter of the

Table 9.1. *Results of general elections 1977–1996, Congress of Deputies (percentage of total valid votes)*

Party	1977	1979	1982	1986	1989	1993	1996
PSOE	28.9	30.5	48.4	44.1	39.6	38.7	37.7
UCD	34.0	35.1	6.3	–	–	–	–
CDS	–	–	2.9	9.2	7.9	–	–
AP/PP	8.0	6.1	26.6	26.1	25.8	34.8	38.9
PCE/IU	9.2	10.8	4.1	4.7	9.1	9.5	10.6
PDC/CiU	2.8	2.7	3.7	5.0	5.0	4.9	4.6
PNV	1.7	1.7	1.8	1.5	1.2	1.2	1.3
Others	15.6	13.1	6.3	8.7	10.6	10.7	6.9

Key:
PSOE   Partido Socialista Obrero Español and Socialistes de Catalunya
UCD   Unión del Centro Democrático and Centristes de Catalunya, (CC–UCD)
CDS   Centro Democrático y Social
AP/PP   Alianza Popular (1979), Coalición Democrática (1982–1986), Partido Popular (1989–1996)
PCE/IU   Partido Comunista Español and Partit Socialista Unificat de Catalunya (1977–1982), and Izquierda Unida (1989–1996)
PDC/CiU Pacte Democràtic per Catalunya (1977) and Convergència i Unió (1979–1996)
PNV   Partido Nacionalista Vasco
Source: Gunther, Sani, and Shabad (1986: 402); Cotarelo (1996: 218–221).

votes and established itself as a viable, conservative alternative. The UCD came in a distant third, winning only 6.3 percent of the votes – just 2.2 percent more than the Communists.

For most analysts, though the 1978 Constitution officially institutionalized Spanish democracy, it was the 1982 elections that marked the "end" of the Spanish transition.[26] With the victory of the socialists, a genuine party (rather than a transitional coalition) came to power; and power was transferred successfully. Yet, the striking electoral turnaround in 1982 cries out for explanation. How could the party that "brought democracy to Spain" suffer such a brutal defeat so shortly thereafter? What happened to the Spanish "center" of the two previous national elections?

Most analysts attribute the fall of the UCD to the serious ideological divisions that had been inherent in the UCD from the beginning. For instance, while Gunther, Sani, and Shabad acknowledge that all of the major Spanish parties faced serious ideological divisions in the transitional period, they maintain that the PSOE and the AP faced their internal ideological divisions "earlier" and thus had come much closer to resolving these conflicts by the time of the 1982 elections.[27]

Yet, this explanation is problematic. If centrist leaders were in fact so "pragmatic" (as they were deemed in the early transition period), why did these leaders fail to contend with their ideological differences in order to make the UCD a united party for the 1982 elections? Once again, we see that if elites do pact or resolve their differences, their motivation is deemed strategic. If elites fail to pact or resolve their differences, structural impediments are called up, or their interests are deemed simply "irreconcilable."

From a culturalist perspective, most interesting is the fact that it was the unabashedly consensual parties – the PCE and the UCD – that were devastated in the 1982 elections. Recall that the Union of the Democratic Center (UCD), in particular, was born not as a party at all, but as a coalition of groups (including the traditional right; a democratic right with a conservative Christian ideology; and a reformist sector).[28] Though it professed to having no "ideology," the ideology of the UCD was clearly the core representations of the transition. The UCD was *the* center party, and "center" meant not "gray, lead weight" but moderation, democratic compromise, and national reconciliation. The problem with relying on the core transitional symbols for ideology, however, was that after the transition was "over," i.e. after the core symbols were institutionalized in the 1978 Spanish Constitution, the effervescence of the core symbols receded. With institutionalization the core symbols began to be taken for granted; they tended to evoke the preceding periods of separation and liminality, rather than the "new" one of democratic reaggregation. Thus, just as Suárez was "the right man for the transition but not the right man for democracy,"[29] the UCD was the party of the transition, but not the party of the new parliamentary democracy. As Arango states, the UCD "appeared to be more the dull reflection of politics past than the bright image of politics to come."[30]

The good, the bad and the ugly: the era of "Felipe" (1982–1996)

After the Socialists' victory in 1982, Spain's position in the world strengthened and stabilized. The gap between the Spanish and European standards of living narrowed; spending on education grew considerably; and adult literacy grew to nearly 100 percent.[31] In 1986, Spain joined the European Community (now the European Union) – which was touted not merely as joining the European Community as an organization, but as "joining Europe." The "coming out" of the new Spain was celebrated on a global scale in 1992, when Spain hosted both the summer Olympics and the "Expo" World Fair (which included the debut of a new high-speed "bullet train" from Seville to Madrid).

But if "joining Europe" was the "good" in the era of Felipe, the "bad" in the era of Felipe was the unemployment that plagued the Socialist government from its inception; and the "ugly" was the "epidemic" of sleaze and corruption which became the most serious challenge to the legitimacy of the Socialist government. Specifically, when the Socialists took over in 1982, 16 percent of the Spanish population was unemployed, and González pronounced with confidence that the Socialists would create hundreds of thousands of new jobs. But unemployment rose to over 21 percent in 1985, and has oscillated between 16 and 24 percent of the active population since them. This is twice the average level of unemployment in Europe, and three times that of the United States.[32]

The PSOE had boasted *cien años de honradez* (one hundred years of honesty/honor) in the 1979 elections (which coincided with their hundredth anniversary); and, poised for victory three years later, the PSOE emphasized that theirs would be an era of honesty (*siglo de honradez*).[33] But as early as 1983, scandals began to emerge which challenged the government's self-stylized democratic imagery. These various scandals became the launching pad for a new newspaper, *El Mundo*, founded in 1989. *El Mundo* began a campaign of uncovering various incidents of corruption, not exclusively but primarily within the Socialist government.[34]

The first major scandal uncovered by *El Mundo* was that of the GAL, or Grupos Antiterroristas de Liberación, a death squad created to wage a "dirty war" against ETA separatists. The infamy of the GAL resided not so much in the fact of its existence (for many Spaniards had grown exasperated with legal attempts to stem ETA violence), but because Socialist top brass, including the Minister of the Interior, José Barrionuevo, were allegedly directly involved, and because GAL mercenaries were allegedly paid with public funds. Moreover, the public became even more incensed when rumors began to abound that as many as nine of the GAL's twenty-seven victims may have had nothing to do with terrorism.[35]

Still, many analysts maintain that the GAL affair would have been shortly forgotten if it was not for the emergence of a whole new series of government scandals. Certainly the most poignant drama to unfold was that of Luis Roldán, the Director General of the Civil Guards, who managed to accumulate millions of dollars in personal foreign bank accounts, on an annual salary of approximately $80,000.[36] The Roldán case evolved from just another scandal to a suspense-filled saga when Roldán mysteriously disappeared in the midst of the investigation. For ten whole months Spaniards followed various rumors of Roldán's whereabouts (and the news magazine *Cambio 16* offered a million pesta reward), until finally, in February 1995, Roldán was apprehended in Laos.[37]

The Socialist government tried to portray these scandals as isolated incidents, but as the number of cases mounted, this illusion was hard to maintain. Moreover, the incidents started to hit closer and closer to the center of power. In March 1991, Deputy Prime Minister Alfonso Guerra resigned in the midst of a scandal involving his brother, Juan Guerra. Juan Guerra was accused of amassing a personal fortune as a result of "influence trafficking" (using the PSOE offices in Seville for private business). Though most of the charges against Juan Guerra were dropped, the resignation of Alfonso Guerra was a major blow to the legitimacy of the González government. The González–Guerra partnership went all the way back to their days as activists with the Young Socialist group in Seville, and Guerra had been Deputy Prime Minister since the very beginning of the Socialist era.[38]

By the early 1990s, government ministers were resigning right and left. Scandals embraced the Minister of the Economy, Miguel Boyer, the Minister of Agriculture, Vicente Albero Silla, and Health Minister Julián García Valverde (among others).[39] In April 1993, student protestors yelled "corruption," "sleaze," and "Italy" while Prime Minister Felipe González attempted to give a speech at Madrid University.[40] In a survey conducted in 1994, more than half of the voters who had abandoned the PSOE in the parliamentary elections cited "corruption" as the main reason.[41]

The "Second Transition"

With the legitimacy of the Socialist Party rapidly declining, new opportunites for the conservative opposition emerged. In 1988, the Popular Alliance (AP) led by Manuel Fraga was "refounded" as Partido Popular (PP, Popular Party); and under the direction of the young José Maria Aznar, president of the Castile-Leon regional government, the PP began to try to shake off its old authoritarian image. In the 1989 general elections (the first under its new name and image), PP won nearly 26 percent of the votes; this percentage climbed to 34.8 percent in 1993 (see Table 9.1). This meant that the Socialists became a minority government, relying on the Catalan conservative nationalist party Convergència i Unió (CiU), led by Jordi Pujol, for a working majority in parliament.

The Partido Popular won the European Parliamentary elections in June 1994; and in March 1996, the PP won the Spanish general elections. Thus, the peaceful alteration from center-right to left in 1982 was finally succeeded by the peaceful transfer of power from left to right in 1996 – a shift Aznar calls Spain's "Second Transition."[42]

Yet, the Partido Popular did not win by as much as many analysts thought. As shown in Table 9.1, the Socialists garnered nearly 38 percent of the vote, and Felipe González continues to be popular, especially in his native Andalusia. Moreover, according to a recent poll, many Spaniards continue to be wary of the right, despite the Partido Popular's highly pro-claimed shift to the "center."[43]

In part this is because despite the recent epidemic of socialist corruption and scandal, "sleaze" in Spain is linked not so much to the Socialist Party per se, but to the incessant problem of Spanish political elitism. And while corruption is clearly a multipartisan problem today, it is also a problem with strong historical roots in Spanish authoritarianism.[44] This is why no matter the unsavory practices in which they are involved, the Socialists continue to portray themselves as the bearers of (sacred) modernity and democracy – in symbolic opposition to (profane) authoritarianism.

Of course, another source of concern in this on-going period is the continuing regional autonomy (and ETA) issue. The Constitution of 1978 gave the autonomous regions (seventeen, in all) significant latitude in making laws and spending funds for culture, infrastructure, and government services; but this latitude means that there has been constant negotiation and bargaining between the center and the regions. Indeed, in March 1997, yet another legislative debate on autonomy was "opened up" by a dramatic assassination by ETA. The death of prison psychologist Francisco Gómez Elosegi brought the ETA victim count to seven in the first two-and-a-half months of 1997, thereby surpassing the number of victims in all of 1996.[45]

Clearly, resolving Spain's economic, regional and political dilemmas will not be easy. The future of Spain (as elsewhere) is open. However, no matter what happens next, one thing about Spain's past is certain: the recent Spanish post-Franco transition is an exemplar of peaceful transformation from authoritarianism to democracy. And intertwined in the political lessons from the Spanish case are critical cultural lessons. In sum, in illuminating the role of culture in this complex case of social change, my intent has not been to ignore politico-economic or existential concerns, but to "plunge into the midst of them."[46]

Notes

1 Introduction

1 McNamara (1995).
2 See Wagner-Pacifici and Schwartz (1991) for an excellent analysis of the history and meaning of the Vietnam memorial. Interestingly, among the "things left behind" at the Vietnam Memorial are the ashes of "Robert Strange McNamara's book" (and accompanying photos of a man burning the book in a barbecue pit). See the *New York Times Magazine* (11–12–95: 83–85).
3 Tusell (1986).
4 Preston (1988:14).
5 By the "success" of the Spanish transition I mean, first, that unlike other moments of transition in Spanish history, the death of Franco in 1975 did not result in a civil war, military coup, or even the purging of Francoists; and secondly, that the Francoist authoritarian system was effectively replaced by a self-sustaining democracy. By "self-sustaining democracy" I mean one in which there is (1) a real possibility of partisan alternation in office, and (2) a real possibility of reversible policy changes resulting from alternation in office, and (3) effective civilian control over the military (see Przeworski 1991). As will be discussed shortly, the crucial exception in terms of the "smoothness" or "uneventfulness" as well as the "success" of the recent Spanish transition to democracy, however, is the Basque and corresponding centralist violence and terrorism which plagued the new democratic regime, and continues to be the most threatening and divisive issue in Spain.
6 Carr (1980: 1); see also Payne (1973; 1985).
7 As Esenwein and Shubert (1995: 64) point out, Spain's contributions to the political vocabulary in the nineteenth century – *guerrilla*, *caudillo*, and *pronunciamiento* – reflect its history of militarism quite clearly.
8 Esenwein and Shubert (1995: 1).
9 Significantly, the military itself was also divided. In Madrid, Valencia, and Barcelona, the army stood by "the people" against the rebel officers. And in four-fifths of the navy's ships the sailors and petty officers executed and then

replaced their rebellious commanders (Vilar, 1967: 107). See also Esenwein and Shubert (1995), Ellwood (1991), and Browne (1983), among others.

10 Esenwein and Shubert (1995: 104–108).

11 The expression "ley de la transición para la transición" was coined by Iñigo Caver, "Soberanía y elecciones constituyentes," *Informaciones políticas*, 9–18–76, as cited by P. Lucas Verdu in "Derecho político y transformación política española," *Revista de la Facultad de Derecho de la UCM*, 55, Winter 1979, p. 22, as cited by del Aguila and Montoro (1984: 38).

12 Carr and Fusi (1979: 244).

13 Payne (1985: 25).

14 Huntington (1991).

15 Gunther (1992).

16 An important exception here in one respect is Poland. As Kubik (1994), among others, points out – and the saying "ten years" (Poland) vs. "ten days" (Romania) attests – post-totalitarian culture in Poland long preceded post-total-itarian politics, which allowed rapid mobilization.

17 This is also true for the other "southern European" cases of transition: Portugal and Greece.

18 See Bunce and Csanadi (1993). Verdery (1993) takes this argument even further. She maintains that under state socialism the "real" self was meaningful and coherent only in relation to the public or official self; people's senses of identity required the "enemy" party, the "them," to complete it. With the end of the party rule, the "other" was abolished, which produced a crisis in self-conception; and nationalisms – with their clear "other" – became very appealing. Verdery's interpretation does not necessarily contradict the notion that eastern Europeans *wanted* to avoid the project of creating a blueprint for a new society, i.e. it was precisely that experience that they wanted to escape.

19 The implication of an inevitable end is precisely the problem with the terms "transition to democracy" and "democratic transition." As Bunce and Csanadi (1993) point out, these terms call our attention to an (idealized) future state, rather than the present uncertainty. This problem is especially apparent in elite and rational choice models, discussed in chapter 2.

20 Marías (1990: 413).

21 The eminent historian Stanley Payne (1987a: 8) argues that the threat from the Spanish military was little more than a "paper tiger" because "the Spanish mili-tary historically only revolts against *unpopular* regimes." The problem with this assertion is twofold. First, the first post-Franco government of Carlos Arias Navarro was not particularly popular. Indeed, Arias Navarro alienated both the Francoist bunker and the democratic opposition, and in 1976 he was forced by the king to resign. Secondly, if we take seriously the notion that reality is a social construction, it becomes obvious that military leaders could easily have per-ceived the dissatisfaction of Spaniards. In point of fact (rightly or wrongly), many analysts and journalists believed that Spaniards became "disenchanted with their democratic experiment" in the late 1970s and early 1980s (see, for

example, McDonough and López Pina, 1984: 365). See Agüero (1995) for a more detailed analysis of the role of the military in the Spanish transition.

22 As Valerie Bunce first pointed out to me, one of the few advantages the post-communist states had over Spain was that they were not burdened by a history of military *pronunciamientos*.

2 Theories of transition and transitions in theory

1 Of course, these are general trends in sociology, and there are important exceptions as well as much disagreement among those classified under the same rubric.

2 Lipset (1963); Almond and Verba (1989); Pye and Verba (1965).

3 See Prager (1986: 8–10; 227–229) for more on the political culture tradition in sociology. As Prager (p. 228: n.20) notes, there are, however, important exceptions to sociology's weak understanding of political culture. Most importantly, Walzer's *Revolution of the Saints* (1964) remains an exemplar on the empirical interrelations between culture and politics; and Eisenstadt's *Revolution and the Transformation of Societies* (1978) formally advances our understanding of the interaction between culture and politics and links them to patterns of change.

4 Poulantzas (1976); Gunder Frank (1967); Tilly (1978).

5 Somers (1995) points out the conceptual weaknesses of the political culture concept, which, along with the rise of more radical alternatives, led to the concept's demise.

6 Burton and Higley (1987, 1989); Przeworski (1986, 1991); O'Donnell and Schmitter (1986); Diamond, Linz, and Lipset (1988).

7 There are a handful of "pactwomen" (e.g. Nancy Bermeo, Andrea Bonime-Blanc, and Eva Etzioni-Halevy), but I will continue to use the term "pactmen" instead of pactmen and pactwomen or "pactpeople" for brevity, and because – although it is outside the scope of this book to discuss it here – the legitimacy of the Western individualistic theoretical orientation (and rejection of "subjectivity") is related to its links to "masculinity."

8 As Alexander (1982) first pointed out, every social theory is implicitly cross cut by specific presuppositions as to the rationality of action and the nature of social order. The central question that every social theory addresses is to what degree action is rational. Is action guided by ends of pure efficiency? Are goals calculated? Or are goals produced by the substantive ideal contents of norms themselves? The problem of order is the problem of how individual units, of whatever motivation, are arranged in non-random social patterns. Every theory must adopt a solution to the order problem, just as it must also address the problem of action and motivation.

9 Przeworski (1991). Similarly, O'Donnell and Schmitter (1986: 3) maintain that their work "involves an effort to capture the extraordinary uncertainty of the transition." Theirs is an inquiry "into the problem of 'underdetermined' social change, of large-scale transformations which occur when there are

insufficient structural or behavioral parameters to guide and predict the outcome."

10 See Alexander (1987: 162).

11 Higley and Burton (1989: 17–32).

12 According to Burton and Higley (1987: 295), elite settlements are "broad compromises among previously warring elite factions that result in political stability, and are a precondition for democracy."

13 See Colomer (1991) and Przeworski (1991, ch. 2) for game theoretic perspectives. See O'Donnell and Schmitter (1986) for perhaps the most developed game/metaphor analogy – O'Donnell and Schmitter discuss "playing coup poker" and devote the entire conclusion of their book on transitions to "the metaphor of the multi-layered chess game." Baylora (1987) and Share (1986), among others, also adopt a chess parlance, discussing the "opening moves" and "endgame" of transition.

14 See Gunther (1992).

15 Przeworski (1986: 61); Share (1986; 1987; 1989).

16 Wert Ortega (1985: 77, emphasis added).

17 Gunther, Sani, and Shabad (1986: 118–119, emphasis added); Giner (1986: 14).

18 Maravall and Santamaría (1986: 86); see also Bonime-Blanc (1987: 54–60).

19 Morlino (1987: 65). This deterministic conceptualization of "experience" is so common, it is taken for granted and generalized in the pact school. For example, Medhurst (1984: 40) maintains that "the shared experience of *dictatorship*" as well as the civil war "left its mark on the quest for consensus" (emphasis added).

20 Share (1986: 120).

21 Medhurst (1984: 40).

22 Share, for example, ignores the Basque issue in *The Making of Spanish Democracy* (1986).

23 Gilmour (1985: 221).

24 Gunther, Sani, and Shabad (1986: 338).

25 See Gunther, Sani, and Shabad (1986: 104).

26 Przeworski (1991).

27 Gilmour (1985: 221–222). In addition, Gilmour states:

> The PNV leadership was hampered all along by the attitude of the party's radicals . . . The intransigence of the *sabiniano* group [i.e. followers of Sabino Arana] in the PNV made it practically impossible for the party to take an unambiguous stance on anything other than police brutality. Arzallus was a fine orator and an able man, but he did not have the character, and perhaps not the will, to fashion a coherent programme for his party. Throughout the critical period of the transition, the PNV leadership lacked the courage to state unambiguously where it stood on the vital issues of terrorism and eventual independence.

28 Gunther, Sani, and Shabad (1986: 120).

29 Gunther, Sani, and Shabad (1986: 119). When Gunther et al. (pp. 117–8) broach

the issue from the other side (and attempt to explain the success of the Spanish politics of consensus), even they realize that their argument borders on tautology:

> The most important ingredients of the politics of consensus were the historical memories, basic values, political objectives and behavioral styles of the relevant sets of party elites. Care must be given to avoid tautological arguments involving these kinds of variables, but it can be stated in the abstract that negotiations involving pragmatic political figures, whose historical memories lead them to perceive potential threats to system survival and who wish to preserve important features of that system, are more likely to culminate in satisfactory conflict resolutions than will negotiations among dogmatic individuals, who are unaware of the fragility of the system or who have no stake in its preservation.

30 Maravall and Santamaría (1986: 91).
31 Burton and Higley (1987: 295). Similarly, Higley and Burton (1989: 19) maintain that "over time, most elites achieve their most basic aims and are therefore inclined to view the totality of decisional outcomes as positive-sum."
32 López Pintor (1982: 17). States López Pintor (1982: 52), "the majority of Spaniards were to be witnesses – not without fear and anxiety – to how the Government and opposition put themselves more or less peacefully in agreement in order to sign the social contract."
33 Gunther, Sani, and Shabad (1986: 117).
34 López Pintor (1982); McDonough and López Pina (1984: 365–396); Share (1987: 536); Maravall and Santamaría (1986: 91). See also McDonough, López Pina, and Barnes (1981) and McDonough, Barnes, and López Pina (1994).
35 López Pintor (1982); McDonough and López Pina (1984: 365–396).
36 Fishman (1990); Przeworski (1991). Tarrow (1995) quite rightly points out that "elitist" accounts of the Spanish transition ignore the period of "prolonged struggle" before the historic period of consensus (1976–1978) . Yet, by highlighting the role of the mass public only in the earlier "prolonged struggle," Tarrow implicitly affirms that the "period of consensus" was indeed an "elite" phenomenon. However, as Fishman (1990: 217) points out, an important problem in the elite argument is that the peak of strike activity in Spain was actually attained in 1979, *"after the alleged demobilization had already taken place"* (emphasis in original).
37 Fishman (1990: 227).
38 Fishman (1990: 227).
39 Foweraker (1987: 2). Yet, though Fishman and Foweraker distinguish themselves from their fellow pactmen by acknowledging the role of workers in the Spanish transition, neither challenges the theoretical presuppositions of the pact school. On the contrary, Fishman (1990: 248) embraces pact school atheoreticism – which he calls the "Weberian tradition" of "answering broad analytical questions" with "historically specific conclusions" – and, not surprisingly, ends

up relying on the same subjective residual categories seen previously in the pact school. Similarly, Foweraker (1987: 2) skirts, rather than confronts, the theoretical implications of his argument: "my intention is not to contest or confirm extant accounts of the [Spanish] transition per se . . . [though] I confess my dissatisfaction with studies . . . which limit democratic achievement to changes of regime at government level." The problem with Lachmann's (1990) "elite conflict theory" is different: Lachmann bridges elite and conflict concerns, while demonstrating that both elite and conflict theory lack a coherent conceptualization of culture.

40 Alexander (1982: 24).

41 Alexander and Colomy (1990: 6–10). Specifically, Alexander and Colomy note that structuralists such as Skocpol and Finegold (1982), and Sewell (1980), have begun to bring subjectivity into their analyses; general theorists such as Giddens (1984), Collins (1981), and Habermas (1984) have all moved away from one-sided polemics of earlier theoretical work; micro-sociologists such as Goffman (1974), Lewis and Smith (1980), and Fine (1990) have challenged Blumer's emphasis on individualistic contingency; and Cicourel (1981), Schegloff (1987), and Heritage and Greatbatch (1986) seek to establish micro–macro links. Of course, as the diversity in these citations reveals, despite the trend toward synthesis, there is no consensus as to the theoretical and methodological form multidimensional analyses should take. Moreover, this is a general trend and there are important exceptions. For instance, in direct contrast to Lipset's (1985) attempts to bridge the consensus/conflict divide, political scientist Gabriel Almond (1990, especially pp. 142, 234, and 251–253) laments his discipline's divisions, but continues to lambast statists, Marxists, and dependency theorists.

42 For example, Swidler (1986) argues for culture's opening to contingency, Archer (1988) for culture's sensitivity to change, and Eisenstadt (1986) for its link to material force and institutional life (Alexander and Colomy, 1990: 8).

43 See Wagner-Pacifici (1989), Wagner-Pacifici and Schwartz (1991), Zelizer (1979; 1994), and Crane (1994) for exemplars in the new cultural sociology/sociology of culture. Of course, the recent cultural turn has additionally taken place outside sociology. See Laitin (1977) and Kertzer (1988) for two exemplary new approaches to political culture in political science and anthropology, respectively.

44 Alexander (1997).

45 Pérez Díaz (1993: 3).

46 Pérez Díaz (1993: 3, emphases added).

47 Pérez Díaz (1993: 13; 36, emphasis added).

48 In precisely the same way, Rodríguez Ibañez (1987: 125) maintains that the "erroneous perception of democracy" as "'salvation administration' was dissolved once the negative consequences of generalized apathy were seen" – which implies that democratic perceptions are "really" just calculations about utility, and again, results in determinism. Of course, this type of of instrumentalization of subjectivity is quite standard in political science. It is readily apparent in Wiarda's (1996) recent book, *Iberia and Latin America: New Democracies, New*

Policies, New Models, as well as in two of the most highly acclaimed recent "political cultural" works of the last few years: Robert Putnam's *Making Democracy Work: Civic Traditions in Modern Italy* (1993), and Francis Fukuyama's *Trust* (1995). By contrast, in their study of Spanish transitional political discourse, del Aguila and Montoro (1984) do not simply instrumental- ize subjectivity, assert "meaning" or deny its existence. On the contrary, del Aguila and Montoro thoroughly investigate "meaning" in the Spanish transi- tion. Yet, though they purport to explain "the interconnected play (*"juego"*) between ideology and reality" (p. 2), in the end, del Aguila and Montoro confess that their goal has been merely descriptive (to have offered "the most rich and complete vision of the structure of political discourse" possible). Thus they beg the critical theoretical question: how did this transitional discourse actually impact the events and the outcome of the Spanish transition?

49 Swidler (1986).

50 Eco (1976: 124).

51 Eco does not discuss the extraordinary racialization in his example (i.e. beauti- ful, long, *white* neck), but clearly one of the most important arenas for cultural analysis today is race and representation. See Prager (1982) and hooks (1992) for two seminal works in this regard.

52 Eco (1979: 78).

53 Giddens (1986: 537).

54 For instance, the "swan" metaphor above relies on the existence of a "white" standard of beauty, a predominant, oftentimes hegemonic cultural pattern. But the existence of this cultural pattern does not mean that it is unilaterally inter- nalized as a static "value" for any particular person or group. It can be upended, distorted, made fun of, etc.; but, ironically, in its very reversal, the original cul- tural pattern is *recognized* and thereby oftentimes reaffirmed.

55 Ricoeur (1971).

56 I could also have used interview data as the texts for analysis. But only inter- views done at the time could possibly reveal the actual symbolic configurations of the Spanish cultural system during the transition. Moreover, in asking sub- jects to articulate their views, interviews always contain a problematic "norma- tive" dimension. Interviews reported in the media are included in this study, but they are not considered substantively different from other media discourse.

57 Durkheim (1912) ambiguously used "profane" to mean both negatively charged symbols, and non-sacred (uncharged) signs. Callois' (1959) first modified Durkheim's sacred–profane dichotomy into a threefold classification, which I use in this study. See Alexander (1988); also Mary Douglas (1966), who notes that the profane is often the pollution of the sacred.

58 Graham (1984: 230).

59 Quoted by Maxwell (1983: 17). Similarly, van Noortwijk (1995) argues that the news magazine *Triunfo* was part and parcel of a "culture of resistance" before Franco's death; and that this reconstruction of "democratic reason" abetted the Spanish transition.

60 Maxwell (1983: 17); Graham (1984: 228).

61 Quoted by Maxwell (1983: 17). According to Graham (1984: 228):

> Not long after taking office, Felipe González sent a circular to all the ministries insisting that no one read *El País* before midday. The Prime Minister was concerned that his ministers and senior civil servants might allow the newspaper to make up their minds on policy decisions rather than using their own judgement. The story is told with relish at *El País* and dismissed airily at the Prime Minister's office.

As this story reflects, while there is no question that the Spanish media played an important role in the transition, the media has often been accused of exaggerating its influence. See Giner (1983) and Martínez Soler (1980).

62 *El Alcázar* ("The Fortress") is a far right newspaper, unabashedly nostalgic, focusing heavily on the military. Interestingly, the circulation of *El Alcázar* declined between 1970 and 1975, but more than quadrupled between 1975 and 1980 (Maxwell, 1983: 48; Graham, 1984: 245). *El Socialista* ("The Socialist") is the official newspaper of the Spanish Socialist Workers' Party (PSOE) and its union affiliate, the Unión General de Trabajadores (UGT). It re-emerged in 1978 after having been eradicated under Franco (Roldán Ros, 1985: 256). The Suárez government legalized the Spanish Communist Party in April 1977, and the official organ of the PCE, *Mundo Obrero,* came out on the streets after years of underground publication shortly thereafter. *Mundo Obrero* aspired to be like the French *Humanité* or the Italian *Unità,* but it never carried much weight outside the party, and collapsed in 1980 (Graham, 1984: 245). The first Basque newspaper to emerge in the Basque country after Franco's death was *Deia,* of Bilbao, which published its first edition on June 8, 1977, just in time for the first democratic elections. The less moderate *Egin,* of San Sebastián, followed shortly thereafter, in September 1977. As Coca et al. (1993: 23–24) point out, both *Egin* and *Deia* emerged directly out of the political arena, rather than from either professional journalists or American-style "editors." *Deia* is closely tied to the Basque Nationalist Party (PNV), and *Egin* to ETA–KAS Koordinadora Abertzale Socialista–(HB) Herri Batasuna. See also Pascual (1995: 526).

63 Ricoeur (1971).

64 Turner (1969). Alexander (1988) points out that Turner never acknowledged his debt to Durkheim.

65 Turner (1969: 94–95).

3 Spain: a history of divisions and democracy

1 There are many excellent works on Spanish history. This chapter relies heavily on the classic works of Crow (1963) and Vilar (1967), as well as recent works by Payne (1993), and Esenwein and Shubert (1995). In terms of political analysis of late nineteenth- and early twentieth-century Spain, see Linz (1964; 1967; 1973a; 1973b; 1978; 1980a; 1980b).

2 The Roman geographer Strabo observed that the peoples of Spain are "bad

mixers who are difficult to unite" (Geoffrey J. Walker, Introduction to the English edition of *Catalan Nationalism*, by Albert Balcells, 1996).

3 Crow (1963: 41).

4 Crow (1963: 79).

5 Crow (1963: 182).

6 As Crow (1963: 151) points out, Catholic, Castilian centralization is epitomized in the year 1492, perhaps the most extraordinary year in Spanish history. In 1492, the war against the Moslems was won; the Spanish Inquisition turned its full force against the religious minorities in Spain; the Spaniard Rodrigo Borgia was made Pope in Rome (thus giving Ferdinand and Isabella a strong ally inside the Church); Christopher Columbus touched shore in the New World; and *Castilian Grammar*, by Antonio de Nebrija, was published – the first grammar book of any modern European tongue, and a clear reflection and affirmation of the hegemony of the Castilian region, as well as Castilian language and literature.

7 Balcells (1996: xiii).

8 According to Vilar (1967), the terms "political and economic imperialism" and "nation-state" are perhaps more applicable to Catalonia between 1250 and 1350 than to any other European country.

9 The Catalan national anthem, *Cant dels Segadors* ("Song of the Reapers"), recounts the *Corpus de Sang* ("Corpus of Blood") insurrection (Balcells, 1996: 13). See also Díez Medrano (1995: ch. 1).

10 Crow (1963: 255–256); see also Carr (1980: 3). As Crow points out, plagued by a full-blown Carlist war in the north, the revolt in Cuba, the collapse of discipline among the military and the splintering of the liberals, the wonder is not why the Republic failed, but how the Republic got established at all.

11 Díez Medrano (1994).

12 Esenwein and Shubert (1995: 88–90).

13 Anarchism was first introduced in Spain in 1868, and the first labor congress was held in Barcelona in 1870. After the First World War, anarchism merged with French revolutionary syndicalism and became a mass movement firmly rooted in the working class, known as anarchosyndicalism. See Esenwein and Shubert (1995: 79–80).

14 Esenwein and Shubert (1995: 79–80).

15 Esenwein and Shubert (1995: 37–43).

16 See Ullman (1968: 326) and Read (1978: 174).

17 Esenwein and Shubert (1995: 80).

18 Payne (1993: 22).

19 Payne (1993).

20 A coalition of Catalan leftists, called the Esquerra Republicana de Catalunya ("Republican Left of Catalonia"), had agreed to support the Republican–Socialist coalition in return for the promise that once the monarchy was defeated, the Catalan Generalitat would be re-established. See Read (1978: 185); also Esenwein and Shubert (1995: 55).

21 Esenwein and Shubert (1995: 44).

22 Crow (1963: 305). Yet, the Church's perspective was confirmed when merely a month after the elections anti-clerical violence broke out. Six churches in Madrid and fifteen more in various southern cities were burned. See Sánchez (1987).

23 Esenwein and Shubert (1995: 10–13).

24 Esenwein and Shubert (1995: 16–17); Payne (1993: 179).

25 Esenwein and Shubert (1995: 17).

26 Esenwein and Shubert (1995: 15).

27 See Esenwein and Shubert (1995: 84), as well as Payne (1993: 220, and fn. 68, pp. 430–431), which includes a bibliography of works on the October revolution. As Payne (1993: 222) notes, historians are nearly unanimous in viewing the revolutionary resurrection of 1934 as either the "prelude to" or the "first battle of" the Civil War.

28 Payne (1993: 222).

29 Payne (1993: 281–287); Sánchez (1987: 8).

30 Esenwein and Shubert (1995: 121) quite rightly point out that this revolutionary side of the Civil War has received scant attention in Civil War literature and films.

31 Esenwein and Shubert (1995: 124–5).

32 Esenwein and Shubert (1995: 132); Sánchez (1987).

33 Esenwein and Shubert (1995: 179).

34 Most analysts agree that though international aid was important to both sides, Franco's troops would not have won without the help of nearly fifty thousand Italian militiamen and munitions and support from Germany. See Esenwein and Shubert (1995, ch. 10).

35 Rodríguez Armada and Novais, "¿Quién mató a Julián Grimau?" (1976), as cited by Preston (1988: 17).

36 Preston (1988: 12–13). As Preston (1988: 17) notes, the Valle de los Caídos ("Valley of the Fallen") took nearly 20 years to complete, even with the use of 20,000 Republican prisoners.

37 Carr and Fusi (1979: 52).

38 Payne (1987b: 418).

39 See Lancaster (1989: 25–31).

40 Carr and Fusi (1979: 54).

41 See Lancaster (1989).

42 Martinez (1993: 114).

43 Carr and Fusi (1979: 58).

44 Graham (1984: 165–166). As Marías (1990: 407) points out, unlike the previous "Europeanization" of Spain in the 1800s, the recent Europeanization of Spain has been not merely an "elite" but also a "mass" phenomenon.

45 Carr and Fusi (1979: 29).

46 Payne (1987b: 421).

47 Payne (1984: 194–195).

48 Escarrré stated:

We do not have behind us twenty-five years of peace but only twenty-five years of victory. The victors, including the Church which was obliged to fight on their side, have done nothing to abolish this division between victors and vanquished: this represents one of the most lamentable failures of a regime which calls itself Christian, but whose state does not follow the basic principles of Christianity.

Interview published in *Le Monde* (1963), and reproduced in Jacques Georgel, *El Franquismo: historia y balance 1939–1969* (1971), as cited by Gilmour (1985: 56).

49 Carr and Fusi (1979: 154). As Carr and Fusi point out, the far right did not take well to the appointment of Tarancón, and throughout the early 1970s Cardinal Tarancón was often greeted with the slogan "Tarancón al paredón" ("Tarancón to the firing squad").

50 Payne (1984: 202).

51 Payne (1984: 207–208).

52 Cooper (1975: 33–40); Payne (1984: 204).

53 Foweraker (1987; 1989); see also Belda (1977). The workers' commissions would present a particular demand to employers; if the demand was successfully negotiated, the commission would disband. Significantly, employers were often willing to comply with initiatives regarding wages and conditions of work in order to bypass the more repressive and intransigent official channels. Foweraker (1987: 107).

54 Maravall (1982).

55 Carr and Fusi (1979).

56 Sainz Rodríguez, *Un reinado en la sombra* (1981), as cited by Gilmour (1985: 89).

57 Carr and Fusi (1979: 166); Gilmour (1985: 100–101).

58 Maravall (1982: 9). See also Foweraker (1987); and Gilmour (1985: 58; 91).

59 Payne (1987b: 376). As will be discussed in chapter 8, the military trial of the *etarras* in the old Castilian city of Burgos turned into a public relations nightmare for Franco. European journalists published the defendants' detailed accounts of torture and condemned the Franco regime for the violation of internationally recognized principles of due process. When six of the defendants were sentenced to death, European intellectuals and, more importantly, the Pope, appealed to Franco for clemency. In the end, Franco relented and signed reprieves on the six death sentences.

60 This "spiral of violence" was particularly ominous because, as will be discussed further in chapter 8, the purpose of ETA violence was not to push the regime toward moderate democratic reforms, but to incite a "spiral" of violence–repression–violence, etc., which would lead to mass rebellion, civil war, and ultimately Basque secession. Clark (1990: 8–9).

61 *Pueblo* (2–6–68), as cited by Carr and Fusi (1979: 32).

62 The 1969 appointments of Carrero Blanco as vice president and Juan Carlos as Prince of Spain were motivated by a sharp decline in Franco's health. Indeed, analysts such as Carr and Fusi (1979: 189) and Preston (1994: 749–751) suggest

that though Carrero Blanco was officially head of state for only six months in 1973, he had virtually acted as prime minister since 1969, when he was appointed vice president.

63 Carr and Fusi (1979: 199).

64 Carr and Fusi (1979: 201).

65 Carlists, who had hoped to see the Carlist Pretender, Don Javier, returned to the throne, were continually disappointed by Franco. Nevertheless, one of the reasons often given as to why Don Juan would allow his son to be educated by Franco is the supposition that if he did not, Franco might exclude his family altogether in favor of a Carlist claimant to the throne.

66 Payne (1987b: 496). Franco first handed over his powers to Juan Carlos when he seemed to be on his deathbed in the summer of 1975; but Franco then recovered and took his powers back. After Franco died, this incident was memorialized by *Saturday Night Live* with the recurring line, "and . . . Franco is *still* dead."

67 *La Vanguardia* (4–10–77), cited by Carr and Fusi (1979: 210).

68 See Huneeus (1985: 88).

69 Arango (1985: 99).

4 The spirit of consensus: the core representations of the Spanish transition

1 Alexander (1988); see also Tiryakian (1967).

2 Hunt (1984).

3 Turner (1969: 96).

4 Santiago Carrillo, who had a penchant for catchy phrases as well as popular sentiment, entitled one of his books, *Después de Franco, ¿Qué?* (1965).

5 *El País* (4–26–77: 13).

6 *El País* (4–24–77: 9).

7 *El País* (5–17–77: 11). The transcendence of the symbol "new generation" is also readily apparent in *The Return of Civil Society* (1993), which begins with the "personal observation" that Pérez Díaz is a member of the "new generation" – i.e. that "generation of Spaniards who first assumed professional and political responsibilities in the late 1950s and 1960s" – which believed not in "the institutional framework of Francoism," but in "solving Spain's problems in a spirit of freedom, justice and creativity."

8 *El País* (5–18–77: 9).

9 *El País* (4–28–77: 1).

10 *El País* (6–9–77: 9). Indeed, as will be discussed shortly, the Communist Party began talking about a non-violent strategy as early as 1948, and officially adopted the "Policy of National Reconciliation" in 1956.

11 Turner (1969: 96).

12 *El País* (5–8–77: 9).

13 See Benson (1967), Hart (1988), Kaplan (1992: 177–187), and Monteath (1994).

14 Spender, "Guernica," in Murray Sperber, ed., *And I Remember Spain*, (1974: 151–152), as cited by Kaplan (1992: 184).

15 Western writers, such as Malraux (*L'espoir*), Regler (*The Great Crusade*), and Hemingway (*For Whom the Bell Tolls*), however, tended to emphasize the political dimensions of the war more; they saw the Civil War as a struggle between fascism and human dignity.

16 See Fisch (1988: 62–64) for a comparison of *The Third of May, 1814* and *Guernica*. As Fisch notes, one of the fundamental similarities is that both are large murals with life-size or larger than life-size figures, which adds to the total impact of the paintings.

17 Kaplan (1992: 179).

18 Fisch (1988: 23).

19 Fisch (1988: 23).

20 Indeed, as many analysts have pointed out, the Spanish Civil War (1936–1939) is not particularly noteworthy on an historical, geographical, or technological scale. It was the fourth civil war in Spain since the 1830s, and, as British Hispanicist Raymond Carr bluntly states, although horrific, the bombing of the Basque city of Guernica seems a "minor act of vandalism" compared with the horrors of Hiroshima or Dresden (cited by Preston 1986b: 1).

21 By contrast, the American Civil War, the First World War and the Second World War were interpreted largely as Good (freedom, democracy) conquering Evil (slavery, fascism). See Fussell (1975) for a seminal account of "the Great War" and modern memory.

22 Sánchez (1987: 8–11). According to Sánchez, approximately 25 percent of the male clergy behind Republican lines was killed; and approximately 10 percent of the deaths caused by the Republicans were clerical deaths.

23 Preston (1988).

24 See Kaplan (1992).

25 See, for example, López Pintor (1982) and McDonough, López Pina, and Barnes (1981).

26 Marías (1990: 402).

27 See Aguilar Fernández (1995) for a more detailed analysis of the memory of the Spanish Civil War.

28 According to Fisch (1988: 18), "Soviet workers even had to sacrifice one-half percent of their monthly wages to show their solidarity with the Popular Front of Spain."

29 There were also harsh schisms between committed Stalinists (most importantly, Dolores Ibárruri, La Pasionaria) and "traitors" such as Gabriel León Trilla, who was not only expelled from the PCE in 1945, but, allegedly, executed. See Comín Colomer, *Historia del Partido Comunista en España* (1965–1967: 52), as cited by Hermet (1971: 57, 85, fn. 34).

30 Hermet (1971: 56); Bell (1979: 12).

31 Hermet (1971: 66).

32 Cooper (1975); see also Sánchez (1987: 112–113).

33 Cooper (1976: 61).

34 "Reconocemos humildemente y pedimos por ello perdón, por no haber sabido ser, cuando fue necesario, verdaderos ministros de la reconciliación."

Significantly, the Asemblea Conjunta de Obispos y Sacerdotes is a type of assembly now accepted by the post-conciliar Church, but previously forbidden. See Cooper (1975).

35 Cooper (1975: 40). See also Belda et. al. (1977) and Urbina (1977: 11–84).
36 Mujal-León (1983: 99–100).
37 *El País* (5–6–77: 16).
38 *El País* (5–6–77: 16).
39 *El País* (6–12–77: V).
40 *El País* (5–19–77: 22).
41 *El País* (6–3–77: 9).
42 Aguilar Fernández (1995: 465).
43 *El País* (6–11–77: 18).
44 *El País* (5–18–77: 15).
45 *El País* (5–15–77: 33).
46 *El País* (4–15–77: 8). Similarly, the general director of the local administration in Madrid said he would like to be dynamic, but "we live in a period of transition and one person cannot impress their stamp on the public action; the epoch of triumphalism has past" (*El País*, 4–24–77: 15).
47 *Ya* (4–27–77).
48 The profane character of "violence" is also apparent in such comments as, "the violence, that feeds on defenseless persons, produces in me indignation and disgust" (*El País*, 4–19–77: 9).
49 Herr (1971: 28–32).
50 Maxwell (1983).
51 Recall that the editor-in-chief of *El País*, Juan Luis Cebrián, was only thirty-one when he was chosen to be editor, and was clearly a member of "the new generation"; and *El País* shareholders ranged from the conservative ex-Francoist minister Manuel Fraga to the communist economist Ramón Tamames, which reflected the new transitional ideal of national reconciliation. Interestingly, the link between the "new beginning" and "Europeanization" is also readily apparent in Pérez Díaz's (1993: 1) opening "new generation" remarks discussed previously (see note 7):

> I belong to a generation of Spaniards who first assumed professional and political responsibilities in the late 1950s and early 1960s, in the belief that the institutional framework of Francoism was both inimical to us and an impediment to solving Spain's problems in a spirit of freedom, justice, and creativity. We believed then that, for all its limitations and internal tension, and with all the reservations that our own youthful maximalism advised, western Europe and the western world as a whole provided us with keys to a better understanding of our situation and a better future for our country.

52 *El País* (5–25–77: 21).
53 *El País* (5–27–77: 29).
54 *El País* (5–4–77: 8).

55 *El País* (4–23–77: 15).
56 The lack of sacrality of the monarchy at the time of Franco's death is reflected in Santiago Carrillo's famous (albeit erroneous) witticism that Juan Carlos would be "Juan the Brief." Cited by Gilmour (1985: 138).
57 *Arriba* (5–15–77).
58 As Turner (1969: 96) notes, liminality is characterized by the "communion of equal individuals who submit together to the general authority."
59 *Información Política* (4–12–77).
60 *El País* (4–28–77).
61 *El Alcázar* (4–23–77: 6).
62 *El Alcázar* (6–15–77: 1). The day that Franco died, November 20, 1975, is also the day of the death of José Antonio Primo de Rivera, who was executed in 1936. Hence many Spaniards speculate that Franco might have in fact "died" before that day, but been sustained in some sort of technological "hibernation." According to Ellwood (1987: 131, n. 43), the Falangists were especially incensed that Franco apparently usurped the sacred iconography of the founder of the Falange.
63 *El Alcázar* (6–13–77: 2).
64 *El Alcázar* (4–14–77: 2).
65 *El Alcázar* (4–29–77: 1).
66 *El Alcázar* (4–11–77: 16).
67 *El Alcázar* (5–7–77: 5).
68 *El Alcázar* (6–15–77: 3).

5 The curtain rises: the first democratic elections

1 This chapter relies extensively on Gunther, Sani, and Shabad (1986) and Huneeus (1985).
2 Gunther et al. (1986: 37–38).
3 Linz et al. (1981: 163).
4 The most important reason for the discrepancy between the poll and election results is that 40 percent of those surveyed were undecided in the April poll, and in addition, Suárez had not yet joined the Center Party. In any case, the poll results underscore the high level of uncertainty prior to the first elections.
5 Huneeus (1985: 88).
6 Huneeus (1985: 90–95).
7 Huneeus (1985: 98).
8 *Informaciones* (7–9–76), as cited by Huneeus (1985: 98).
9 Gunther et al. (1986: 93).
10 Gunther et al. (1986: 94).
11 Gunther et al. (1986: 95).
12 Gunther et al. (1986: 96).
13 Gunther et al. (1986: 98).
14 Gunther et al. (1986: 99–100).
15 Gunther et al. (1986: 104).

16 For instance, Juan Linz (1967: 267) stated that, "inevitably, whatever party system [adopted] in Spain will revolve around two dominant tendencies, socialism and Christian democracy"; see also Huneeus (1985: 175).
17 Gunther (1986: 107–108).
18 Linz et al. (1981: 163).
19 Gunther et al. (1986: 108–109).
20 Gunther et al. (1986: 110–111).
21 Huneeus (1985: 182).
22 Huneeus (1985: 180).
23 *El País* (6–12–77: xxiv).
24 Gunther et al. (1986: 59).
25 Bell (1983: 68); Gunther et al. (1986: 70).
26 Gunther et al. (1986: 66).
27 Bell (1983: 68).
28 *El País* (4–15–77: 12).
29 *Mundo Obrero* (4–20–77: 4–5).
30 The Spanish Communist Party abandoned the phrase "dictatorship of the proletariat" in time for the 1977 elections, but as Bell (1983: 64–70) points out, the absence of this phrase is neither new nor a significant guide to future behavior – the French, Portuguese, and British Communist Parties had also abandoned this phrase and nevertheless acted in "hard-line" ways. The dropping of Leninism from the statutes by the Ninth Congress in April 1978, however, was crucial, as it reflected the consolidation of the moderate Eurocommunist line.
31 Gunther et al. (1986: 70).
32 Esenwein and Shubert (1995: 210–211). As Esenwein and Shubert note, Ibárruri borrowed these slogans from previous wars, namely the First World War and the Mexican Revolution.
33 For example, "Guadalajara: José Sandoval. Born in Gijón. Painter. After having lived in exile, he spent 10 years in prison. Member of Executive Committee." Interestingly, all candidates listed have exile and/or prison to their credit. *Mundo Obrero* (6–8–77: 2).
34 "Con motivo de eso de la edad," by Rafael Alberti was reprinted in *Mundo Obrero* (6–29–77: 3):

> Quisiera en este momento,
> el más joven de mi vida,
> no ser sólo una perdida
> partida de nacimiento.
>
> Que como la libertad
> el hombre cuando está vivo
> en la luz no tiene edad.
>
> Y yo estoy vivo, aunque viejo
> y nadie me va a decir
> que soy ya un muerto pellejo.

Ni en mi ver la pretensión
de ser un sabio niñito
de primera comunión.

Sentirse joven no es ser
joven, es sólo sentir
la ilusión de amanecer.

Y como la luz, yo entiendo
que cuando va a anochecer
ya está casi amaneciendo.

Y mientras arda la luz,
negros o albos los cabellos,
arderá la juventud.

35 Gunther et al. (1986: 155).
36 See also Bell (1983).
37 *Mundo Obrero* (6–22–77: 2).
38 *Mundo Obrero* (6–8–77: 7).
39 Gunther et al. (1986: 70).
40 Gunther et al. (1986: 72–73).
41 Gunther et al. (1986: 72–73).
42 Nash (1983: 33).
43 Gunther et al. (1986: 74).
44 At the Suresnes Congress of 1974, the party declared itself opposed to "any reform, continuation or transformation of the [Franco] regime" (Gunther et al., 1986: 73).
45 Buse (1984: 160).
46 Gunther et al. (1986: 73, emphasis added), as quoted from socialist activist and author José Maravall.
47 *El País* (5–25–77: 21). The goal of Europeanization was also reflected in the PSOE electoral program, which emphasized that "to vote PSOE is to vote for democracy, liberty and better conditions of life," and listed seven goals:

> 1) end unemployment and emigration, 2) establish free public education and equal opportunities for all, 3) integrate Spain in Europe and the world, 4) elaborate a democratic Constitution that guarantees individual and collective rights and liberties, 5) . . . agricultural reform, 6) . . . fiscal reform that assures a more just distribution of wealth, 7) reform of the pension system (*El País,* 5–29–77: 26).

48 Gunther et al. (1986: 73).
49 Gunther et al. (1986: 75).
50 As PSP leader Raúl Morodo stated:

> While the PSOE, through its connection with the Socialist International, which is a social-democratic International, has great and intimate ties

especially to German social democracy, the PSP maintains a very independentist line, a line more of the Mediterranean, more of the socialism of the south (Alfaya, 1977 as cited by Gunther et al., 1986: 77).

51 Gunther et al. (1986: 78–79).
52 Gunther et al. (1986: 79).
53 Huneeus (1985: 68).
54 *El País* (5–7–77: 16).
55 Ramírez (1977), as cited by Gunther et al. (1986: 91).
56 Gunther et. al (1986: 91).
57 Gunther et al. (1986: 91).
58 *El País* (6–9–77: 1).

6 The 1977 Mondoa Pacts and the ritualization of communality

1 Maravall (1982: 120–121).
2 Aguilar et al. (1984: 125–127).
3 Maravall (1982: 121).
4 Gilmour (1985: 189); Maravall (1982: 12–13, 53, 60). Maravall notes that this data from the British Ministry of Labour published in *El País* (2–1–81) refer only to mining, manufacturing industries, building and transport, in order to standardize the industrial structures of the different countries.
5 Gilmour (1985: 188–190).
6 Coverdale (1979: 92).
7 Coverdale (1979: 92).
8 PSOE (1977).
9 Coverdale (1979: 93).
10 *El País* (10–9–77: 11).
11 *El País* (10–9–77: 11).
12 *El País* (10–26–77: 12).
13 *El País* (10–29–77: 11).
14 *El País* (10–29–77: 11).
15 Turner (1969: 94–97).
16 *El País* (11–12–77: 10).
17 *El Socialista* (10–16–77: 6).
18 *El País* (11–2–77: 12).
19 The only parliamentary opposition to the economic pacts was that of Francisco Letamendía, the deputy of the leftist Basque party Euzkadiko Ezkerra (EE). See *El País* (10–30–77: 11). The "Basque exception" in the politics of consensus will be discussed in chapter 8.
20 *El Alcázar* (10–26–77: 1).
21 In response to Fraga's reconciliation with Carrillo, a few right-wing members of AP, who were tied to the Unión Nacional Española and the Unión del Pueblo Español, resigned. Some analysts believed, however, that AP welcomed their departure. See *El País* (11–4–77: 14).
22 *El País* (11–2–77: 1).

23 *El País* (11–5–77: 12).
24 *El País* (11–10–77: 14).
25 Gilmour (1985: 191). The moderation of Santiago Carrillo was vital to the completion of the Moncloa Pacts, but not all Spanish communists favored Carrillo's "moderate" Eurocommunist strategy. Internal conflict between more and less "moderate" members of the PCE was exacerbated by the Moncloa pacting, but it would come to a head at the the the Ninth PCE Party Congress in April 1978. While previous congresses had been unanimous, in a vote of 248 for Leninism, 968 for Carrillo, and 40 abstentions, the word "Leninist" was now officially removed from the Communist Party program (Alba, 1983: 417).
26 *Mundo Obrero* (10–13–77: 5).
27 *Mundo Obrero* (10–20–77: 11).
28 *Mundo Obrero* (11–2–77).
29 *Mundo Obrero* (11–10–77: 3).
30 *El País* (10–19–77: 14).
31 *El País* (10–19–77: 14).
32 The Partido Socialista Popular (PSP) and the PCE were the only parties to favor a government of concentration.
33 *El País* (10–19–77: 14).
34 Gilmour (1985: 191).
35 Gilmour (1985: 192).
36 *El Socialista* (11–3–77).
37 Cited in *El País* (10–25–77: 7).
38 *El País* (10–21–77: 12).
39 *El Socialista* (10–16–77: 6)
40 *El Socialista* (11–6–77: 17). The powerful business organization Confederación Española de Organizaciones Empresariales (CEOE) also rejected the pacts, in large part because they excluded business from the negotiations. See *El País* (10–13–77: 43).
41 *El Socialista* (10–23–77: 20).
42 *Mundo Obrero* (10–20–77: 11).
43 *El País* (10–6–77: 9).
44 *El País* (10–21–77: 12).
45 *El Socialista* (10–30–77).
46 *El País* (10–22–77: 14).
47 *El País* (10–29–77: 11).
48 See Gillespie (1989: 337).

7 Democratic reaggregation and the 1978 Constitution

1 Prager (1986: 68–71).
2 The constitutional document itself has been extensively examined by Aguirre (1978), Alzaga (1978), Hernández Gil (1982), Peces-Barba and Prieto Sanchis (1981), and Predieri and García de Enterria (1981), among others.
3 Though it is cumbersome and appears oxymoronic, here I use the term "regional

nationalism" to refer to "nationalism" within a particular region of Spain. As we will see shortly, however, "regional nationalists" generally consider themselves "nationalists," while other Spaniards reject the "nationalist" label for any particular Spanish "region," maintaining that there is only one "nation" ("Spain"). I do not use the terms "center" and "periphery" because these terms are ideologically loaded and particularly misleading in the case of Spain. "Periphery" tends to imply industrially backward, economically disadvantaged, and/or culturally unimportant to the larger nation. This applies somewhat to Galicia, but the "peripheral" regions of Catalonia and the Basque Country are among the most industrial, wealthy, and influential parts of Spain.

4 This section relies heavily on Bonime-Blanc (1987).

5 Bonime-Blanc (1987: 53).

6 *El País* (3–16–78), as reported by Bonime-Blanc (1987: 57).

7 Bonime-Blanc (1987: 59).

8 Bonime-Blanc (1987: 61).

9 Bonime-Blanc (1987: 42, 62). Many politicians and journalists were disappointed that only 67 percent of Spaniards voted, although less than 8 percent rejected the Constitution. Most blamed the rainy weather for the lack of voter turnout. As discussed in the following chapter, however, the situation was quite different for the Basque provinces. Turnout was as low as 43 percent, owing largely to the PNV's campaign for abstention. See *El País* (12–7–78; 12–8–78).

10 *El País* (12–7–78: 12).

11 *El Socialista* (12–10–78: 14–15).

12 *El País* (11–24–78: 13).

13 *El Socialista* (11–26–78: 5).

14 *El País* (12–1–78: 12).

15 *El País* (12–3–78: 10)

16 *Mundo Obrero* (12–5–78: 2).

17 *El Alcázar* (12–1–78: 9).

18 *El País* (12–3–78: 16).

19 *El País* (10–6–78: 10).

20 *El País* (10–6–78: 10).

21 *El País* (10–6–78: 10).

22 *El País* (12–5–78: 13).

23 *Arriba* (12–3–78).

24 *Mundo Obrero* (11–30–78: 13).

25 *El Alcázar* (12–1–78: 9).

26 *El País* (12–6–78: 1).

27 *El País* (11–28–77: 14).

28 The articles on the monarchy and the economic system were also particularly volatile. The Socialists were reluctant to accept the term "monarchy" because it had long symbolized the negation of liberating change in Spain. The UCD softened their position, and emphasized the parliamentary dimensions of the new "parliamentary monarchy," however. Specifically, unlike the old monarchy, the

new monarchy would "accept popular sovereignty as its ultimate reference"; and it would not function as the supreme executive, but would play a purely symbolic role (López Pina, 1985: 36). In terms of the new economic order, the polemic issue was "free-market" vs. "planned" economies. In the end, a compromise was reached such that both free-market and planned systems are explicitly recognized in the Constitution. Specifically, article 38 states:

> Free enterprise is recognized within the framework of a market economy. The public authorities shall guarantee and protect its exercise and the safeguarding of productivity in accordance with the demands of the economy in general and, as the case may be, of its planning.

Meanwhile, article 128.2 recognizes:

> public initiative in economic activity. Essential resources or services may be restricted by law to the public sector, especially in the case of monopolies. Likewise, intervention in companies may be decided upon when the public interest so demands.

Finally, according to article 131:

> the state, through the law, shall be able to plan general economic activity in order to meet collective needs, balance and harmonize regional and sectorial development, and stimulate the growth of income and wealth and its more equitable distribution (López Pina, 1985: 38–40).

Thus, the legislature can choose a market-economy model or a more centrally planned economy – both are constitutional.

29 See note 3 above.
30 Gunther and Blough (1981: 366); Esenwein and Shubert (1995).
31 Gunther and Blough (1981: 370–371).
32 Gunther and Blough (1981: 371).
33 Gunther et al. (1986: 220–221).
34 Bonime-Blanc (1987: 57).
35 AP leader Manuel Fraga was in the United States when Silva Muñoz announced that the AP would withdraw from the committee. Upon his return, Fraga promptly reversed Silva's decision. Silva Muñoz was one of the five AP representatives to vote against the 1978 Constitution, and subsequently resign from the AP to form the Derecha Democrática Española ("Spanish Democratic Right"), a party to the right of the AP. Gilmour (1985: 195–201).
36 Gilmour (1985: 195).
37 *El País* (10–26–78: 9).
38 *El País* (10–20–78: 16).
39 *El País* (9–23–78: 11).
40 *El País* (10–6–78: 12).
41 Gunther et al. (1986: 116–118).
42 *El País* (3–8–78: 9).

43 *El País* (3–10–78: 1,14).
44 Gunther and Blough (1981: 374).
45 Gunther and Blough (1981: 374).
46 Gunther and Blough (1981: 374).
47 Arango (1985: 119).
48 Gunther and Blough (1981: 377).
49 Fraga (1982: 147).
50 Alzaga (1978: 185), as cited by Gunther and Blough (1981: 378).
51 *El País* (3–18–78: 11); Gunther and Blough (1981: 372).
52 Gunther and Blough (1981: 372–373).
53 Gilmour (1985: 198).
54 Carr and Fusi (1979: 156).
55 There were a few important exceptions in terms of cultural and linguistic repression under Franco. For instance, early-morning mass in rural areas was permitted in Basque in order to serve the needs of monolingual Basques (most of whom were elderly). Yet, as we will see in the following chapter, even these small slivers of space became critical moral and organizational resources for the Basque opposition.
56 Bonime-Blanc (1987: 81).
57 As Johnston (1991: 43) points out, Franco abhorred everything Catalonia represented: social revolution, the Communist Party, the Republic, anti-clericalism, cultural pluralism, and regional political autonomy.
58 Johnston (1991: 2).
59 Balcells (1996: 164–5). States Balcells, "the fact that the *Assemblea* printed 20,000 copies of each of its leaflets gives some idea of the extent of its influence."
60 Pi-Sunyer (1985: 260); see also Elliot (1963) and Payne (1973).
61 Woolard (1989: 46); Solé-Tura (1974).
62 Brandes (1991: 65–66).
63 Cited by Brandes (1991: 66).
64 Of course, this inclusive definition of "Catalan" is an ideal. As Woolard (1989) points out, alongside the overtly inclusive definition of "Catalan" are intricate social mechanisms for distinguishing "Catalan Catalans" from others. Moreover, parallel to the "melting pot" debate in the United States, another interpretation of the inclusive definition of "Catalan" is that it is only a thinly disguised veil for forced assimilation.
65 The European orientation of Catalonia was readily apparent in the 1992 Olympics in Barcelona. The three official languages were English, French and Catalan, (not Spanish); and tourists were greeted with signs that read, "Catalonia: A Country in Europe" (Gies, 1994).
66 In 1954, the President of the Generalitat in exile, Josep Irla, resigned on the grounds of serious health problems. Under the Statute of Self-government, Serra i Moret should have automatically become president, but Tarradellas maintained that the new president should be chosen by the members of the

Catalan parliament. Thus Tarradellas himself was elected president from exile in Mexico, with twenty-four votes out of twenty-six votes (Balcells 1996: 137).

67 Gilmour (1985: 216); Balcells (1996: 172).

68 *Mundo Obrero* (11–23–78: 5).

69 However, the main reason that the percentage of negative votes was higher in Spain as a whole (than in Catalonia) is because the far right, which is centered in Madrid, also voted "no" in the referendum.

70 *El País* (2–25–78: 7).

71 *El País* (1–6–78: 10).

72 *El País* (10–26–78: 9).

8 The Basque exception: questions of communality and democracy

1 While a few Basque activists have been French Basques, and Spanish Basque nationalists have often found refuge on the French side of the Pyrenees, the French Basque population does not enter significantly into the dynamics of Spanish Basque politics, and they will not be considered here.

2 Castresana Waid (1987).

3 Castresana Waid (1987: 15).

4 Castresana Waid (1987).

5 There are significant provincial differences in the Basque language (*Euskera*), and it was not until the cultural and linguistic recovery movement of the 1960s that *Euskera* became somewhat standardized. See Tejerina (1992).

6 Coverdale (1985).

7 Carlism was not exclusively a Basque movement, however.

8 General Espartero of the Centralist Forces allegedly promised, "Do not worry, Basques, your *Fueros* will be respected and preserved; and if anyone were to move against them, my sword would be the first to be unsheathed in their defense," Manuel Estomba and Donato Arrinda, *Historia general del País Vasco* (1980: 179), as cited by Castresana Waid (1987: 17).

9 Díez Medrano (1994: 554; 1995).

10 Díez Medrano (1994: 546; 1995).

11 Díez Medrano (1994: 546–547; 1995).

12 One of the most poignant accounts of Basque fraternal division is "The Tragedy of Carlos" by Zulaika (1985: 309–331). This is the true story of two "milk brothers," Carlos and Martin, from the Guipúzcoan village of Itziar (population 1,100). Carlos' family was of Carlist persuasion and sided with the anti-Republican forces of Franco. Martin's father fought for the PNV on the Republican side, and two of his uncles were socialists. While the menfolk were battling each other on the war front, Carlos and Martin were both being nursed by Carlos' mother (because Martin's mother's milk had dried up); and as they grew up, Martin and Carlos were close friends. In the 1950s, both became dedicated members of the Catholic organization *Baserri Gaztedi* ("Basque Youth"). But later the Catholic group split into militant *abertzale* and conservative (pro-

Franco) sectors. Martin became a militant for ETA; Carlos gained the reputation of a *chivato*, or police informer. One Saturday morning in 1975, two ETA militants pulled Carlos off the road, yelled "you are a dog" *("hi txakur bat haiz")*, and shot him dead. Five other political killings occurred in Itziar between 1975 and 1980. Martin died of natural causes in 1981.

13 Lewis, "The Spanish Ministerial Elite 1938–1969," *Comparative Politics* (1972: 102–103), as cited by Coverdale (1985: 362, fn. 11).

14 See Zulaika (1988: 40–41), and Sullivan (1988: 34–35).

15 Clark (1984: 44–53); Zirakzadeh (1991: 143).

16 Sullivan (1988: 161; 196).

17 See Linz et al. (1981: 522) and Zulaika (1988: 100).

18 As Sullivan (1988: 94) notes, the Burgos 16 were fairly representative of the social base of ETA throughout its existence. Nearly all came from Vizcaya or Guipúzcoa. Most held lower-middle-class positions, such as technicians, teachers, and clerks; two were priests and several were ex-seminarists. None was a farmer, though they came from smaller towns, rather than cities. Most were quite young, and had not been members of ETA at the time of the 1966–1967 Fifth Assembly.

19 Zirakzadeh (1991: 184–185).

20 The Burgos 16 had publicly declared their Marxist orientation, and decried members of the less militant *Branka* group and ETA-V as "traitors" and "right-wing Basques" who distributed folklore calendars and wrote novels while committed patriots relentlessly worked toward Basque liberation (Zirakzadeh, 1991: 184).

21 For example, Gilmour (1985: 134) states that "moral considerations aside, the murder of Carrero was probably the only thing the Basque guerrillas ever did which furthered the cause of Spanish democracy."

22 See Clark (1990: 8–9).

23 Although ETA-pm was originally the more radical of the two in the ideological sense, through the mid and late 1970s the more radical members of ETA-pm grew more restive and left ETA-pm to join the more dramatic (and by this time more dangerous, disruptive and activist) ETA-m. By the beginning of the 1980s, ETA-m members outnumbered those of ETA-pm by about three to one (Clark, 1984: 80–81). The decline of ETA-pm was also spurred by the disappearance and presumed death of ETA-pm leader "Pertur" in 1976, allegedly killed by the militant ETA faction, the Berezi commandos. Pertur supporters resigned from ETA-pm and formed a new organization, EIA (Euskao Iraultzale Alderdia, the "Basque Revolutionary Party") explicitly devoted to non-violent action (Clark 1990: 75–77).

24 Pérez-Agote et al. (1987: 4).

25 In their survey of Basque nationalists, del Campo, Navarro, and Tezanos (1977: 220) found that no single defining characteristic of Basque identity (e.g. birth, adoption of customs, residence, linguistic ability, etc.) was adopted by as many as half of the sample (cited by Clark, 1984: 222). In terms of autonomy, Clark

(Table 19, 1984: 245) found that support for outright independence was rejected by most Basques, although over half favored some form of autonomy. Support for the most "radical" solutions was most prevalent in the province of Guipúzcoa, where one-third favored independence – by either violent or peaceful means.

26 "Hoy estrenamos democracia" (*Deia,* 6–15–77: 1).

27 *Deia* (6–16–77: 32).

28 *Deia* (6–15–77: 2). Similarly, in their campaign in favor of the 1978 Constitution, Basque Communists acted out the "death" of Francoism by throwing a coffin "of Franco's Fundamental Laws" into the Nervión river (*El País,* 12–5–78: 15). While, on the one hand, this ritual act reaffirms the symbolic opposition of (sacred) democracy/Constitution vs. (profane) dictatorship/Fundamental Laws discussed previously (and illustrated in Figure 7.1), on the other, it not only seemingly celebrates "death" (rather than "rebirth"), but seemingly celebrates not a "natural" death, but murder. Thus, this act conjures up (profane) images of "violence," "confrontation," etc. obviously at odds with "*convivencia*" and "national reconciliation."

29 *Deia* (6–14–77: 5).

30 *Deia* (6–15–77: 2).

31 *El País* (5–18–77: 9).

32 Similarly, an editorial in *Deia* (11–19–78: 14) described autonomy as "establishing an enclosed place [*encaje*] in which the Basque nation can practice their own rights, in solidary *convivencia* with other peoples" ["*en convivencia solidaria con los restantes pueblos*"]. And *Deia* columnist García Olano maintained:

> The peoples of Spain must be able to recognize their own political, social and cultural personalities, the right to be how they are and how they want to be. Without cultural invasions, living alone but fraternally with other peoples, in a diversity enriched by that which each one has the right to be.
> (*Deia,* 6–11–77: 2)

33 *El País* (5–29–77: 11).

34 *Deia* (6–14–77: 9).

35 *Deia* (6–9–77: 32).

36 *Deia* (6–9–77: 32).

37 This article, titled "Demócratas de última hora" (*Deia,* 6–8–77: 2) goes on to state: "we have the obligation to strip off the false skin of [false] democrats and expose their true dictatorial hides" – thus affirming the symbolic opposition between genuine (sacred) "democracy" and false (evil) dictatorship.

38 *Deia* (6–10–77: 2).

39 As one of ETA's first pamphlets published in the 1960s states, "Among Basques, democracy has not been either a discovery or a bloody conquest; it has been a practice centuries old . . . the Basque democratic system was based on the *etxeko-jaun* 'lord of the house' as the holder of active suffrage" (ETA, 1979: 2: 68), as cited by Zulaika (1988: 135).

40 *Deia* (6–8–77).

41 *Deia* (6–15–77: 2).
42 This same division as to the role and meaning of the king was evident throughout the transition. For example, in February 1981, deputies of Herri Batasuna (HB) "shouted down" King Juan Carlos during his speech at the Casa de Juntas (Basque parliament) in Guernica, and gave an impromptu rendition of the Basque national anthem. After order was restored, the king declared: "Against those who make a practice of intolerance, who are contemptuous of *convivencia* and who have no respect for our institutions, I proclaim my faith in democracy and my confidence in the Basque people" – for which the king received a standing ovation from the PNV and other members of the Basque parliament. Thus, the king dichotomizes (profane) HB/ intolerance/intransigency, and (sacred) "democracy" and "*convivencia*," and attempts to link himself (and the monarchy) – as well as the Basque people – to the sacred side of this symbolic equation. Yet, if the intent of HB was to incite a "spiral of violence," in fact, they partially succeeded. The military was appalled that the king and queen even visited the Basque Country let alone that they were "shouted down"; and a few weeks later, military outrage erupted in the infamous aborted coup d'état, known as "23–F."
43 *El País* (10–3–78: 14); Gunther et al. (1986: 123).
44 *El País* (10–1–78: 1).
45 *Informaciones* (8–9–78: 2); *ABC* (8–17–78: 18); Gunther et al. (1986: 123).
46 *Deia* (11–25–78: 4).
47 Gunther et al. (1986: 119–120). As Gunther et al. point out, without a Basque representative in the *Ponencia*, it was difficult for the Basque nationalists to accept any of the *Ponencia* texts. Indeed, a PNV deputy interviewed in 1981 maintained, "We would not approve the Constitution, in fact, ever . . . because it is a *Spanish* Constitution."
48 Gunther et al. (1986: 123–124).

Conclusion and epilogue

1 Although de Esteban and López Guerra (1985: 48) admit that "Spain's experience yields up no magic formula for transforming dictatorships into democracies" and that "the Spanish recipe is almost certainly not exportable"; de Esteben and López Guerra nevertheless set out to explain "the reasons for Spain's *easy* political transition" (emphasis added).
2 Przeworski (1991).
3 Gunther et al. (1986: 178).
4 With the dissolution of the AP federation in late 1978, Manuel Fraga instigated the creation of the Coalición Democrática (CD). In addition to the AP, the main components of CD were: José Maria de Areilza's Acción Ciudadana Liberal (ACL), Alfonso Osorio's tiny Christian Democratic Partido Democrata Progresista (PDP), the Partido Popular de Cataluña, Renovación Española, Reforma Social Española, and segments of the Democratas Independientes Vascos (Gunther et al., 1986: 173).
5 Gilmour (1985: 209).

6 Gunther et. al. (1986: 414–416).

7 Preston (1986a: 164).

8 While Preston (1986a: 162) maintains that the UCD's reflex of massaging the military ego was "understandable" in light of "deafening" rumors of a coup, other analysts, such as Boyd and Boyden (1985: 108) maintain that "for many members of the [UCD], the argument that military pressure made restraint a necessity was a convenient excuse for their own lack of enthusiasm for democratic principles."

9 Gilmour (1985: 249–50).

10 *Cambio 16* (October 19, 1980: 21).

11 Clark (1984: 103–105, 252).

12 López Pintor (1985: 293).

13 Gilmour (1985: 273).

14 Gilmour (1985: 230).

15 Gilmour (1985: 231).

16 Gilmour (1985: 235–6); see also Agüero (1995, chapter 5).

17 Gilmour (1985: 230).

18 Calvo Sotelo had been nominated by King Juan Carlos for the premiership. But on February 22, 1981, Calvo Sotelo had failed in his first attempt to receive the necessary majority vote – a failure in part attributable to the abstention of the seventeen deputies belonging to regional parties.

19 Lt. Gen. Jaime Milans del Bosch was an outspoken Franco loyalist, who had been transferred to Valencia from his position as the commander of the elite armored division (DAC) Brunete number 1 outside Madrid, as a precaution, in September 1977 (Boyd and Boyden, 1985: 109).

20 Though Tejero had initially ordered all televising to be stopped, one cameraman had cut the image on the monitor, but did not cut the transmission. After a few moments, a suspicious Civil Guard ordered that the cameraman focus on the floor. The last thing heard on the tape (while the picture was dark) was Captain Jesus Muñecas' announcement that, "Within a quarter of an hour or twenty minutes, or maybe more, competent military authority will come here and explain what will happen" (*El Periódico de Catalunya*, 1985).

21 Juan Carlos concluded his speech:

> Y finalmente, reitero a todos mi petición de colaboración leal y desinteresada, superando diferencias secundarias en beneficio de una identificación en los más grandes y fundamentales problemas del país, para que podamos consolidar nuestra democracia dentro del orden, la unidad y la paz.   (*El Periódico de Catalunya*, 1985: 271–272)

22 *El País* (2–28–81), as cited by Agüero (1995: 175).

23 Interestingly, the term "strategy of cooperation" is similar to the previous term "strategy of consensus" in that they both connote (sacred) peaceful dialogue and moderation, in symbolic opposition to (profane) violence and confrontation. But, whereas "consensus" implies agreement in values and/or ideals/policies, "cooperation" suggests perhaps a more pragmatic awareness of differences.

24 Preston (1986a: 194–204). Unfortunately, the ceasefire offered by ETA-pm following 23–F was not emulated by ETA-militar. And although the *concertación* resulted in the successful drafting of the *Ley Orgánica de Armonización del Proceso Autonómico* (LOAPA), the law – which was subsequently frozen by appeals made to the Supreme Court by the Basque and Catalan regional governments – only escalated regional–national tensions. While the government interpreted 23–F as evidence that the anti-terrorist campaign should be intensified and the process of regional autonomy slowed down, Basque and Catalan nationalists argued that the weak, emasculated concessions of LOAPA only meant that the far right was actually achieving some of its aims. Indeed, regional nationalists' claim that the far right did not suffer much as a result of the aborted coup was not unfounded. Several of the minor participants in 23–F were simply released, and though Colonel Tejero was sentenced to thirty years, he was allowed to receive gifts as well as visitors in his "five-star cell" in the outskirts of Madrid. Moreover, from his "cell" Tejero and his adulators organized a new political party, *Solidaridad Española*, and Tejero even stood as a candidate in the 1982 elections (Gilmour, 1985: 265–266).

25 Gunther et al. (1986: 401).

26 See, for example, Mujal-León (1985), Gunther et al. (1986), and Gilmour (1985). Interestingly, former Prime Minister Felipe González pegs the "end" of the Spanish transition as Spain's incorporation into the EC – which, conveniently enough, links González and the PSOE to this sacred moment of modernization and democratic reaggregation. States González, "It does not seem risky to me to predict that when historians try, some day, to signal a final date to the end of the period of transition and our completeness as a democratic and free nation the elected date will be January 1, 1986 . . . on this day, the incorporation of Spain into the European Communities will be consummated" (El Periódico de Catalunya, 1985: 307).

27 Gunther et al. (1986: 402).

28 Maravall (1982: 64).

29 *Cambio 16* (October 19, 1980: 21).

30 Arango (1985: 172). Of course, as Durkheim (1912) first pointed out, symbols inevitably lose their effervescence; thus the need for periodic collective reaffirmation through ritual. In the case of Spain, the decline in symbolic effervescence was embodied in the perception and discussion of a so-called *desencanto* (disenchantment) following the drafting of the 1978 Constitution. See, e.g., Montero (1993), and McDonough, Barnes, and López Pina (1986).

31 Chislett (1996: 32).

32 Alcaide, Inchausti Julio, "La alta tasa de paro española y sus expectativas a plazo media," (*Cuadernos de información económica* 105: 21–28, December 1995), as cited by Pérez Díaz (1996: 135). Pérez Díaz notes that the underground economy is not reflected in these figures, which probably takes off about 3 percent from the unemployment statistics.

33 Amodia (1994: 177).

34 Heywood (1995: 728) reports that in April 1994 even *El País* began a regular section on "political scandals," which by the end of the year was headlined "corruption and political turmoil."

35 Valls-Russell (1995).

36 Gies (1996: 404).

37 Pérez Díaz (1996: 108).

38 Gillespie (1993: 83); Heywood (1995: 728).

39 Significant "casos" (cases) included: Filesa, Ibercorp, Salanueva, Renfe, Nasiero, and Sarasola. See Pérez Díaz (1996), Cotarelo (1996), Gies (1996), and Heywood (1995).

40 González tried to appease student protestors by telling them that he too had boycotted the visit of a government official (Manuel Fraga) as a student protestor under the Franco regime. But González's "touch of nostalgia" had little effect. Apparently, González did not realize that Fraga himself (now a representative from Galicia) had spoken at the University of Madrid without problem a few weeks earlier. See Pérez Díaz (1996: 90–91).

41 Chislett (1996: 37).

42 Aznar (1994).

43 *La Vanguardia electrónica* (3–16–97).

44 Wiarda (1996) provides a coherent account of the persistence of Spanish authoritarian political culture, although his thesis is based on gross oversimplification. Heywood (1995: 757) quite rightly underscores the need for better anti-corruption legislation in Spain. According to Heywood, in 1991 the World Economic Forum deemed Spain second only to Italy in the developed world in the inadequacy of its anti-corruption measures (ibid). Pérez Díaz (1996:211–212) observes that perhaps the lesson to be learned from the recent difficult years is that "politics is too serious of a subject to leave to professional politicians." Pérez Díaz (1996: 212) calls for a stronger "European civil society," though he realizes that "there is no [functional] 'need' to have it [European civil society]. If some day we have it, it will be the result of . . . many individual acts of liberty."

45 *La Vanguardia electrónica* (3–16–97). Interestingly, President Aznar opened the Senate session on autonomy by once again calling up the symbolic opposition between (sacred) democracy/rationality/non-violence and (profane) irrationality/violence, stating that the fight against terrorism would be "won" by the democrats and "by reason, liberty and peaceful *convivencia*" (*El Periódico de Catalunya on-line*, 3–16–97). See Ross (1996) for an excellent recent analysis of Basque and Catalan nationalism and party competition.

46 Geertz (1973: 30).

References

Abel, Christopher, and Nissa Torrents, eds. *Spain: Conditional Democracy*. London: Croom Helm, 1984.

Aguila, Rafael del, and Ricardo Montoro. *El discurso político de la transición española*. Madrid: Centro de Investigaciones Sociológicas, 1984.

Agüero, Felipe. *Soldiers, Civilians and Democracy: Post-Franco Spain in Comparative Perspective*. Baltimore, MD: Johns Hopkins University Press, 1995.

Aguilar Fernández, Paloma. *La memoria histórica de la Guerra Civil Española: un proceso de aprendizaje político*. Ph.D. thesis, Universidad Nacional de Educación a Distancia, Spain, 1995.

Aguilar, Salvador, Alfons Barteló, Bernat Muniesa, Albert Regio, and José María Vidal Villa. "Notes on the Economy and Popular Movements in the Transition," in Abel and Torrents, eds., *Spain: Conditional Democracy*. London: Croom Helm, 1984, pp. 125–135.

Aguirre, Joaquín Bellver. *Así se hizo la Constitución*. Valencia: s.n., 1978.

Alba, Victor. *The Communist Party in Spain*. New Brunswick, NJ: Transaction Books, 1983.

Alexander, Jeffrey C. *Theoretical Logic in Sociology, Volume I: Positivism, Presuppositions, and Current Controversies*. Berkeley: University of California, 1982.

Twenty Lectures in Sociology. New York: Columbia, 1987.

Durkheimian Sociology: Cultural Studies. London: Cambridge, 1988.

After Neofunctionalism. Oxford: Blackwell, 1997.

Alexander, Jeffrey C., and Paul Colomy. "Neofunctionalism Today: Reconstructing a Theoretical Tradition," in George Ritzer, ed., *The Frontiers of Social Theory*. New York: Colombia, 1990, pp. 33–67.

Alfaya, Javier. *Raúl Morodo*. Madrid: Editorial Cambio 16, 1977.

Almond, Gabriel. *A Discipline Divided: Schools and Sects in Political Science*. Newbury Park, CA: Sage, 1990.

Almond, Gabriel, and Sidney Verba. *The Civic Culture Revisited*. Newbury Park, CA: Sage, 1989.

Alzaga, Óscar. *La Constitución Española de 1978.* Madrid: Foro, 1978.

Amodia, José. "A Victory Against all Odds: the Declining Fortunes of the Spanish Socialist Party," in Richard Gillespie, ed., *Mediterranean Politics,* vol. I. London: Farleigh Dickenson University, 1994, pp. 171–190.

Arango, E. Ramón. *Spain: From Repression to Renewal.* Boulder, CO: Westview Press, 1985.

Archer, Margaret. *Culture and Agency: the Place of Culture in Social Theory.* Cambridge: Cambridge University Press, 1988.

Aznar, José-María. *La segunda transición.* Madrid: Espasa-Calpe, 1994.

Balcells, Albert. *Catalan Nationalism.* New York: St. Martin's Press, 1996.

Baylora, Edward, ed. *Comparing New Democracies: Transition and Consolidation in Mediterranean Europe and the Southern Cone.* Boulder, CO: Westview Press, 1987.

Belda, Rafael. "La iglesia y el sindicalismo vertical," in R. Belda et al., eds., *Iglesia y sociedad en España 1939–1975.* Madrid: Editorial Popular, 1977, pp. 205–239.

Belda, Rafael, J. Bigordá, A. Duato, C. Martí, E. Martínez, J. M. Rovira, and J. M. Totosaus, eds., *Iglesia y sociedad en España 1939–1975.* Madrid: Editorial Popular, 1977.

Bell, David S. *Eurocommunism and the Spanish Communist Party.* Sussex: Sussex European Research Center, 1979.

Bell, David S., ed. *Democratic Politics in Spain.* New York: St. Martin's Press, 1983.

Benson, Frederick. *Writers in Arms: the Literary Impact of the Spanish Civil War.* New York: New York University, 1967.

Bermeo, Nancy. "Sacrifice, Sequence, and Strength in Successful Dual Transitions: Lessons from Spain," *Journal of Politics* 56: 601–627, 1994.

Bonime-Blanc, Andrea. *Spain's Transition to Democracy: the Politics of Constitution-Making.* Boulder, CO: Westview Press, 1987.

Boyd, Carolyn, and James M. Boyden. "The Armed Forces and the Transition to Democracy in Spain," in T. Lancaster and G. Prevost, eds., *Politics and Change in Spain.* New York: Praeger, 1985, pp. 94–124.

Brandes, Stanley. "Catalan Expressive Culture and Catalan National Identity," in Milton M. Azevedo, ed., *Contemporary Catalonia in Spain and Europe.* Berkeley: University of California Press, 1991, pp. 62–69.

Browne, Harry. *Spain's Civil War.* London: Longman Group, 1983.

Bunce, Valerie, and Maria Csanadi, "Uncertainty in Transition: Post-Communism in Hungary," *East European Politics and Societies,* 7(2): 241–275, Spring 1993.

Burton, Michael, and John Higley. "Elite Settlements," *American Sociological Review* 52: 295–307, 1987.

Buse, Michael. *La nueva democracia española.* Madrid: Union Editorial, 1984.

Callois, Roger. *Man and the Sacred.* New York: Free Press, 1959 [1939].

Campo, Salustiano del, Manuel Navarro, and José Felix Tezanos. *La cuestión regional española.* Madrid: Cuadernos para el Diálogo, 1977.

Carr, Raymond. *Modern Spain.* Oxford: Oxford, 1980.

Carr, Raymond, and Pablo Fusi. *Spain: Dictatorship to Democracy.* London: George Allen, 1979.

Carrillo, Santiago. *Después de Franco, ¿Qué?* Mexico: España Popular, 1965.

Castresana Waid, Gloria. "Euskadi-Spain: Linguistic, Social and Political Contexts," *Journal of Basque Studies* 8: 13–28, 1987.

Chislett, William. *Spain 1996.* Madrid: Central Hispano, 1996.

Cicourel, Aaron, "Notes on the Integration of Micro- and Macro-Levels of Analysis," in K. Knorr-Cetina and A. Circourel, eds., *Advances in Social Theory and Methodology.* New York: Methuen, 1981, pp. 51–80.

Clark, Robert P. *The Basque Insurgents: ETA, 1952–1980.* Madison: University of Wisconsin, 1984.

"Dimensions of Basque Political Culture in Post-Franco Spain," in W. Douglass, ed., *Basque Politics: a Case Study of Ethnic Nationalism.* Reno: University of Nevada, 1985, pp. 217–263.

Negotiating with ETA. Reno: University of Nevada, 1990.

Clark, Robert P., and Michael L. Haltzel, eds. *Spain in the 1980s.* Cambridge: Ballinger Publishing, 1987.

Coca, César, F. Martínez Aguinagalde, and O. Bezunartea. *Los medios de la comunicación en el País Vasco.* Bilbao: University of the Basque Country, 1993.

Collins, Randall. *Sociology Since Midcentury.* New York: Academic, 1981.

Colomer, Josep. "Transitions by Agreement: Modeling the Spanish Way," *American Political Science Review* 85: 1283–1302, 1991.

Comín Colomer, Eduardo. *Historia del Partido Comunista en España.* Madrid: Editora Nacional, 1965–1967.

Cooper, Norman. *Catholicism and the Franco Regime.* Beverly Hills, CA: Sage Research Papers Series 90–019, vol. III, 1975.

"The Church: From Crusade to Christianity," in Paul Preston, ed., *Spain in Crisis.* London: Harvester Press, 1976.

Cotarelo, Ramón. *El alarido ronco del ganador.* Barcelona: Grijalbo, 1996.

Coverdale, John. *The Political Transformation of Spain After Franco.* New York: Praeger, 1979.

"Regional Nationalism and the Elections in the Basque Country," in H. Penniman and E. Mujal-León, eds., *Spain at the Polls, 1977, 1979, and 1982.* Durham, NC: Duke University Press, 1985, pp. 226–252.

Crane, Diana, ed. *The Sociology of Culture.* Oxford: Blackwell, 1994.

Crow, John. *Spain: The Root and the Flower.* Berkeley: University of California, 1963.

Diamond, Larry, Juan J. Linz, and Seymour Martin Lipset, eds. *Democracy in Developing Countries.* Boulder, CO: Lynne Rienner, 1988.

Díez Medrano, Juan. "Patterns of Development and Nationalism: Basque and Catalan Nationalism before the Spanish Civil War," *Theory and Society* 23: 541–569, 1994.

Divided Nations: Class, Politics and Nationalism in the Basque Country and Catalonia. Ithaca, NY: Cornell University Press, 1995.

Douglas, Mary. *Purity and Danger.* London: Penguin, 1966.

Durkheim, Emile. *The Elementary Forms of Religious Life*. New York: Free Press, 1912.

Eco, Umberto. *A Theory of Semiotics*. Bloomington: Indiana University Press, 1976.

The Role of the Reader. Bloomington: Indiana University Press, 1979.

Edles, Laura Desfor. "Rethinking Democratic Transition: a Culturalist Critique and the Spanish Case," *Theory and Society* 24: 355–384, 1995.

Eisenstadt, S. N. "Culture and Social Structure Revisited," *International Sociology* 1: 297–320, 1986.

Revolution and the Transformation of Societies: a Comparative Study of Civilizations. New York: Free Press, 1978.

Elliot, J. H. *The Revolt of the Catalans*. Cambridge: Cambridge, 1963.

Ellwood, Sheelagh. *Spanish Fascism in the Franco Era*. London: Macmillan, 1987.

The Spanish Civil War. Oxford: Blackwell, 1991.

Esenwein, George, and Adrian Shubert. *Spain at War: The Spanish Civil War in Context 1931–1939*. London: Longman, 1995.

Esteban, Jorge de, and Luis López Guerra. "Electoral Rules and Candidate Selection," in H. Penniman and E. Mujal-León, eds., *Spain at the Polls, 1977, 1979, and 1982*. Durham, NC: Duke University Press, 1985.

Estomba, Manuel, and Donato Arrinda. *Historia general del País Vasco*. Bilbao: La Gran Enciclopedia Vasca, 1980.

ETA. *Documentos*. San Sebastián: Hordago, 1979–1981.

Fine, Gary Alan. "Symbolic Interactionism in the Post-Blumerian Age," in G. Ritzer, ed., *Frontiers of Social Theory: the New Syntheses*. New York: Columbia, 1990.

Finegold, Kenneth, and Theda Skocpol. *State and Party in America's New Deal*. Madison: University of Wisconsin, 1995.

Fisch, Eberhard. *'Guernica' by Picasso*. Cranbury, NJ: Associated University Press, 1988.

Fishman, Robert. *Working Class Organization and the Return to Democracy in Spain*. Ithaca, NY: Cornell University Press, 1990.

Foweraker, Joseph. "The Role of Labor Organizations in the Transition to Democracy in Spain," in R. Clark and M. Haltzel, eds., *Spain in the 1980s*. Cambridge, MA: Ballinger, 1987, pp. 97–122.

Fraga, Manuel Iribarne. *España: entre dos modelos de sociedad*. Barcelona: Planeta, 1982.

Fukuyama, Francis. *Trust*. New York: Free Press, 1995.

Fussell, Paul. *The Great War and Modern Memory*. Oxford: Oxford University Press, 1975.

Geertz, Clifford. *The Interpretation of Cultures*. New York: Basic Books, 1973.

Georgel, Jacques. *El Franquismo: historia y balance 1939–1969*. Ruedo Ibérico, 1971.

Giddens, Anthony. *The Constitution of Society*. Berkeley: University of California, 1984.

"Action, Subjectivity and the Constitution of Meaning," *Social Research* 53: 3, Autumn, 1986.

Gies, David. "A Country in Spain," *The Wilson Quarterly* 18: 70–76, 1994.

"Spain Today: Is the Party Over?," *The Virginia Quarterly Review* 17: 392– 407, 1996.

Gillespie, Richard. *The Spanish Socialist Party.* Oxford: Clarendon, 1989.

"'Programa 2000': The Appearance and Reality of Socialist Renewal in Spain," *Western European Politics* 16: 78–96, 1993.

ed. *Mediterranean Politics.* London: Farleigh Dickenson University, 1994.

Gilmour, David. *The Transformation of Spain,* London: Quartet Books, 1985.

Giner, Juan. "Journalists, Mass Media, and Public Opinion in Spain ," in Kenneth Maxwell, ed. *The Press and the Rebirth of Iberian Democracy.* Westport, CT: Greenwood, 1983, pp. 33–54.

Giner, Salvador. "Political Economy, Legitimation, and the State in Southern Europe," in G. O'Donnell, P. Schmitter, and L. Whitehead, eds., *Transitions from Authoritarian Rule: Southern Europe.* Baltimore, MD: Johns Hopkins University Press, 1986, pp. 11–44.

Goffman, Erving. *Frame Analysis.* New York: Harper Colophon, 1974.

Graham, Robert. *Change of a Nation.* London: Michael Joseph, 1984.

Gunder Frank, Andre. *Capitalism and Underdevelopment.* New York: Monthly Review Press, 1967.

Gunther, Richard. "Spain: the Very Model of Elite Settlement," in John Higley and Richard Gunther, eds., *Elites and Democratic Consolidation in Latin America and Southern Europe.* Cambridge, 1992, pp. 38–80.

Gunther, Richard, and Roger A. Blough. "Religious Conflict and Consensus in Spain: a Tale of Two Constitutions," *World Affairs* 143(4): 366–412, Spring 1981.

Gunther, Richard, Giacomo Sani, and Goldie Shabad. *Spain After Franco: The Making of a Competitive Party System.* Berkeley: University of California Press, 1986.

Habermas, Jürgen. *The Theory of Communicative Action, vol. I: Reason and the Rationalization of Society.* Boston: Beacon Press, 1984.

The Theory of Communicative Action, vol. II: Lifeworld and System. Boston: Beacon Press, 1984.

Hart, Stephan, ed. *No Pasarán! Art, Literature and the Spanish Civil War.* London: Tamesis Books, 1988.

Heritage, John, and David Greatbatch. "Generating Applause: A Study of Rhetoric and Response in Political Party Conferences," *American Journal of Sociology* 92: 110–157, 1986.

Hermet, Guy. *The Communists in Spain.* London: Brown and Knight, 1971.

Hernández Gil, Antonio. *El cambio político español y la Constitución.* Barcelona: Editorial Planeta, 1982.

Herr, Richard. *Spain.* Englewood Cliffs, NJ: Prentice-Hall, 1971.

Herz, John H., ed. *From Dictatorship to Democracy.* Westport, Connecticut: Greenwood Press, 1982.

Heywood, Paul. "Sleaze in Spain," *Parliamentary Affairs* 48: 726–737, 1995.

Higley, John, and Michael Burton. "The Elite Variable in Democratic Transitions and Breakdowns," *American Sociological Review* 54: 17–32, 1989.

Higley, John, Michael Burton, and Lowell Field. "Elite Theory Defended," *American Sociological Review* 55: 421–426, 1990.

Higley, John, and Richard Gunther, eds.. *Elites and Democratic Consolidation in Latin America and Southern Europe*. Cambridge, 1992.

Homans, George. *Social Behavior: Its Elementary Forms*. New York: Harcourt, Brace and World, 1991.

hooks, bell. *Black Looks: Race and Representation*. Boston: South End Press, 1992.

Huneeus, Carlos. *La Unión del Centro Democrático y la transición a la democracia en España*. Madrid: Centro de Investigaciones Sociológicas, 1985.

Hunt, Lynn. *Politics, Culture and Class in the French Revolution*. Berkeley: University of California Press, 1984.

Huntington, Samuel. *The Third Wave: Democratization in the Late Twentieth Century*. Norman: University of Oklahoma, 1991.

Johnston, Hank. *Tales of Nationalism: Catalonia, 1939–1979*. NJ: Rutgers, 1991.

Kaplan, Temma. *Red City, Blue Period*. Berkeley: University of California, 1992.

Kertzer, David. *Ritual, Politics and Power*. New Haven, CT: Yale University Press, 1988.

Kubik, Jan. *The Power of Symbols Against the Symbols of Power*. University Park: Pennsylvania State University Press, 1994.

Lachmann, Richard. "Class Formation without Class Struggle: an Elite Conflict Theory of the Transition to Capitalism," *American Sociological Review* 55: 398–414, 1990.

Laitin, David. *Politics, Language and Thought: The Somali Experience*. Chicago: University of Chicago Press, 1977.

Lancaster, Thomas D. *Policy, Stability and Democratic Change*. University Park: Pennsylvania State Press, 1989.

Lancaster, Thomas D., and Gary Prevost, eds. *Politics and Change in Spain*. New York: Praeger, 1985.

Lewis, David, and Richard Smith. *American Sociology and Pragmatism*. Chicago: University of Chicago, 1980.

Lewis, Paul H. "The Spanish Ministerial Elite 1938–1969," *Comparative Politics* 5: 83–106, 1972.

Linz, Juan J. "An Authoritarian Regime: Spain," in Erik Allardt and Yrjo Littumen, eds., *Cleavages, Ideologies and Party Systems*. The Westermarck Society, 1964, pp. 291–341.

"The Party System of Spain: Past and Future," in S. M. Lipset and S. Rokkan, eds., *Party Systems and Voter Alignments*. New York: Free Press, 1967, pp. 197–282.

"Early State-building and Late Peripheral Nationalism against the State: the Case of Spain," in S. N. Eisenstadt and Stein Rokkan, eds., *Building States and Nations*, Vol. II. Beverly Hills, CA: Sage, 1973a, pp. 32–112.

"Opposition In and Under an Authoritarian Regime: The Case of Spain," in

Robert Dahl, ed., *Regimes and Oppositions*. New Haven, CT: Yale University Press, 1973b, pp. 171–259.

"Politics in a Multi-Lingual Society with a Dominant World Language: The Case of Spain," in J. G. Savard and R. Vigneault, eds., *Multilingual Political Systems: Problems and Solutions*. Quebec: Les Presses de l'Univ. Laval, 1975, pp. 367–444.

"From Great Hopes to Civil War: The Breakdown of Democracy in Spain," in J. J. Linz and Alfred Stepan, eds., *The Breakdown of Democratic Regimes: Europe*. Baltimore, MD: Johns Hopkins University Press, 1978, pp. 142–215.

"The New Spanish Party System," in Richard Rose, ed., *Electoral Participation. A Comparative Analysis*. London: Sage, 1980a, pp. 101–189.

"Religion and Politics in Spain: From Conflict to Consensus above Cleavage," *Social Compass* 27. 255–277, 1980b.

"The Legacy of Franco and Democracy," in Horst Baier, Hans Mathias Kepplinger, and Kurt Reumann, eds., *Offentliche Meinung und sozialer Wandel* [*Public Opinion and Social Change*]. Opladen: Westdeutscher Verlag, 1981, pp. 126–46.

Linz, Juan J., Manuel Gómez-Reino, Francisco A. Orizo, and Darío Vila. *Informe sociológico sobre el cambio político en España, 1975–1981*. Madrid: Fundacion FOESSA, 1981.

Lipset, Seymour M. *The First New Nation*. New York: Basic Books, 1963.

Consensus and Conflict. New Brunswick, NJ: Transaction Books, 1985.

López Pina. "Shaping the Constitution," in H. Penniman and E. Mujal-León, eds., *Spain at the Polls, 1977, 1979, and 1982*. Durham, NC: Duke University Press, 1985, pp. 30–47.

López Pintor, Rafael. *La opinión pública española: Del franquismo a la democracia*. Madrid: Centro de Investigaciones Sociológicas, 1982.

"The October 1982 General Election and the Evolution of the Spanish Party System," in H. Penniman and E. Mujal-León, eds., *Spain at the Polls, 1977, 1979, 1982*. Durham, NC: Duke University Press, 1985, pp. 293–313.

Malefakis, Edward. "Spain and Its Francoist Heritage," in John Herz, ed., *From Dictatorship to Democracy*. Westport, CT: Greenwood Press, 1982, pp. 215–230.

Maravall, José M. *The Transition to Democracy in Spain*. London: Croom Helm, 1982.

"The Socialist Alternative: The Policies and Electorate of the PSOE," in H. Penniman and E. Mujal-León, eds., *Spain at the Polls, 1977, 1979, 1982*. Durham, NC: Duke University Press, 1985, pp. 129–159.

Maravall, José, and Julian Santamaría, "Political Change in Spain," in G. O'Donnell, P. Schmitter, and L. Whitehead, eds., *Transitions from Authoritarian Rule: Southern Europe*. Baltimore, MO: Johns Hopkins University Press, 1986, pp. 71–108.

Marías, Julián. *Understanding Spain*. San Juan: University of Puerto Rico Press, 1990.

Martinez, Robert. "Business Elites and Political Change," in Richard Gunther, ed.,

Politics, Society and Democracy: the Case of Spain. Boulder, CO: Westview Press, 1993, pp. 113–139.

Martinez Soler, José Antonio. "The Paradoxes of Press Freedom: the Spanish Case," in Anthony Smith, ed., *Newspapers and Democracy.* Cambridge: MIT, 1980, pp. 153–173.

Maxwell, Kenneth, ed. *The Press and the Rebirth of Iberian Democracy.* Westport, CT: Greenwood Press, 1983.

Maxwell, Kenneth, and Steven Speigel. *The New Spain: From Isolation to Influence.* New York: Council on Foreign Relations, 1994.

McDonough, Peter, and Antonio López Pina. "Continuity and Change in Spanish Politics," in R. Dalton, S. Flanagan, and P. Beck, eds., *Electoral Change in Industrial Democracies.* Princeton, NJ: Princeton University Press, 1984, pp. 365–396.

McDonough, Peter, Antonio López Pina, and Samuel H. Barnes. "The Spanish Public in Political Transition," *British Journal of Political Science* 11: 49–79, January 1981.

McDonough, Peter, Samuel Barnes, and Antonio López Pina. "The Nature of Political Support and Legitimacy in Spain," *Comparative Political Studies* 27: 349–380, October 1994.

McNamara, Robert. *In Retrospect: the Tragedy and Lessons of Vietnam.* New York: Times Books, 1995.

Medhurst, Kenneth. "Spain's Evolutionary Pathway from Dictatorship to Democracy," in Geoffrey Pridham, ed., *The New Mediterranean Democracies: Regime Transition in Spain, Greece and Portugal.* London: Frank Cass, 1984, pp. 30–50.

Monteath, Peter. *The Spanish Civil War in Literature, Art and Film: an International Bibliography of Secondary Literature.* Westport, CT: Greenwood Press, 1994.

Montero, José Ramón. "Revisiting Democratic Success: Legitimacy and the Meanings of Democracy in Spain," in R. Gunther, ed., *Politics, Society and Democracy: the Case of Spain.* Boulder, CO: Westview Press, 1993, pp. 140–168.

Morodo, Raúl. *La transición política.* Madrid: Tecnos, 1984.

Morlino, Leonardo. "Democratic Establishments: A Dimensional Analysis," in Edward Baylora, ed., *Comparing New Democracies: Transition and Consolidation in Mediterranean Europe and the Southern Cone.* Boulder, CO: Westview Press, 1987, pp. 53–78.

Mujal-León, Eusebio. *Communism and Political Change in Spain.* Bloomington: Indiana University Press, 1983.

"The Spanish Communists and the Search for Electoral Space," in H. Penniman and E. Mujal-León, eds., *Spain at the Polls, 1977, 1979, and 1982.* Durham, NC: Duke University Press, 1985, pp. 160–187.

Nash, Elizabeth. "The Spanish Socialist Party since Franco," in David Bell, ed., *Democratic Politics in Spain.* New York: St. Martin's Press, 1983, pp. 26–62.

Noortwijk, Annelies van. "La contribución de *Triunfo* a la restauración de la democracia en España," in Alvaro Soto Carmona and Javier Tussell, eds.,

Historia de la transición y consolidación democrática en España (1975–1986). Madrid: UNED, 1995, pp. 493–500.

O'Donnell, Guillermo, and Philippe Schmitter. *Transitions from Authoritarian Rule: Tentative Conclusions about Uncertain Democracies*. Baltimore, MD: Johns Hopkins University Press, 1986.

O'Donnell, Guillermo, Philippe Schmitter and Laurence Whitehead, eds. *Transitions from Authoritarian Rule: Southern Europe*. Baltimore, MD: Johns Hopkins University Press, 1986a.

O'Donnell, Guillermo, and Philippe Schmitter. *Transitions from Authoritarian Rule: Comparative Perspectives*. Baltimore, MD: Johns Hopkins University Press, 1986b.

Pares I Maicas, Manuel, ed. *Approach to Catalonia*. Barcelona: Universitat Autonoma de Barcelona, 1985.

Partido Socialista Obrero Español (PSOE), Secretaria Federal de Organización. *Este viejo y nuevo partido*; and *Análisis de los acuerdos económicos y políticos*. Madrid: Editorial Pablo Iglesias, 1977.

Pascual, Pedro. "La Prensa construyó la democracia," in Alvaro Soto Carmona et al., eds., *Historia de la transición y consolidación democrática en España (1975–1986)*. Madrid: UNED, 1995.

Payne, Stanley. *A History of Spain and Portugal*, vols. I– II. Madison: University of Wisconsin, 1973.

Spanish Catholicism. Madison: University of Wisconsin, 1984.

"Representative Government in Spain: the Historical Background," in H. Penniman and E. Mujal-León, eds., *Spain at the Polls, 1977, 1979, 1982*. Durham, NC: Duke University Press, 1985, pp. 1–29.

"The Armed Forces in the Transition," in Robert Clark, ed., *Spain in the 1980s*. Cambridge, MA: Ballinger Publishing, 1987a, pp. 79–96.

The Franco Regime. Madison: University of Wisconsin, 1987b.

Spain's First Democracy. Madison: University of Wisconsin, 1993.

Peces-Barba, Gregorio, and Luis Prieto Sanchis. *La Constitución española de 1978: un estudio de derecho y política*. Valencia: Fernando Torres, 1981.

Penniman, Howard, and Eusebio Mujal-León, eds., *Spain at the Polls, 1977, 1979, 1982*. Durham, NC: Duke University Press, 1985.

Pérez-Agote, Alfonso. *La reproducción del nacionalismo: El caso vasco*. Madrid: Centro de Investigaciones Sociológicas, 1984.

Pérez-Agote, Alfonso, J. Azkona, A. Gurrutxaga, and F. Llera. *El nacionalismo vasco a la salida del franquismo*. Madrid: Centro de Investigaciones Sociológicas, 1987.

Pérez Díaz, Victor. *The Return of Civil Society in Spain*. Cambridge, MA: Harvard University Press, 1993.

España: puesta a prueba (1976–1996). Madrid: Alianza, 1996.

El Periódico de Catalunya: Enrique Arias Vega, director; Raimundo Castro et al., textos. *Desatado y bien desatado*. Barcelona: El Periódico de Catalunya, 1985.

Pi-Sunyer, Oriol. "Catalan Nationalism: Some Theoretical and Historical Considerations," in E. Tiryakian and R. Rogowski, eds., *New Nationalisms in the Developed West*. Boston: Allen and Unwin, 1985, pp. 254–276.

Poulantzas, Nicos. *Crisis of the Dictatorships: Portugal, Greece and Spain*. London: New Left Books, 1976.

Prager, Jeffrey. "American Racial Ideology as Collective Representation," *Ethnic and Racial Studies* 5: 99–119, January 1982.

Building Democracy in Ireland. Cambridge: Cambridge University Press, 1986.

Predieri, Alberto, and E. García de Enterria, *La Constitución española de 1978: estudio sistemático*. Madrid: Editorial Civitas, 1981.

Preston, Paul. *The Triumph of Democracy in Spain*. London: Methuen 1986.

The Spanish Civil War. New York: Grove Press, 1986b.

"The Legacy of the Spanish Civil War," in Stephen Hart, ed. *No Pasarán! Art, Literature and the Spanish Civil War*. London: Tamesis Books, 1988, pp. 11–19.

Franco. New York: Basic Books, 1994.

ed. *Spain in Crisis*. Sussex: Harvester Press, 1976.

Pridham, Geoffrey, ed. *The New Mediterranean Democracies: Regime Transition in Spain, Greece and Portugal*. London: Frank Cass, 1984.

Przeworski, Adam. "Some Problems in the Study of Transition," in G. O'Donnell, P. Schmitter, L. Whitehead, eds., *Transitions from Authoritarian Rule: Comparative Perspectives*. Baltimore, MD: Johns Hopkins University Press, 1986, pp. 46–63

Democracy and the Market. Cambridge: Cambridge University Press, 1991.

Putnam, Robert. *Making Democracy Work: Civic Traditions in Modern Italy*. Princeton, NJ: Princeton University Press, 1993.

Pye, Lucian, and Sidney Verba. *Political Culture and Political Development*. Princeton, NJ: Princeton University Press, 1965.

Ramírez, Pedro. *Así se ganaron las elecciones*. Barcelona: Planeta, 1977.

Read, Jan. *The Catalans*. London: Faber & Faber, 1978.

Redero San Roman, Manuel, ed. *La transición a la democracia en España*. Madrid: Ayer, 1994.

Ricoeur, Paul. "The Model of the Text: Meaningful Action Considered as a Text," *Social Research* 38: 529–562, 1971.

Rodríguez Armada, Amandino, and José Antonio Novais. "¿Quién mató a Julián Grimau?" Madrid: Ediciones 99, 1976.

Rodríguez Ibañez, José Enrique. *Después de una dictadura: cultura autoritaria y transición política en España*. Madrid: Centro de Estudios Constitucionales, 1987.

Roldán Ros, Juan. "The Media and the Elections," in H. Penniman and E. Mujal-León, eds., *Spain at the Polls, 1977, 1979, 1982*. Durham, NC: Duke University Press, 1985, pp. 253–273.

Ross, Chris. "Nationalism and Party Competition in the Basque Country and Catalonia," *West European Politics* 19:3: 488–506, 1996.

Sainz Rodríguez, Pedro. *Un reinado en la sombra*. Barcelona: Planeta, 1981.

San Sebastián, Koldo. *Historia del Partido Nacionalista Vasco*. San Sebastián: Editorial Txertoa, 1984.

Sánchez, José Maria. *The Spanish Civil War as Religious Tragedy*. Notre Dame, IN: University of Notre Dame, 1987.

Santamaría, Julian, ed. *Transición a la democracia en el sur de Europa y América latina*. Madrid: Centro de Investigaciones Sociológicas, 1982.

Schegloff, Emanuel. "Between Macro and Micro: Contexts and Other Connections," in J. Alexander, B. Giesen, R. Munch, and N. Smelser, eds., *The Micro–Macro Link*. Berkeley: University of California, 1987, pp. 207–236.

Sewell, William. *Work and Revolution in France: the Language of Labor from the Old Regime to 1848*. Cambridge: Cambridge University Press, 1980.

Share, Donald. *The Making of Spanish Democracy*. New York: Praeger, 1986.

"Transitions to Democracy and Transition through Transaction," *Comparative Political Studies* 19: 525–548, 1987.

Dilemmas of Social Democracy. New York: Greenwood Press, 1989.

Skocpol, Theda. *States and Social Revolutions*. Cambridge: Cambridge University Press, 1979.

Skocpol, Theda, and Kenneth Finegold. "State Capacity and Economic Intervention in the Early New Deal," *Political Science Quarterly* 97: 255–278, 1982.

Solé-Tura, Jordi. *Catalanismo i revolución burguesa*. Madrid: EDICUSA, 1974.

Somers, Margaret. "What's Political or Cultural about Political Culture and the Public Sphere: Toward an Historical Sociology of Concept Formation," *Theory and Society* 13(2): 113–144, July 1995.

Soto Carmona, Alvaro, and Javier Tusell, eds. *Historia de la transición y consolidación democrática en España (1975–1986)*. Madrid: UNED, 1995.

Spender, Stephen. "Guernica," in M. Sperber, ed., *And I Remember Spain*. New York: Macmillan, 1974, pp. 151–152.

Sullivan, John. *ETA and Basque Nationalism: the Fight for Euskadi, 1890–1986*. London: Routledge, 1988.

Swidler, Ann. "Culture in Action: Symbols and Strategies," *American Sociological Review* 51: 273–286, April 1986.

Tarrow, Sidney. "Mass Mobilization and Regime Change: Pacts, Reform, and Popular Power in Italy (1918–1922) and Spain (1975–1978)," in Richard Gunther, P. N. Diamandouros, and H. Puhle, eds., *The Politics of Democratic Consolidation*. Baltimore, MD: Johns Hopkins University Press, 1995, pp. 204–230.

Tejerina, Benjamin. *Nacionalismo y lengua*. Madrid: Centro de Investigaciones Sociológicas, 1992.

Tezanos, José Felix. *Sociología del socialismo español*. Madrid: Tecnos, 1983.

Tilly, Charles. *From Mobilization to Revolution*. Reading, MA: Addison-Wesley, 1978.

Tiryakian, Edward. "A Model of Societal Change and Its Lead Indicators," in Samuel Klausner, ed., *The Study of Total Societies*. New York: Praeger, 1967, pp. 69–67.

Turner, Victor. *The Ritual Process*. Chicago: Aldine, 1969.

Tusell, Javier. *La oposición democrática al franquismo*. Barcelona: Planeta, 1977. *Los hijos de sangre*. Madrid: Espasa Calpe, 1986.

Ullman, Joan Connelly. *The Tragic Week*. Cambridge, MA: Harvard University Press, 1968.

Urbina, Fernando. "Formas de vida de la Iglesia en España: 1939–1975," in R. Belda et al., eds., *Iglesia y sociedad en España 1939–1975*. Madrid: Editorial Popular, 1977, pp. 9–120.

Valls-Russell, Janice. "Terror and Politics in Spain," *The New Leader*, 9–11–95: 7–8.

Verdery, Katherine. "Nationalism and National Sentiment in Post-Socialist Romania," *Slavic Review* 52(2): 179–203, 1993.

Vilar, Pierre. *Spain: A Brief History*. Oxford: Pergamon Press, 1967.

Wagner-Pacifici, Robin. *The Moro Morality Play*. Chicago: University of Chicago, 1989.

Wagner-Pacifici, Robin, and Barry Schwartz, "The Vietnam Veterans Memorial: Commemorating a Difficult Past," *American Journal of Sociology* 97: 376–420, 1991.

Walzer, Michael. *Revolution of the Saints: a Study in the Origins of Radical Politics*. Cambridge, MA: Harvard University Press.

Wert Ortega, José Ignacio. "The Transition from Below: Public Opinion Among the Spanish Population from 1977 to 1979," in H. Penniman and E. Mujal-León, eds., *Spain at the Polls, 1977, 1979, and 1982*. Durham, NC: Duke University Press, 1985, pp. 73–87.

Wiarda, Howard. *Iberia and Latin America: New Democracies, New Policies, New Models*. London: Rowman and Littlefield, 1996.

Woolard, Kathryn. *Double Talk: Bilingualism and the Politics of Ethnicity in Catalonia*. Stanford, CA: Stanford University Press, 1989.

Ysàs, Pere. "Democracia y autonomía en la transición española," in Manuel Redero San Roman, ed., *La transición a la democracia en España*. Madrid: Ayer, 1994, pp. 77–108.

Zelizer, Viviana. *Morals and Markets*. New York: Columbia University Press, 1979. *The Social Meaning of Money*. New York: Basic Books, 1994.

Zirakzadeh, Cyrus. *A Rebellious People*. Reno: University of Nevada Press, 1991.

Zulaika, Joseba. "The Tragedy of Carlos," in William Douglass, ed., *Basque Politics: A Case Study in Ethnic Nationalism*. Reno: University of Nevada, 1985, pp. 308–331. *Basque Violence: Metaphor and Sacrament*. Reno: University of Nevada Press, 1988.

Newspapers and Periodicals

ABC, 1977–1979. Madrid.
El Alcázar, 1977–1982. Madrid.
Cambio 16, 1977–1982. Madrid.
Deia, 1977–1982. Bilbao.

Egin, 1978–1982. San Sebastián.
Informaciones, 1977–1978. Madrid.
Mundo Obrero, 1978–1983. Madrid.
El País, 1976–1982. Madrid.
El Socialista, 1978–1982. Madrid.
Triunfo, 1977–1978. Madrid.
La Vanguardia, 1977–1982. Barcelona.

Index